The
Architecture
of All
Abundance

The
Architecture
of All
Abundance

Creating a Successful Life in the Material World

Lenedra J. Carroll

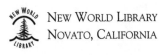 NEW WORLD LIBRARY
NOVATO, CALIFORNIA

New World Library
14 Pamaron Way
Novato, California 94949

The Architecture of All Abundance:
Creating a Successful Life in the Material World
Copyright © 2001 by Lenedra J. Carroll

Cover photograph by West Kennerly
Cover design by Mary Ann Casler
in collaboration with Chad Farmer of Lambesis Agency
and Berne Smith of Mani Management Group
Text design and typography by Mary Ann Casler
Interior photographs by David Owen Kniffen
Photograph on page 301 courtesy of Photonica

Library of Congress Cataloging-in-Publication Data
Carroll, Lenedra J.
Architecture of all abundance : creating a successful life in the
material world / Lenedra J. Carroll.
p.   cm.
Includes index.
ISBN 1-57731-189-2 (alk. paper)
1. Spiritual life. I. Title.

BL624 .C348 2001
291.4'4—dc21   2001002480
                                                                              CIP

First Printing, September 2001
ISBN 1-57731-189-2
Printed in Canada on acid-free paper
Distributed to the trade by Publishers Group West

10 9 8 7 6 5 4 3 2 1

*T*his book — like my life — is dedicated to the understanding of the Divine excellence within each of us that, when lived, uplifts our humanity and moves us beyond our current limitations and difficulties and into the revolution of the Soul and its certain transformation of our individual lives, our planet, and our species.

CONTENTS

THE Architecture OF THE Workplace

THE Architecture OF Health

THE Architecture OF Love

THE Architecture OF THE Soul

Preface

I have lived elements of a "rags to riches" life. I have experienced times of severe lack but I now live a gracious and abundant life filled with the financial resources and possessions that most people long for. However, I did not achieve them by yearning after those things. This book contains the understandings, values, and principles that have allowed me to develop a generative prosperity in my life and by which I have developed businesses that reflect those values.

Key to my accomplishment is a learned ability to source the depth of my being and to follow a passion that drives my life. This passion underlies my experience — the lessons, defeats, victories, and struggles — my humanity. This passion is the essence of my purpose and my joy. It is in all the moments that led me to new methods, profound knowledge, and a vastly providential life.

This passion has been central in the development and management of the career of my daughter, Jewel, as a singer-songwriter, actress, author, and humanitarian. It is the principal impetus behind the development of the international companies for which I am responsible.

In *The Architecture of All Abundance*, I share the nature of this passion, the factors that have shaped it, and its integration into my life. In the process, I speak of Spirit, the Source, faith, the Soul.

And I speak of God, having finally given up any argument about words and my frustrations with language as a means for discussing a power beyond the individual and collective human life. I have thrown up my hands at the attempt to pinpoint this and have chosen language I am personally familiar and comfortable with. I invite you to do the same.

All of the stories are from my experience and are in fact true — some have been altered in consideration of the privacy of those involved; a few are composite stories. They reflect different ages and stages of growth, including the voice of my childhood and youth, the confusion and pain of lessons of the young adult, and the wisdom of experience and Spirit. The observations, ideas, and conclusions are mine. They are presented to provide a landscape on which you, the reader, may construct your own understanding.

At its basis, this book derives from my realization that I have lived a life in which I have remembered to a greater and greater degree that there is a force within us that has the potential to move mountains. This is what I have been dedicated to: remembering. Remembering who we are in our essence and discovering that essence to be profoundly powerful and grace-filled.

We are called to be architects of our future, not its victims.

— R. Buckminster Fuller

DAYSONG

Daysong flickers out.
Hushed ones creep forward
as earth turns over.

Light flees as wind flies
and night rises up to
moisten day with shadow.

At length night pauses,
moon rises, laughing,
and chases illusive dawn.

Lenedra J Carroll

THE
Architecture
OF A
Life

WHAT IS A DEEPLY SATISFYING HUMAN LIFE, AND HOW DO WE
DESIGN ONE? HOW DO WE SHARE THAT INFORMATION WITH
EACH OTHER? WHAT ARE WE MEANT TO DO HERE TOGETHER,
AND WHAT ARE WE TRULY CAPABLE OF IN THE REALM OF HUMAN
EXCELLENCE?

THE ANSWERS TO THESE QUESTIONS ARE NOT MYSTERIES BEYOND
OUR REACH. FULFILLMENT OF THE PROMISE OF OUR SOUL'S
NATURE IS POSSIBLE. IT IS WHY WE ARE HERE. IT IS OUR BIRTH-
RIGHT. THE ANSWERS ARE FOUND IN THE INNER FRONTIERS OF
BEING. THIS IS MY JOURNEY INTO THOSE FRONTIERS.

1

THE Last Frontier

e didn't like what she had done
so the man leaned down into the face of the little girl and hollered in a
very mean tone,

"Who on earth do you think you are?"

She felt a response to the tone and volume of his voice and the mes-
sage of his body language and words. She felt fear and confusion; she also
felt offended. Yet at the same time she thought, "This is a very important
question. I will think about it when I am alone."

Who do you think you are?

She often asked herself versions of this question as she grew older.
There were many answers. Depending.

The winds blew across the pristine glaciers and mountains, over
the waters of Kachemak Bay on the Kenai Peninsula to the remote
Alaskan village of Homer. The tides brought the salmon running up
the rivers; the midnight sun glinted as red as the countless fireweed
flowers that covered the Homer hills behind our house. High in the
winter sky the curtain of Northern Lights seemed to crackle on
frosty Arctic nights. The land and the latitude accessed in me a sub-
tlety that matched the wild but spare landscape. I experienced the
courage and persistence of living things, the strength of the majes-
tic peaks, the stability of the fertile bench of land bordering our bay,

the rapid wax and wane of the short northern seasons, the reclusive energy of long winters, and the thrust of endless summer days. I knew the uncertainty and limitations of the life cycle, and the fragility of human beings in harsh environs. From the extraordinary energy of the land I learned the lessons of nature's silence and observed the power and wisdom of whole, natural systems.

CHILDHOOD VALUES

It was the allure of a new frontier and the wide-open wilderness that drew my parents, Jay and Arva Carroll, to interior Alaska in 1941. They joined my father's adventurous brother, Ward, at his cabin on an island in the Piledriver River, near Fairbanks. My mother's Utah family was aghast, thinking them lost to the dangerous wilds where they could not be reached by car or even telephone. For these early pioneers, amenities were nearly non-existent. The population was sparse and the environment so harsh that good judgment, common sense, and creativity were vital for survival. Hard work, sustainability, the integrity of one's word, and full cooperation with surrounding people and the environment were also essential. These were the values of my childhood.

For my parents it was an exciting life, but not an easy one. The rest of the United States seemed very removed and was referred to as the "lower forty-eight" or "outside." Basic supplies were ordered quarterly, few luxuries were available; most people had a strong reliance on gardens and the local game and fish. Self-sufficiency was the necessity. Roads were primitive or nonexistent; communication systems were often unreliable with mail infrequent and telephones rare. Dwellings, too, were basic. I recall Mom telling me that my oldest brother once slipped out of her arms as she was trying to dry him from a bath. He became a mud ball as he rolled on the dirt floor of their tiny one-room log cabin with its sod roof.

Dad was a very resourceful and inventive man. In Wrangel, Alaska, he hunted and trapped and had a dogsled and team. He later managed the utility company in Seward, Alaska, where he designed and oversaw the building of a power station that became a model for others in the lower forty-eight states. At one point, he wanted a better alternative to the snowshoe so he created a snowmobile long before they became commercially available. He produced many inventions born of necessity. Some of my fondest memories are of him sharing his ideas and his inventive processes with me.

In the early fifties, Dad built an airplane and, with a neighbor, taught himself to fly it. I was eight when he moved us from Seward, the small Alaskan town of my early years, to the village of Homer, population: one thousand. He used his savings to purchase a small rural air service and gradually built it up to include six airplanes. Eventually he added a marine fuel dock at the boat harbor, as well as a service station in town. During summers I worked with him and his partner in their air service, answering the citizens band radio and phones or penciling figures into the ledger.

Dad flew locals and visitors to hunting and fishing areas, and delivered mail and supplies to people in the remote regions of south central Alaska. He was often the only person that these isolated pioneers saw in the course of a year and he would visit — sharing a glass of their homemade dandelion wine or elderberry brandy and stories of close calls with a bear, or the moose that ate the garden. He might leave them with the part they needed to fix their tractor as well as the enjoyment of a little human contact.

I often flew with my father. Our peninsula had a breathtaking beauty. A massive and deep saltwater bay dominated the landscape. On one side of the bay, a long green bench of rich land held our settlement. Across the bay, glacier-filled mountains fell straight into the water. The land was undeveloped and a high degree of skill was required to set the small planes down on the uncertain terrain that passed for landing strips. I loved landing on water in the float planes, but it was also fun to land on beaches and glaciers or in a wilderness clearing.

> Climb the mountains and get their good tidings.
> Nature's peace will flow into you as sunshine flows into
> trees. The winds will blow their own freshness into you,
> and the storms their energy, while cares will drop away
> from you like the leaves of Autumn.
>
> — John Muir

NATURAL ORDER

My greatest joys were the endless hours spent experiencing nature.
Over time I realized that nature is of immense value for its ability to
express pure Being. For me, and later for my children, nature was not
only a vital presence but also a great solace and influence. I had a
favorite place under a stand of Sitka spruce trees near a beautiful
creek where I sat for hours simply observing and being part of nature.
I encountered there a pervasive peace, a purposefulness, and an order
— even in the chaos, destruction, and death observable in nature.

I also observed that there was not just one type of anything —
not one right kind of tree, no singular type of plant or animal, no
sole body of water. I saw, instead, an endless variety of expressions
of peace, beauty, and purposefulness and God. This affected my
view of religion, for I became unable to imagine that there could be
only one right version of God. Each religion seemed to be but one
of many converging paths.

As a child I hungered for information about how things *really*
are, the keys and secrets of life. I sensed that there was vital information that I lacked; I sensed that it was available. I imagined the
impact of such information on people's lives: on our communities
and work, our learning and our loving. My most fervent wish was to
understand these things.

THE RABBIT AND THE CHICKEN

In fifth grade they call it "Health," but in sixth grade it's
"Science." The last part of fifth grade the teacher says we're going

to finish the year with a little science. I guess they're getting us ready for next year. I'm just glad we are getting away from making clay models of the digestive system, which seems like art class to me. I'm hoping that we can get to the hard stuff — microscopes, dissecting things, embryos in jars, lab experiments and explosions.

The teacher, Mr. C., says science is all about noticing and noting things and careful notes are important. "Pioneering the frontiers of science," he said. Well, I'm good at noticing and pretty good at getting it down so I figure I might become a scientist; I'll see. I like the pioneering part anyway. So the first day of science I'm there with my notebook and high expectations. All in all, school just isn't that interesting, you have to really work at it to learn anything very gripping. But I have hope for science.

And I'm not disappointed either. Right off the bat I learn the most amazing thing. Mr. C. tells us about certain experiments. One involves a bunch of dogs that drool every time a bell rings, which is somewhat cool, though in my experience dogs drool a lot anyway.... He tells us about a couple more of these experiments with some rats, and well, okay, I can pretty much see what they were getting at. But then he wraps up the hour with the one that tops everything. He tells us about how some scientists took a baby rabbit away from its momma just as soon as possible. They put it in a nest with a hen because hens are known to accept the young of other animals. Which is interesting in itself. Well, the bunny grows up with the hen and learns a lot of chicken habits. It pecks its food. It roosts with the chickens every evening. It hops funny, sort of chickenlike.

What happens next is the best part. When it's grown, the scientists take the rabbit away from the hen and put it back with the other rabbits. Now, right here I'm getting pretty excited. I'm thinking this is really going to be great. The rabbit is all of a sudden going to understand that it's a rabbit, not a chicken, and it's going to be really happy about that. But no! The rabbit cowers in the corner of the hutch and won't have a thing to do with the other rabbits. It's so upset that it even quits eating and drinking. After a while they put it back with the chickens so it won't die. It perks right up and is very glad to be back home. Mr. C. explains that what the scientists learned here was that all animals, and people too, learn their behaviors when they are young. They are taught. He tells us about some studies that showed that humans need this too — babies in orphanages and stuff like that. He says it's the way we all learn how to be. Somebody shows us, or tells us. Now this is truly amazing. It's by far the most amazing thing I've learned in school so far. It seems as important to me as knowing that the world isn't flat. I can't imagine why they haven't taught us about this sooner!

I'm bored quite a lot so I really appreciate a story that can capture the mind and hold it fast for a good period of time. This is the perfect story for thinking; there are tons of possibilities and questions to mull over. This story is like a secret treasure. At the bus stop I think about it while I wait. I think about it in class when Mr. C. gets stuck teaching the stuff you know you'll never need to think about again, like all those wars that were always going on hundreds of years ago. I think about it at home when nothing much is happening, which is most of the time. What if a person was raised by a hen? Would they like a chicken roost better than a bed? Do animals ever raise people? How do they learn to talk then? Mr. C. tells me it has happened a few times and the person usually couldn't ever adjust to living with people or even learn language. This seems very strange and leads me to a lot of thoughts that start to bother me. What if someone was raised in a box and wasn't taught the right stuff? What if someone taught them all the wrong stuff on purpose, or even accidentally? Would you know it was the wrong stuff? Would you ever figure it out?

This starts me wondering what I am being taught. So I begin to pay attention. That's when I begin to get scared. At home, I don't know if anyone is teaching me anything. At least nothing really important about what it means to be a human being. How will I know the ways to be? How will I know how to have a good human life?

I hit on the idea that maybe it's what they're teaching at school, only I just wasn't noticing before. It must be, after all that's where I learned the story about the rabbit and the chicken! Luckily I know how to do a scientific study — notice and take notes. So I go to school really excited. In my notebook I write HOW TO BE A HUMAN BEING at the top of a page. I'm determined to take really good notes on what they're teaching us about being human. After a few days I'm discouraged. Almost nothing. Lots about human problems in history, but no clear lessons really. No important tips or little wisdoms to guide me, a ten-year-old girl, to grow up right.

I worry about it a while then suddenly I figure it out. It's church! That's where they teach you the right stuff. It makes a lot of sense. I take my notebook to church, certain I will fill it soon. I notice a lot of rules: a lot of "right and wrong," "good and bad" information. More history. A few good ideas like "treat others the way you want to be treated" and so on. But mostly guilt and fear and rules, it seems to me. This isn't so much what I'm looking for. Nobody is talking about being human. About *being*. I'm shocked. Maybe it's a secret you only get to learn at a certain age. Maybe it's hidden information that you have to figure out. Maybe everyone has forgotten. I begin to look for people who have really interesting and happy lives. I start reading biographies and autobiographies in the school library. I read every one they have. I make lots of notes about living, pursuing this interest fiercely and, I imagine, scientifically. I'm on the watch for all the clues about a really great human life. What does it mean to be a human being, in the best sense? And how do you be one? The desire to know this becomes my mission.

※◎ ◎※

THE NATURE OF OUR BEING

In the fall of 1990, I flew in a small aircraft to the remote Alaskan volcano St. Augustine to spend a week alone on the island. During the flight, the pilot of the small plane nudged me and pointed to the water. He tipped the wing allowing me to look more directly below; I was amazed to see what appeared to be a giant jellyfish. I was familiar with this type of jellyfish, having seen them washed up on the beaches by the hundreds when I was a child — opaque white center in the shape of a loose star, more transparent toward the outside, a white band defining their outer edge, eight to ten inches in diameter. But the one I looked down on seemed a hundred feet across! Loose white star becoming more translucent away from the center; ringed with white ... but huge. Huge. The pilot laughed at my reaction and hollered at me over the engine noise, "School!"

It was a group of jellyfish migrating together, but this was still amazing. How did they manage to appear from above to be one large jellyfish? Each seemed to know its place in the formation ... and their group movement was the same undulating movement of the individual jellyfish I saw when I was young.

As I watched I marveled at this group moving together. Does instinct prompt their formation? What awareness do they have of their direction, their movement and destination?

I couldn't help wondering if humans also move intuitively as a group toward a purpose only vaguely sensed, but visible from above.

> Look deep, deep into nature, and then you will understand everything better.
>
> — Albert Einstein

THE DAWN OF THE SOUL

The incident of the jellyfish and the story about the rabbit and the chicken illustrate a passion and a quest that has remained key in my life, driving my actions and growth; re-forming my understandings. What does it mean to be a human being in the highest sense? What is the deepest nature of our being?

I began to be possessed by a gripping curiosity and longing to understand what happens when an individual heeds the urgings of the soul rather than having the soul subject to the ego. It seemed to me that tangible information regarding these things would profoundly impact all areas of our lives — the workplace, our health, our families, and communities.

I have discovered that we are not left without access to this knowledge — fulfillment of the promise of our soul's nature is possible. Indeed, it is what we are here for: to enter the realm of our greater potentiality. The answers are found in the individual and collective journey into our Being and in the stillness that leads us there.

> What seems true to reason and sense perception is not always true in fact. The only sure way to know truth is to realize it intuitively.
>
> — Paramahansa Yogananda

VOICELESS ONE

Voiceless One
I hear you as lapping waves upon the shore
with your lap lap lulling rhythm
bringing my sodden eyelids down
pulling me, heavy with your gravity,
  down
  down upon my knee bones
  curling my spine
and pressing my weighted head to my chest
forcing my hands inward
  to my bosom
  inward furled
until I too am lapping at the shore
growing with the fern and bud
and young green blade
singing from full golden breast
and feathered throat
Rising and falling on the surface
  uncurling
  back curving up
  arms arcing
  neck arching
  head lifting
my eyes have glimpsed your roaring depths
and my heart trumpets your full unending glory

Lenedra J Carroll

THE
Architecture
OF
Stillness

STILLNESS IS THE SPRING THAT ALL RIVERS FLOW FROM AND THE
OCEAN THAT ALL RIVERS FLOW BACK INTO. STILLNESS UNDER-
LIES ALL MOVEMENT, INFORMS ALL LIFE. IT IS THE VITALITY THAT
CREATES US, SURROUNDS US, AND SUPPORTS US. THE SOURCE OF
STILLNESS IS THE SOURCE OF ALL CREATION. IT IS THE ESSENCE
IN WHICH WE LIVE AND BREATHE AND HAVE OUR BEING.

2

INTO THE Silence

*T*he greatest event is that sudden stroke of grace which shows us who and what we are, beyond the world of appearances, beyond conditions and circumstances, beyond fear and resistance, beyond desire and fulfillment, beyond the images and beliefs of the mind. The most wonderful event is to collide with the unifying silence beyond all this, untouched by all this. Here in this silence we encounter our truest potential, already realized. Here in this silence. This silence, which, while beyond all things, is ever present, surrounding us, holding us, sustaining us, feeding us. Entering the deep forests of this silence is the greatest and most wondrous of events.

— Robert Rabbin

It is the journey into silence that leads to a stillness that can inform our actions and our lives with peace and with abundance. Just as there are many roads to the Divine, there are many routes inward: prayer, meditation, nature, solitude, contemplation, workshops, sacred writings, dance, ceremony, poetry, music, chanting, gardening, the practice of religion. A wealth of information about the use of any of these tools for spiritual development is readily available. The method is not nearly as important as the commitment and the practice. It is the repeated journey into silence that brings the rewards of stillness.

Returning often, we learn that each journey is different; each reveals something new. Each time there comes forth some discovery that informs the body and informs the mind about the platform upon which we have built our lives. Therein is grace. There is our identity that surpasses all identities. There are we reinforced and reinspired with knowledge of why we have taken form at this time upon our planet. There, in the grace, in the stillness, all other considerations, identities, fears, and hopes are erased — they are no more. There, in the place of stillness, our soul is completed in its aim of reincorporating into this body the exquisite expression of stillness. In that place comes the knowledge that more communication occurs in the spaces between words than in the words themselves. There we connect with the infinite intelligence in which all answers are found and there we come to know the fullness of our birthright.

COMING TO KNOW

We just moved to Homer. I like our new house and my third-grade class. It snows a lot more here and I really like to play in it. So I've been rolling snowballs around the yard, making trails. I can't make them as big as I want. I wish my brothers were here to help make giant ones and then lift them up on each other to make a snowman. Once they made one that was as tall as our house! I content myself with carving balls into different shapes. I go into the house and get a bucket of water and some crepe paper left over from Christmas. Outside again, I wet the crepe paper, and press it on the snow forms. It leaves bright swaths of red and green color. I patiently wet and pat, wet and pat. My mittens get soggy so I take them off. Soon I have a red heart with white lace, and a green duck with red bill and feet. I'm pretty satisfied when I'm done, but my hands ache. They are pretty numb, in fact, kind of grayish and waxy looking, and puffy. I go in the house to show my mom.

Something must be wrong because she looks alarmed and grabs me by the arm, bouncing me along behind her as she urgently drags me back outside. She doesn't even put her coat on.

What's wrong? Am I dying? If I die how will they dig a hole to bury me, I wonder, the ground is too frozen. If I die will I miss anyone? I imagine everyone cherishing my frozen red and green artistry until it sadly melts in the spring, leaving no trace of me behind.

Mom breaks into my dark wondering by thrusting my hands down and scrubbing them with snow. First one, then the other, back and forth. It hurts! I yelp and jerk my hands away but she takes them again and rubs. I pull them away; she pulls them back. We get pretty caught up in the tug-of-war. "Give me your hands," she says. "This is important!"

"No!" I cry. "It hurts!"

I am holding them behind my back now so she can't get them. "Nedra Jewel Carroll!" she says sharply, so I'll know she means business. "You have frostbite and it can be very serious. It can damage the nerves so your hands ache all the time. You can even lose fingers — we have to rub them with snow to help them."

While she tells me this she is shaking a little from concern and frustration and from the cold.

"No!" I insist. "It doesn't help, it doesn't!"

She tells me forcefully that it's what the doctors say to do for frostbite. "The doctors are wrong!" I yell.

Now she's very upset. She straightens up and puts her hands on her hips. "Well then, miss smarty-pants, if you know so much, you figure out what to do!"

"Okay, I will," I say. "I will!"

She rolls her eyes and stomps into the house and I stomp after her. I'm not usually so much trouble, but I'm feeling really agitated here. I plunk down on the couch and gaze at my hands. Mom's challenge to figure out what to do ricochets in my brain. I don't for a minute think that the doctors have the right idea. I am consumed with the thought that I could know. Even though I'm only nine. *It's my body*, I think, *I can figure this out*. What is the right thing to do? I can tell the answer is somewhere near. I peer at my hands, wondering fervently what the answer is. Then something happens and I see what to do. I see it! My hands become shimmering matter! In them I see little round things filled with liquid. I understand that the liquid has sort of become frozen and the walls of the little blobs are very fragile and when they get rubbed hard, they can break each other and leak. I understand that what needs to happen is for them to be warmed very slowly.

Quickly I place my hands in my armpits but they begin to sting. Too hot, too fast, I realize. I go to my mom. "Mom." She's still annoyed with me and looks away. "Mom!" I press for her attention and she responds to the urgency.

"Mom, there's little round things in my hands, I saw them! They are filled with liquid and when they are frozen their edges get fragile and leak the fluid out and stuff like that. They need to be warmed slowly and gently. I put them in my armpit but that was too hot. They stinged."

She looks at me oddly for a long moment. "There are cells in your hands," she says thoughtfully, then is quiet. We stand in the kitchen; the clock ticks loudly. She walks to the sink and gets a drink, which is what she always does when she's disturbed or needs to think. As she turns from the sink she says, "I know. Let's run some cool water in the sink and put your hands in it, then we'll warm the water gradually."

This is just the right idea, I can tell, and I excitedly push a chair over to the sink and climb up. I plunge my hands in the water and slowly Mom warms it: no stinging. Soon my hands soften, lose their puffiness, and return to their normal pinky flesh color. I don't have any more trouble with them hurting or anything. Mom says it's amazing and Dad thinks it's very interesting too, but the part that I think is amazing is the part that they don't talk about. They sort of act like, "Oh yeah, good idea you had." They are totally missing the point.

There is a miracle here! I needed to know something; I got quiet and asked. I wondered about it, holding on fiercely to the question no matter what, and it opened itself up to me. I came to know the answer. It just bubbled up from somewhere, from some place where all the answers are. We can know anything! It's all right here. We just have to ask.

This is so amazing! It lays me out. It shivers my timbers. It totally unstrings me. It exults me. The answers are all here, in us, all around us! I have to always remember this, always. I write it in my notebook.

Naturally thoughts about this fill my head for a long time. I turn it around this way and that looking for every morsel I can get out of it. I want to understand how it works and how to do it again. The first thing, I figure out, is that I need to know what the question is. That's when I start to realize how important the question is: If you don't make a question you don't have anywhere to go. What if I had believed what the doctors told Mom? I never would have questioned. So I have to notice when there's a question and not skip over it. Next I have to focus on the question, with a lot of concentration. I discover that straining doesn't work — I have to be still and hold the question kinda quietlike.

Eventually I develop a system. I write it down so I remember the steps. I call it Dream Machine because it's sort of like a time machine and sort of like dreaming. I write it in my book under "How to Come to Know." Here's how it works. I sit down in a snuggly place and stare a while and get kind of dreamy. I imagine I'm floating on a pond. It is a pond as big as the ocean. It has everything in it that is possible to know or feel or think or see. The whole wide world is in it. It is a safe and beautiful pond. I slowly let myself sink down into the pond. I can breathe underwater, just like in my dreams, so I don't get worried about that. Slowly, slowly I sink to the bottom. It is a lovely sandy bottom. There are plants and fish and shells and pretty rocks and I enjoy all of that for a while. Then I look up and see the surface far above me. It shimmers like a jewel in the sunlight. I begin to watch all the things that are floating by on the surface. My thoughts, pictures of things, even people's faces. I just let it all drift by. I am very peaceful. Even if a storm is raging on the surface, something I'm worrying about for instance, I am peaceful here. I know it is just a surface storm and that I am deep in a very calm place that can't be touched by the storm.

Often what drifts by up there on the surface takes on a really sharp focus — the stuff I'm worrying about for instance — and Boink! an answer comes, something adds up, or points in a direction. It comes into my mind as a picture, or a voice, or a thought, often arriving suddenly and completely as a fully formed understanding. I simply come to know something I didn't know the moment before. Other times the answer doesn't come while I snuggle there. It comes later, bit by bit over a few days. I might even find a book with the answer or a person will tell me something that is an answer.

The more I play with this the more I learn that there isn't really anything that we can't come to know for ourselves. Even great wisdom and new ideas are there. Comfort and peace too. And solutions to practical matters like why did my kitty die and things like that. I think this makes things very hopeful. Very hopeful indeed.

Sit quietly, doing nothing. Spring comes, and the grass grows by itself.

— Zen saying

3

Empty Space

*T*hroughout the millennia, all cultures have had various terms for their view of empty space — *chi, qui,* void, *prana, barraka,* ether, *shunyata plenum.* It has typically been seen as a sort of energetic sea that connects man and the cosmos with an underlying power.

In quantum theory it becomes very clear that what we call empty space is not so empty — sub-atomic particles flash in and out of existence, fields fluctuate, expansion and contraction occur. Empty space contains energy that, by conservative calculation, is on the order of nuclear energy. So empty space is a very energetic plenum. When you are thrown back in the seat of your fast car, or knocked down when the bus takes off before you are seated, what is it that shoves you back with such force? It is the energetic power contained in empty space. I recall a *New York Times* headline that reported: "Physicists Confirm the Power of Nothing." It discussed recent experiments successfully measuring the nearly unimaginable energetic power of empty space.

In many Eastern systems of thought there are considered to be five elements: Earth, Air, Water, Fire, and Space. Space is a vital element. The heavens are comprised primarily of space; the stars are few and far between. Most matter is comprised primarily of space. Our bodies are largely comprised of space.

I once heard a scientist say that if all of the space in our body was removed, the remaining physical matter would fit on the head of a pin. Recently I confirmed this in a conversation with a scientist at the University of California. He said, "Matter is the common substance that forms all things, it has always existed and cannot be destroyed. We are indeed primarily space for we are comprised of a very small amount of matter that exists in the form of atoms, electrons, and neutrons — the elemental substances of the body. If you could remove the space and force that give matter its configurations and actions in the body, then the matter would certainly fit on the head of a pin."

We are primarily space — in our muscles, between our organs, the space in and between our cells and atoms. Our bodies cannot function without that space. What creates and maintains the energy of space in us? What is that space responsive to?

Stillness creates space in our thoughts and our embodiments. Without the space that silence, rest, and breath give us, our lives, our bodies, our minds grow tightly compressed. We experience that compression as stress, fatigue, and ill health. Space makes a great energy available to us. Without it we do not receive an element vital to sustain our life energy. Many qualities essential to achieving a high quality of life require space. Love requires space to blossom. Creativity requires space for its development. Time requires space. Abundance also. Genius cannot be accessed without space. Health as well. And magic.

MAKE SPACE FOR MAGIC

The growing season is too short in Alaska for sunflower plants to mature. These valiant seven, however, have contradicted their own requirements and flourish here in the sun against the house. They press against the window where, inside, I am at the white desk in my art gallery in Anchorage.

It's September of 1986, just days before my thirty-sixth birthday. I am on the phone with an artist discussing the work he is sending for a show next month. My left hand doodles in the margins of my notebook, then picks up a small pouch and fiddles with it absently as he talks. The tiny pouch is made of soft, cream-colored leather and is gathered shut with a thin brown cord. As I hold it, I realize I don't remember how it came to me. I've had it a very long time, I think, but I haven't seen it in many years. Recently I discovered it in an old box of treasures and placed it on my desk. I pull the string that opens it. Out tumble several small stones. One is a small rose quartz egg. Another, translucent blue, is a double pyramid, and the third is some sort of gold metal — a perfect little square. The last one rolls out onto my desk blotter: a lovely pale yellow stone shaped like a pyramid capstone.

Who gave these to me? Where did the pouch come from?

As I wonder this, something in me startles, sharpens; the voice on the phone recedes. A flush buzzes up my body, causing a feeling of nausea, and blood pounds at my brain stem; my eyes blur with light-headedness. I hastily end the phone call and lay my head on the desk. A memory returns swiftly and fully, so vivid that it seems immediate. I am remembering the man who gave me the pouch!

Sitting up, slightly dizzy still, I lean back in my chair in recollection. It's a few days before my twelfth birthday. There is a man at church that no one has seen before, not at church and not in town. This is odd because in a village everyone knows all about everything. We all stare at him. He sits in our row and smiles at me during the service. I can tell he's a grown-up who knows the secrets children know. I've been thinking about this because I've just noticed that people seem to forget all the magic when they grow up. It's been worrying me. I can tell he hasn't forgotten — kids can tell — it's in his eyes, which are wonderfully kind and deep. I think he looks very wise. His skin is rough and brown — he's an Indian! Even though he wears jeans and a plaid shirt, I imagine him in feathers and leather leggings and I hope he has a rattle or a drum in the bag at his feet. I know about Indians from books and movies. He winks at me and my brother, making the "how" sign. Grinning, he makes other signals with his hands. Indian sign language! We laugh and signal back. Mom nudges us to be still.

After church he approaches us and speaks to my mother. "I understand you have rooms to rent, Mrs. Carroll."

This idea is very funny to my brother and me because we never have company. Never! Dad doesn't allow it. "Well, no . . . ," Mother begins uncomfortably.

"Great!" he says, just as if she had said yes instead of no. "I could use a place for a few nights. I sure appreciate your hospitality." Mom blinks. We all do. He follows us to the car and climbs in. Mom lets him. I can't believe it!

We don't have much room — I sleep on the couch in the living room, my little sister in an alcove. My four brothers are all in the unfinished basement and he's going to sleep with them down there. I lurk about, watching him put the sheet and blanket on the old army cot he will sleep on, hoping to catch a glimpse of the contents of his bag. After practically forever he opens it. Out come brushes and paints and colored pencils. He explains that he's an artist, which isn't as exciting to me as a dancing, drumming, whooping Indian, but when he offers to paint my picture I guess that might be interesting. He stays three nights. It turns out that my dad is away the whole time with a group of hunters he is guiding. So it all works out.

During the day he sketches and tells me stories. I wasn't wrong about him remembering the secrets. He talks about all the unseen things that kids know about but grown-ups don't seem to see — wood spirits, and angels, and what the wind can tell you, and what the animals know. He knows all this and lots more. At night he helps make up my bed on the couch and sits by me holding my hand, talking about me. He understands a lot about me. He asks me about my dreams, too, and has me tell him stories. He tells me I am an artist just like him, which is exciting to me. One evening, he puts his hand over my throat for a while. His hand really heats up and my throat starts to ache and tears come to my eyes.

"It's okay to cry," he says. "It's good to let the tears come so they don't block your voice."

So I sit there in the living room crying silently with him for quite a while and it kind of feels good. Then he ties a leather thong around my neck that holds a turquoise stone over my throat. He tells me I will speak and sing to the nations of the world. My mother and brothers, reading near us, pay no attention to me and the odd native man telling stories.

Each morning, I wake excited and wait impatiently for him to have his instant coffee and bring out his pencils. He sketches scenes and tells me about them. He even has me sit very still so he can draw me. For three full days we visit and draw together. He takes me on walks, talking to nature. We talk about God and spirit and the soul. My child heart is affirmed again and again and I deepen in self-trust that I know what matters, what is real.

On the third day it is my twelfth birthday. He says he has to leave now and tells me that he came to be with me and to give me gifts for my birthday. He hands me the pencil portrait he drew of me along with two colored-pencil sketches of places that he says are very important for me. Then he folds a pouch into my little hand and says,

"Remember that you are an artist.

Know that you are more than the things that happen to you.

Always make space for magic to happen."

Something is tap-tapping at the window. I lift my head from the desk and see the sunflowers, whipped by the wind, bumping rhythmically against the pane. I feel like I am coming out of a stupor. I am absolutely fascinated. He was so kind to me. I have seen him numerous times, since childhood, in dreams. Who was he?

I pick up the phone and call my mother. "Mom, I'm just remembering a man who stayed with us when I was twelve. He was there for my birthday; he gave me some drawings..." I tell her what I recall. "Do you remember him?"

"Oh yes. Really, it was such an odd thing. We did meet him at church. He stayed with us a few days. He was very taken with you, even gave you a drawing if I remember right. He was a lovely man.

The oddest thing, though, was how he left. He thanked me for my hospitality and headed down the drive — I was at the kitchen window doing the dishes — and he turned to wave and then he just disappeared right in front of my eyes. I've never seen anything like it. I didn't know what to make of it. I wondered if he was an angel."

After I hang up the phone, I sit entranced. A deep silence seems to fill me. Evening shadow creeps across the sunflowers and into the room. I sit long into the dark. His words to me on my twelfth birthday are the only thoughts repeating themselves, looping again and again in my mind.

"Make space for magic to happen."

> The universe is full of magical things patiently waiting for our wits to grow sharper.
>
> — Eden Phillpots

A few days later, on my birthday, I sit at the breakfast table with my morning coffee and sort through a pile of old papers from my studio. Suddenly I am faced with my innocent twelve-year-old profile, sketched in pencil for me by this loving teacher. My young, open face in the drawing recalls the magic I knew existed then, recalls the wisdom he spoke to me and my hopes and dreams and purpose in the world. These permeate me and I begin to weep.

That afternoon I cut the sunflowers and harvest the seeds, placing them in a pouch. I take my medicine bundle from my altar and leave the city, driving up into the Matanuska Valley. The sun lowers across the river delta, then drops beyond the horizon. Bumping along dirt roads I head for the butte, pursuing the dusk. Night settles in before I reach the foothills of the plateau, but there is a clear, starry sky and a full moon rising. Soon I leave the car and hike across a broad field of waist-high timothy grass that moves like quicksilver in the wind, illuminated by the moonlight. My lungs fill with the sweet breath of earth and sky and night. I begin climbing, moving deeper and deeper into the stillness.

Reaching a flat, jutting overlook at the base of the cliff, I seat myself and spread the contents of my medicine bundle on a red cloth on the ground. The bundle is expertly beaded with large pink and red roses in raised relief; I run my hands over the beads and think of the wonderful teacher, a Lummi Indian woman, who gifted it to me. Then, as I pull the little pouch out of the bundle, my mind fills with the face of the man who placed it in my hand on my twelfth birthday. Smiling, I begin to surrender to the magic that is all creation. I press seven sunflower seeds into the earth in front of me, one from each of my plants. As I pat the rich glacial silt over the seeds, I whisper my gratitude and my blessings to this planet that nurtures me. A dragonfly lights on my leg and then one on my hand, another on my shoulder. More and more follow until these ancient and mystical creatures delightfully engulf me, their iridescent wings reflecting the effulgent moonlight into my eyes. I laugh in delight at the wonder of God and begin my prayers.

It's a magical world, Hobbes, ol' buddy…let's go exploring!
— Calvin's last words,
"Calvin and Hobbes," by Bill Waterson
December 31, 1995

4

Centered IN Being

We fear we are alone and in that aloneness we fear for our safety. Fearing the loneliness, the emptiness, we are afraid we will sail right off the edge of it should we venture forth into the yawning maw. It is an emptiness we seem compelled to fill, willing to pay any price for a fleeting glimpse of security along our barren shorelines. The fear expresses as a longing, a yearning to be full. And this, if we could be assured, is purposeful and good. We should let it be, to irritate and discomfit. If we do not hurry to fill it with a lover, an addiction, an entertainment, or project; if we pause before launching into movement or word or definition, the fear will lead us. If we acknowledge or share our fear with the goal of knowing ourselves and becoming free, it will lead us here and there, in and out, above and below. Left unattended, denied, the fears can become neuroses, but by being conscious of them and using them, they can be important markers for us to follow. Riding our rudderless fears and insecurities, our pitching and tossing compulsions; letting them chart our way we follow them, follow them, to a new land, a promised land. Only there, to our absolute surprise and delight, do we find we are truly safe at last. There is the rest and health and love that we so longed for; there is the blessed safety and the peace we despaired to find. There, we discover, is the source of all knowledge that we sensed but no longer hoped we could claim.

THE WEB OF LIFE

I open my eyes with a sense of dread that I have to get through another day of grief. Tears from my slumber have soaked my pillow and continue to flow down my face. Jewel is gone; she was killed by a fan at one of her shows two weeks ago. The feeling of the grief and loss makes my bones ache, my cells scream. I lie in a hot trough of pain for fully half an hour before I realize it is a dream. My shoulders heave with relief, my throat aches with joy and gratitude. It isn't true! It was only a horribly graphic dream!

I pull myself from bed and move quickly to the little altar in the corner. I light a candle and, from the place of gratitude, I move deep into the center of myself, the core of all that is. In that place I connect to the peace that is in every situation. I affirm our covenant in life and ask that the dream — a powerful portent not uncommon in my dreams — show itself to be dealt with.

Later that morning I contact members of our team, asking them to be alert to any potential security situation. Within two weeks a team member forwards information to me that matches the details of my dream. The feel I get of the man is the same as the one I had awareness of in both the dream and in my silence and prayer following it.

In the investigation that follows, I learn that this troubled man is determined to get to Jewel at a show that summer and propose marriage. If she refuses, he threatens to take the two of them, violently, into the beyond. The details of the situation match my dream precisely. We begin a coordinated effort involving our team and authorities in each town Jewel visits on tour and eventually the man is confronted, the situation resolved, and the danger averted.

This is the first time Jewel and I fully experience the feeling of threat that can attend celebrity. I am certainly grateful that I received such a powerful warning in the dream, but I am not fully comforted by it. This is one of the areas where it is not easy to be an artist's manager and mother simultaneously. I feel a grave responsibility to be constantly aware; to always be able to sense what is going on. What if I miss a beat, am out of "tune," don't get the warning? How, I wonder, can we be safe in this strange new world of celebrity?

I feel frightened. The world wavers uncertainly before me. One afternoon I walk in my garden, pondering the question of safety. The melodious water and bird songs, the radiance of the flowers, the gentleness of the breeze are in sharp contrast to my febrile thoughts.

"Where is the peace in this? How are we safe?" I wonder. "How can I always know what needs to be known?"

Gradually, as always happens, the nature surrounding me begins to lull me into the stillness where all is known. My breath pulls deeply and evenly in and out of me. The questions lose the agitation and float abstractly, quietly, a little distance from me. I walk for a time in this inner silence.

Suddenly, as though at a command, I stop short and look up. Three feet away, illuminated by a wide shaft of afternoon sun, is a very large spider in the center of an enormous web. My approach causes a barely perceivable tremor along the threads. Instantly the spider leaves the center and, waiting at the edge, is poised to flee into the leaves and grasses beyond.

"How does it know? How is it that sensitive to everything that happens around it?" I wonder.

Then comes the reply. The web is that sensitive. Not the spider. The spider needs only to be aware of the web. The web of life reveals all motion.

Another question comes to my mind, "If the spider leaves the center, leaves the web, then how does it know? How do I always stay in that center of knowing?"

Again comes an answer. You cannot move out of your center. It is not possible — it moves with you. You only lose awareness of it. The task is to bring your awareness back to it. You are always in the center of your Being.

A VAST UNIVERSE OF WISDOM

There is so much to access beyond our individual minds, a vast universe of wisdom that is our birthright. It only requires silence, commitment, and practice. It allows the development of an ability to intuit a more universal wisdom that helps us be more secure in our humanity. This intuition is a connection to that which is far more vast, even divine, within us. Developing a higher intuition involves accessing the wisdom of the Soul — becoming responsive to our souls. When one accesses the soul, what comes forth is pure knowingness.

Forging this connection is a simple matter, really. Begin to identify with your soul. Realize you have one, you are one. You are a soul expressing through a physical form. You are not the physical form; it is merely your tool for expression. Honor your soul. Know it is eternal: you existed as a soul before you took physical form; you will do so after you lay your body down for the last time. Feel gratitude and love for its presence, its constant guidance in your life.

Know that your soul is connected to the Source of all that is. It is directly connected. Take moments to quiet yourself, ask for your soul's voice to speak to you, learn to hear it, practice translating its wisdom in your life; you will always know your soul's voice by its quality of peace. Doing this, you will inevitably strengthen your connection with your soul and the Source. You only need to ask, simply ask, no specific rules, no "right" method, prayer, or ritual is necessary. It is a simple matter of consistent application. Forget about the outcome; forget about how long it will take or whether you will be good enough to do it; forget about whether you are doing it right. These are all issues of the personality, the ego; they have no bearing on the soul. With persistence over time the result is assured. You will become familiar with the realm of Being.

THE OCEAN OF BEING

There is an ocean of Being. We are bathed in it. There is nothing that is not in it. It is all things and connects us to all things. It is the pure source of all that is. It is that in which we move and breathe and have our Being. It is the essence of our Being. We can touch, intuit, express, and come to know this seemingly intangible world. In nature it shows itself to us. In the silence it speaks to us. In our life it is made visible.

We live in the world of action that exists within this vast ocean of Being, that envelops all things, permeates all things. This beingness creates and quickens all things. To know its depths is to know our source, the God of all things. It is a limitless ocean, at the depth of which is a still, silent, and unchanging place. Above is the active, ever-changing surface-world of action.

We wonder where the peace is but we are immersed in it. We are like fish swimming in water but thirsting to drink! We long for peace, harmony, rest, abundance; but the distance between us and what we long for is so short that there isn't even room for a path! We feel separate from our Being but we are not. We cannot be, it is not possible. Separateness is in our perception only. As we correct our perceptions and as we journey in silence to visit the depths of Being, we come to know the core of our soul. From this place we can have revealed, in our hearts, the purpose and the destiny of our humanity. In the stillness we come to know that we are each capable of being the love, being the abundance. We can be the peace that we long for.

Lenedra J Carroll

5

Be Peace

I t is my afternoon period of meditation and retreat and I am seated quietly in my sanctuary. On my simple altar a candle burns. The room is filled with the smell of fresh flowers and subtle incense. I am in prayer and meditation about my desire for peace in the world, expressing my hopes, my willingness to participate, asking what I can do to further this aim. Suddenly my perspective shifts, a vision opens before me. I see our world as though from outer space. I feel its life and all life upon it, and my heart fills with a love and awe for that life.

At the same time that I see this broad view, I also seem to see the microcosm. I am shown the millions of people on this planet that are praying for peace. I feel their lives; I know the sincerity of their prayers, the deep longing of their hearts. I have an experience of knowing all those prayers, feeling them, and it is beautiful. My heart swells with excitement at the numbers — there are so many earnestly praying! I become elated and overly excited by what I see and find myself, suddenly, back in my room, thrilled by what I have witnessed. It seems to me that peace must be inevitable if so many millions of hearts yearn for it, pray for it, for I know prayer to be a powerful force.

At this point I am interrupted by the gentle voice of the Indwelling Christ that seems to resonate in the marrow of my bones.

"The prayers for peace are wondrous indeed," the voice says, "and necessary and good they are. But if the prayers were enough there would have been peace upon this planet long ago."

Shocked silence ripples through me, penetrating every atom of my body. A hush falls like dew around me. Time extends without even a heartbeat or breath. Then a wind rises up through me, filling my belly, my lungs, my throat, and my head to bursting.

I cry out, "What is enough?! What will bring about the change we so much desire? How will we ever live in peace?"

The beautiful voice speaks in answer.

"Be peace."

A penetrating love begins a soft pulse through my veins and a bottomless peace engulfs my entire being as though I am held in the very arms of God. Tears drip from my chin, covering my blouse. Information of a wordless nature fills me.

In that moment, I come to know it is the action of peace in every individual life that is the missing part. I understand the vital difference between wanting, praying, or even working for peace, and *being* peace. And, I come to know it is possible to be peace.

Be peace. The wisdom, the necessity, the potential of it fills my chest cavity, expanding in my mind until it transforms all thought. "How?" I wonder. "How can one be peace?"

In answer comes the words, "My peace be with you. My peace be unto you."

I am stunned, then, by the realization that the peace has been within me all along.

Disoriented, I look around me; night has come and the candle guttered out without my notice. I am aware only of a deep gratitude and a profound peace as I sit in the circumambient azure glow that lingers in the darkened room.

IT IS TIME FOR PEACE

In the days that followed this vision, in 1992, I realized that our current perception is that an abiding peace is not really attainable by the average person. This is largely because we have been taught that though we may futilely strive for personal peace, such perfection is beyond our grasp. Peace, we seem to think, is not possible in an active, everyday world.

So we have for the most part delegated the task of peaceful living to good behavior on Sunday mornings, or we leave it entirely to our great spiritual leaders or religious orders living secluded from the world. As a result, our individual lives remain full of fear, anxiety, tension, stress, argument, and disharmony. Our interactions on even the smallest level are very often not peaceful: our mindless but potent anger at another driver on the road, the dueling egos of family members or neighbors, petty gossip about a coworker. This results in the turmoil that creates a world of individuals living in disharmony with each other and all their resources.

When the voice of my vision spoke to me, "Be peace," I knew, then, that it is absolutely possible for me and for every one of us to be peace in our lives, and it is vital to our survival as a species.

With the addition of, "My peace be with you," I realized that peace already existed. It was there, gifted, all around me. I didn't have to try to find it — it dwelt in the stillness within and surrounding me; I needed to learn to access it and to express it.

> Peace is not a relationship of nations. It is a condition of mind brought about by a serenity of soul. Lasting peace can come only to peaceful people.
>
> — Jawaharlal Nehru

PEACE THAT SURPASSES UNDERSTANDING

I made a covenant, in that dim room that evening. It was a covenant between my Soul and that which I know to be God. I do not enter into covenant lightly for it is a sacred and powerful commitment; one I make prayerfully and ceremonially. I covenanted to focus my consciousness and my discipline toward becoming a personification of peace. This propelled me into an exploration of learning to access peace and seeing how a human being could become a pure expression of it in both thought and action. To date, it has been a wonderful and fruitful journey full of surprises and questions, challenges and victories; and one of profound changes in how I relate to myself, to others, with my world, and with my God. There is a peace that surpasses understanding, and it is available to us all.

The opportunity of our times is for each one of us to understand, at a very personal level, that we can have a profound impact on the world in which we live. The greatest possibilities for global transformation exist in the fabric of our individual lives. If we can learn to become our prayers and hopes, expressing them in our daily interactions, then together we can create a more peaceful and loving world.

This vision, and my commitment, changed the very fabric of my life. Every interaction is now an opportunity for transformation — for me as well as my immediate world. I no longer move mindlessly into potentially difficult situations. I bring, instead, a mindfulness and willingness to see what else can be done; I realize I have choice. Since I am the one who dreamed the situation, what does it show me about me? What can I master within myself? How can the process with another be elevated for better results?

Every day we face the choice repeatedly. Will we succumb to road rage or will we require ourselves to notice our strong response and reroute it with a prayer, or deep breaths, or self-compassion? Will we call the difficult sales clerk an idiot or will we exhibit clarity and grace while dealing with him or her? Will we always cling adamantly and fearfully to our own views or will we allow differing opinions and methods to cohabitate with our own? These are the mundane but vital moments where we can choose to pioneer peace into our lives.

PEACEFUL MEANS

For example, there was a woman who held a place of trust in my business. We spent a great deal of time together and she was aware of many details of my business and personal life. She had access to my accounts and sensitive private information. It was a position that required great mutual trust and cooperation. All was well until the woman entered a time of crises and stress in her personal life. In response to her crises, she began to act out certain unhealthy coping behaviors at work that resulted in anxious and, primarily, unconscious misuse of resources at her disposal.

My team noticed that accounts were not balancing and items were being purchased that were not in our inventory. Merchandise was disappearing and petty cash was unaccounted for. We made some changes in our system and her supervision in an attempt to correct matters, but the behavior continued. It was behavior that not only violated her work agreement, but also was legally actionable. In most cases she would have been fired immediately with threat of legal action.

Instead, my team first entered into a period of fact-finding to fully grasp the situation. In this process we discovered that she had falsified her previous experience, covering up a similar situation in a previous employment. When we were sure of the extent of the offense, I met with two of my executive officers to decide our action. We were deeply contemplative together, feeling a genuine concern for this woman as well as the responsibility to our business — the two things were not at odds. We looked at the immediate and big picture, the holistic aspects, and agreed to review how we had helped to create the situation. We discussed how to proceed, looking for methods and timing that would create the least ripples out into our system with the greatest growth for the woman involved.

We agreed it would likely be necessary to terminate her employment but I felt strongly about waiting until we were certain of the moment. This was to allow Spirit a hand in the action: the preparation of the woman for changes in her life and clarifications on our part about what our legal procedure required. We waited until we knew it was the right moment to interact. It was nearly three months before we fired her. During that waiting period, we tightened the system, making it difficult to take advantage; we also gave her further warnings and training and made her aware of our scrutiny of the accounts. The misuse continued, though to a far lesser degree, but the changes and restrictions caused her to feel irritated and she began to grumble and gossip to others about her dissatisfactions. She said many things that were not true in an attempt to gain sympathy with other team members and people in the industry outside of our company. I knew, however, that I have a company strongly committed to more elevated behaviors; the gossip was seen for what it was. I was also secure in my company's reputation in the business; it was sad that she was damaging herself in this way.

I remained even with her in my interactions and thoughts and asked my team to do the same. I felt calm, and certain that I would take the right action at the right moment. I counseled those involved on my management team to maintain a loving, even, and nonjudgmental stance toward the woman. I asked that we not move into typical behaviors such as case building, acting outraged and betrayed, vilifying her to each other or coworkers, or determining to "teach her a lesson." This was not easy for those close to the situation who felt protective of Jewel and me, but it was an important exercise for us all.

TAKING ACTION

When I felt it was timely, I met again with my chief executives for a period of quiet contemplation. During this meeting we assessed all the information, reviewed our legal requirements under the state labor laws, as well as discussed the needs of the company and the soul of the woman.

We set up a meeting with the woman, beginning with a fifteen-minute period of silence together. We presented her with the evidence we had gathered and our view of her situation and our position. While we made it clear that we were terminating her, we offered her choices about the method. She was tearful, frightened, and regretful. We were not accusative or shaming though we took a firm line, speaking very frankly to the problem but in a way that allowed dignity, compassion, and self-assessment. We did not vilify or humiliate her. The meeting was short, but powerful in its ability to effect change.

With a swelling roster of employees, we experience numerous difficult situations; we keep internal discussion of such matters to a minimum. Gossip, backbiting, and judgmental means are prevalent in most companies; these create a great deal of spin in the environment that enormously decreases the creativity, productivity, and satisfaction at the workplace. While we find it necessary to assess and discern situations, we draw a distinction between discernment and being judgmental.

We try to handle each circumstance with comprehensive preparation in silence, and with evenness, compassion, and attention to human dignity. The company and the individual are both served in this way. These methods greatly decrease the stress for all involved, cause the least disturbance in the company, and create the most likely environment for change.

We attempt to hire employees interested in and willing to elevate their methods and interactions in the workplace. This integration of our highest-held values into our actions is where our evolution must take us for our health, happiness, and survival. Taking time to center in the stillness of our Being, we access resources greater than our common tendencies and abilities; it then becomes possible to operate in more elevated ways.

STILLPOINT

Still your self.
Shhh. Grow still.
Hear the silence.
In the quiet
know God.

Lenedra J. Carroll

6

Natural Systems

ithin the world of nature, there are observable rhythms — the order, laws, methods, and the Being that govern all life, including humankind. We can be unaware of them, misunderstand them, or ignore them. However, we can only pretend to act outside of them. In spite of flagrant denial, we are subject to them. We live in a great natural system; conciliation with these forces is necessary to our survival — individually and as a group.

In this natural system everything waxes and wanes, ebbs and flows, advances and retreats. Following that example, understanding that necessity, I am committed to establishing this rhythm in each hour, day, month, and year — in my businesses, my relationships, my home. It is an ongoing commitment, not easy to keep. But it is growing easier as more and more often the fruit of silence is the first hunger of my soul.

For this reason, several times a year I seek solitude in retreat. In this space I can be taught; I can observe the ways of nature, which are my nature. There I can more easily relinquish old ways and I can affirm my place and purpose in the balance of life. Immured in silence, free of distraction, I can commune most freely and fully with my own soul and the Soul of all that is. I retreat into this natural world to rest and recuperate physically, to renew my enthusiasm for life and my covenant with my Soul. At least once a year I require a lengthy period of silence. This has been a vital habit in my life.

~ JOURNAL: THREE WEEKS IN SEPTEMBER 1999 ~

Breaking Free

It's two years since I have been able to manage more than four days of uninterrupted silence. The requirements of artist management, business development, and my personal life set a fast and often rigid pace. I am deeply fatigued and have a growing listlessness; I am ill more often. I feel worn, easily irritated, and almost desperate to get away.

The demands of a growing company make this very difficult but my team has worked hard to reach the point that allows me to step back. We have managed to carve time for me to have three weeks of silence. Their challenge is to get along without me entirely; my challenge is to let them.

I feel called from the depth of myself to learn even more how to bring the silence into all my actions. I sense a breakthrough is possible for me. I have become adept at moving from silence to action, action to silence — back and forth in a comfortable rhythm — but I have begun to sense that I can now learn to stay in the silence in all that I am — my work, my play, under stress, in everything. I hunger to explore this and it is my goal as I arrive at this small country retreat, a health and cleansing center in the rural Midwest, called the Raj.

The Lake at Noon

"You have a lovely room overlooking the lake," they told me on my first day, but the lake is really a pond set in the huge lawn behind the health center. After lunch today I dash out to circumnavigate the lake a couple of times to aid in digesting my simple meal. The fall lawn is dry and tough under my bare feet. The top of my head grows warm in the sun and my hair, fresh from the shower that follows my spa treatment, gently begins to blow dry in the constant but gentle breeze. A swan circles the pond. I gather its feathers as I walk along the shore. Each day I find six or so good ones loosened during preening. My altar in my small room is afroth with my collection.

The pond is set about a foot down into the lawn and is ringed by a narrow mud beach, which I step down onto. The mud is thick between my toes, and cool. My feet make slurping noises as I walk along. The part of me that would prefer not to be messy admonishes me faintly but is soon overwhelmed by the unctuousness of it. Hundreds of little pieces of mud burst alive in flying hops ahead of me as I move forward. They are the many teeny tiny frogs that bask at the water's edge. The size of pennies and the color of earth, they are very difficult to see when still.

Today, a larger frog startles me by flying off the bank, shooting across in front of me into the water with a big ploink. The frog is out of sight in the opaque water. I sit down immediately on the bank, waiting to satisfy my curiosity about how long frogs can stay underwater. Four minutes later it surfaces near my feet and skittles off far behind me in the shallows.

I know where a gigantesque old frog spends his days in the sun. He has requisitioned a fish hole and sits, stoic, over-lording, half immersed in water. When I disturb him today, he jumps far out into the water. I wait to see if he stays under as long as the other frog. Four minutes pass and four more before I catch him at his breathing trick — off to my right, frog lips break the surface of the water, suck air, and disappear, creating barely discernible ripples. He's crafty, which must account for how he has lived to such a grand ol' age.

A favorite part of pond walking is the many little butterflies that prefer the moist earth by the water. They light and bask in the sun in groupings of a dozen or so. Maybe they nibble the wet earth. Why do they swarm along here? Mostly they are yellow but some are white, and there are others that are a lovely pale violet. Sometimes they land on me. Above, on the bank, are larger butterflies in orange and brown — monarchs. There are also mini-dragonflies in vibrant neon blue-violet, darting about in their omnidirectional manner. Dragonflies and butterflies remain favorites: they seem magical, and often mark times of spiritual transition in my life, times like these three weeks.

Here at the pond, walking through hundreds of hopping frog-gies, swirling bitsy butterflies, and teensy dragonflies, I am giddy with the pulse, the Being, of life. All of nature is so glorifying of that One in whom we live and share our Being. In all of life it seems that only humanity separates itself from that quiet glorification.

But I have paused too long counting frog breaths and I am late for my sound therapy so I hurry, guilty, like a child late from recess. I wash my feet in the hose I have discovered at the side of the build-ing, and rush to my room with the swan feather bouquet I have gathered. Placing my earphones on my head, I dial the number for the sounds and settle back on the bed to the murmur of men from India chanting syllables in Sanskrit that are chosen for their healing and cleansing effect. My feet are still wet and swan feathers cover my belly.

The Lake at Dawn

Things are taking on faces. As I bundle up in my room for the chill morning walk, I could swear that the rose on my altar has a face. It captures me with its grace and the subtle sound of its vivid color. Fresh from the deep silence that informs my meditations here, this rose seems to sing to me. And its song moves me to tears that catch at my breath and drip onto my sweatpants as I pull my legs into them. I wipe my face on my shirt as I pull it on, and head out to herald the day.

I don't have much interest in the pond at dawn today. I want to rush headlong into the woods. I take the high road first; it affords a view of the sunrise. The dew is so cold on my bare feet that my legs ache already. My breath puffs out in front of me. Fall is such exul-tation. Moving toward the sun, I flush a pheasant. I grin and gather the little swirl of feathers he leaves in his hurry. I'm hurrying too.

The sky is now palest rose. I want to get down the hill, through the blue wildflowers, and up on the other side of the meadow because there is a wonder there, if I am in time to witness the first sun rays as they hit the slope.

It is the spider fields! On the distant hillcrest, from the intensely pink point where the sun is now rising, beams of light spin out and illuminate the dew that clings to *hundreds* of huge circular spider webs that are attached to the grasses on the incline of both sides of the path. Everywhere there are glittering webs of bright shining glory that dance and sparkle on the morning breeze. In the center of each one is a very large spider, broad belly to the sun! What a sight! I will miss it when I leave. I will remember it. I laugh aloud and stamp out a little dance on the path.

I have been too noisy and I hear the deer flee; they were grazing tentatively nearby. Never mind, I will have another chance to sneak up on them on the low road that leaves the fields and goes deeper into the woods. The owl is there too. The one that I saw my first night here, in a dream. "He is wise who sees action in inaction and inaction in action," the dream voice had said.

On my walk the next morning the owl rose — as it had in my dream — from a huge hollow stump that, though dead, had a young sapling springing from it. I came up out of the dim morning woods and paused, breathless and squinting, before heading across the bright clearing. We startled one another and my soul seemed to go aloft with it as it lifted up into the morning light.

I have learned this in my time here: in the depth of Being is the still point that ripens the fruit of action with its inaction, its stillness. When anchored in it, one can be both still and active — productive from that place. The stillness informs and integrates all, even creating all action. Without the stillness we move into action prematurely, ineffectively, and with much higher cost of our resources.

> The world is not to be put to order; the world is order
> incarnate. It is for us to harmonize with this order.
> — Henry Miller

Days 11, 12, New York City

The only way I could get three weeks away was to interrupt it with a two-day business trip. It gives me a chance to see how the peace can be deeply retained in the whirl of management. So I'm up at 4:30 A.M. to catch a small five-seat airplane, heading for a connecting flight to New York. Jewel is taping a Christmas special for PBS and I'm joining her to handle management details. On this trip I will also sing with Jewel in her TV performance — several songs that I perform with her on the Christmas album.

From the silence of my retreat I reenter the maelstrom that is my life. The day grows long with meetings that are back-to-back without break. I interface with the record label regarding her Christmas album release and with the publishing company about holiday promotion of her poetry book, *A Night Without Armor.* I work out a dispute over song credits with a manager and artist, then meet with the editor of *Vogue* magazine. After these, phone calls about legal matters and contracts, the unrelenting challenge of setting schedules, and many faxes and e-mails cram the day.

By evening we are in a flurry of hair, makeup, and wardrobe and then we are ushered into the soundstage for the taping. Jewel stands at her microphone and I am seated in the front of the audience. She is somewhat unfamiliar with the song arrangements, having done only a few takes of each when recording the album some months earlier. This is her first performance of them. The verses of the holiday music roll in front of her on the monitor. It is certainly not her preferred way to perform, but all goes well. When I join her to sing I feel the deep calm of my time in retreat blended in the tones of my voice.

At midnight, Jewel and I are going over a list of decisions that require her input. That is followed, for me, by a meeting with Ron Shapiro, executive vice president and general manager of Atlantic Records. We grind through the myriad details that precede the press tour and release of her holiday album, *Joy.* By 2:30 A.M. I am finally in bed only to be in a car two-and-a-half hours later headed for the airport. Yet throughout the entire period I feel the humming in my cells, the humming of silence sustaining my energy and interactions; I am elated at seeing what I have learned to hold. And I'm so glad to be able to retreat again and move even deeper into the undiluted Spirit in nature and to integrate stillness more and more into my process.

Eleven Days: The Lake When I'm Gone

I find that the swan, each time I squat down and dip my head to the ground and then stand, will mirror me by dipping its head to the water, drinking and then extending its lengthy neck, bill stretched to the sky. I spend a lot of hours watching it and I'm getting a feel for swanness. It's just fine to be a swan, I'd say. What odd noises it makes, less bird than mammal. It growls, for instance, and it rumbles. I'm particularly happy with how fastidious it is because each time it preens, I get another fistful of feathers. I collect them a couple of times a day and it's fun to see what sizes I'll get. They are quite small with a fair share of four-inchers, some six, and occasionally a little over that. I'm hoping for a couple of long ones before I go, but it's not the time of year when a swan wants to part with tail or wing feathers.

At night there is something that glows in the mud around the edge of the pond. These very small beads of phosphorescence, like single eyes, scatter along the shore. They wax and wane like breath, on the bank, blinking on and off. From my perch I poke them with a twig but they don't move. I've puzzled long moments during the day, trying to see what it is that glows at night, but I'm still wondering. I like to sit on the edge with my feet in the mud whenever I don't feel too well from the cleansing routine I'm here for. The cool clay pulls all the aches right out of me. There are lots of critter tracks at the water's edge. Raccoon. Possum? Definitely deer. And muskrat.

I walk at sunset each day. Nearly three weeks have passed, and the moon is almost full. Now I stand between the rising moon and the setting sun, watching the moon grow less faded as the sky turns red. The sun sinks, transferring its light to the moon, which grows more yellow and distinct. The wisps of cloud that edge it reflect the pink in the sky. The tree I stand under becomes a butterfly tree — it is full of monarch butterflies. So here I am looking back and forth between the dipping sun and the full moon with hundreds of orange-winged monarchs swirling around me. The air is an incandescent realm of flame. Deep, shining joy.

Full moon early this morning. I'm up at 3:30 A.M., taking my bundle from the altar. Swan feathers swirl to the floor. I go out into the moonlit morning. The stars are dim because the moon is so bright. With blanket and pillow I make my way up the hill toward the butterfly tree in the cold dark. The sibilant wind can't pierce me as I sit wrapped to my nose in bedding. I light a candle and enter into ceremony to renew my covenant with the Divine. The wind talks in the leaves, light floods me, the love of pure Being streams down my face. I am that I am. I sleep a few hours until dawn under the fading radiance of moon and stars.

Early evening I take a last turn around the lake. After a time I notice that the swan is persistently swimming back and forth between me and a spot on the far shore. Puzzled, I circle back to the place where the swan waits and find there a delightful gift! Three full-length swan feathers, white and perfect, are tucked into a crevice. I bow to the swan and it dips its head to the water then glides away. I say a prayer of thanks to all the inhabitants of this place — the animals, the wind and sun, the forest and field spirits, all that exult here. With my prayer I express my heartfelt gratitude for the gifts received and I affirm my commitment to stewardship of the earth by leaving an offering of cornmeal and a macaw feather given to me on a recent visit with indigenous peoples in the Amazon region of Peru.

In my weeks here, fall has grown more persistent. The tiny dragonflies are gone, most of the little yellow butterflies, too, and there aren't many of the penny frogs that hop ahead of me in the mud. The leaves are turning; the insistent wind carries them away nearly as soon as they change color. It seems I'm leaving with everything else. My room is emptied into my bags, except for the carnation and the rose, in their vase on my altar. They have lasted noticeably long.

I recall the question posed by philosophers: Does a tree falling in the forest make a sound if no one is there to hear it? Man has such a winsome and youthful arrogance. The question, really, is without bearing: for the pond and the woods, in all their distilled rapture, will continue their muffled witness, unceasingly, when I am gone.

Into the Fray

The next morning I leave for an international conference where I am to speak and sing. Five hundred world leaders have come together to exchange ideas and resources. The press of agendas and networking is furious. The variety of events, of thoughts, cultures, and needs is not possible to assimilate. The demands for my attention and resources are overwhelming. Hotel food is a challenge after the simple fare of my cleanse. The din and roar of the conference rise over the three days. It is a good experience but it is far from the cry of the silence of the pond and forest. I am literally reeling in my attempt to make the transition, to hold my awareness of the quiet core. I do not want to shift out of the still point; I want to walk through this world marketplace in the peace I know is possible.

I develop vertigo as my body is suddenly bombarded with stimuli; it is a struggle even to stand. I wonder how I will speak and, especially, how I will sing from the place of spirit as I have been invited here to do. I gather all my resources to reconcile the action with the inaction, to find the stillness in all of this. I succeed in part and, helped onto the stage, I stand with only a slight waver, speak briefly, and sing. In the song, as I move into Spirit, I come closer to the alignment I desire. Music, like prayer and stillness, is a swift vehicle into Being.

After two days at home I am still wobbly and dizzy, though greatly improved. I glimpse the potential and the process. Now I must leave for New York, where I join Jewel at Net Aid (Netaid.org) — a global multimedia humanitarian event — to debut our humanitarian endeavor, Clearwater Project. The travel is a challenge as I stagger my way through airports and hotels.

As I struggle to find what brings the balance, however, I realize what has occurred: On my retreat I achieved still point at a profound level. This stop-action in myself is what I desired to achieve and to hold. By comparison, the active world seems to be spinning wildly. Slowly I see that it is not necessary to rev up to match the outer world pace. The speed and spinning are perception — more like an illusion or mirage. I will myself to completely comprehend. I experiment with time, space, and movement to find an internal pace that allows me to be deeply grounded and still as I rush about in limousines, meet celebrities, talk with the record company, production people, and the press.

Standing backstage, the energy and sound of seventy thousand people greets the performers in a great roar. The music begins to pulse deafeningly from the speakers near me. For some reason, in this unlikely moment, my careening world rights itself, mutes, elevates. All the layers focus and peace becomes the fabric that my existence filters through. I know a rock-solid pervading calm, and I know that when I lose it I can find my way back as I continue in the practice of stabilizing and fully integrating it into my daily life.

ACCESSING STILL POINT

Time spent in nature, in silence, prayer, meditation, or entranced by music, poetry, yoga, even exercise, or the many other things that take us into and beyond our individual selves gives us familiarity with the stillness that is a necessary element of life. That still point is not accessed only in full retreat, however. It can be accessed in every moment — during feelings of fear or anger, under duress, in chaos and calamity. We can drop out of the rush and the staggering pace, the smothering lack of time, by accessing and remembering the still place that is the true center of our movement in the world. Constantly reminding ourselves to slow, to breathe, to pause, to pace, breaking the circuit by adding space. This shifts us into a far more manageable dimension. It is a dimension immeasurably more provident and rewarding, and one where far, far more, not less, is accomplished.

SURRENDER

How to break the barriers of your confinement?
   Race
to your banquet, famished.
   Devour
all the life laid out for you.
   Plunge
headlong into your deep
            falling upon yourself
            laughing in the face of your folly.
   Throw
open all the doors
let them bang in the wind
that gushes in and sucks out
the whole of your truth.
   Rush
your heights
   Storm
your valleys
            overtaking those impotent fears
            and clamor of cynic voices.
   Bust
into the breadth of your own truth
   Seize
your divine birthright and run
with the madness of the saints
            Abandon reason
            Loosen intellect
surrender
surrender
surrender
            It is far
            more simple
            than it seems.

Lenedra J Carroll

THE
Architecture
OF
Prosperity

I LIVE A GRACIOUS AND ABUNDANT LIFE FILLED WITH THE
FINANCIAL RESOURCES AND POSSESSIONS THAT MOST PEOPLE
YEARN FOR. HOWEVER, I DID NOT ACHIEVE THIS LIFE BY
YEARNING AFTER THOSE THINGS. THE FINANCES AND THE
POSSESSIONS ARE, TO ME, MERELY THE TRAPPINGS OF THE LIFE I
DREAMED OF. FOR I LONGED TO DEEPLY KNOW AND BE IN
HARMONY WITH THE LAWS OF DIVINE PROVIDENCE. WE LIVE
IN A VAST AND SUPREMELY RESPONSIVE UNIVERSE. WITHIN THIS
GREAT BEING, HELD IN DIVINE PROVIDENCE, WE ARE INFINITELY
PROSPEROUS.

7

Lilies OF THE Field

And why take ye thought for raiment? Consider the lilies of the field, how they grow; they toil not, neither do they spin; and yet I say unto you, that even Solomon in all his glory was not arrayed like one of these.

Wherefore, if God so clothes the grass of the field — which today is, and tomorrow is cast into the oven — shall he not much more clothe you, O ye of little faith?

Therefore take no thought, saying, "What shall we eat?" or, "What shall we drink?" or, "Wherewithal shall we be clothed?" for the God of your Being knoweth that ye have need of all these things.

Seek them not, nor be of doubtful mind but rather seek ye first the kingdom of your God, and in his righteousness all of these things shall be added unto you, for it is God's good pleasure to give you the kingdom.

— Matthew 6:28–33; Luke 12:27–31

ANTIDOTE TO GREED

We wake in the morning feeling we didn't get enough sleep, hurry through our day without taking sufficient nourishment, we feel we lack time for our friends, children, obligations, for ourselves. Often we feel insufficiently loved. We think we lack enough money for our dreams. Frequently we feel we don't have enough energy or health for our day. Rest, nourishment, time, love, money, energy, health; these are often deficit in our lives. Insufficiency, lack — isn't there ever enough?

We live in an economy of lack and, feeling so much lacking in our lives, we strain to have more; we cling to what we have, trying to hoard some measure of resources to create a stockpile. We have been taught that this is natural and even wise but this is, in fact, *the economy of greed* at work in each of our lives. The truth is that there is more than enough of everything. There is sufficient for all our requirements and dreams. We are unable to see it, to know it, but providence is there. We suffer a peculiar blindness that is robbing us individually of a satisfying quality of life, one that includes ease and abundance. As a group it is devouring our world's resources in a way that cannot be sustained. What could cause us to have such a fatal blindness? What is the antidote to greed? It is knowing that all we require is already before us; we simply don't see it.

In Lawrence Blair's book *Rhythms of Vision: The Changing Patterns of Belief,* he refers to an accounting of Magellan's first landing at Tierra del Fuego. The explorers were met by the Fuegans, people isolated for centuries by their canoe culture. Though the large hulking ships were in full view in the harbor, the Fuegans were not able to see them. Such ships were so far beyond their experience as to actually be invisible to them. According to another account, it wasn't until the shaman — realizing that the newcomers had arrived in *something* — pondered and divined the matter until he was at last able to see the ship. The shaman then brought it to the attention of the villagers that "the strangers had arrived in something, something which, although preposterous beyond belief, could actually be seen if one looked very carefully." With gestures, drawings, and words he patiently described the ship in the bay again and again until the entire tribe could see it.

The Fuegans, lacking experience, familiarity, or history of ships had no frame of reference — no context — to see the sailing vessels anchored before their eyes. Until they could understand it

— have it discovered and then interpreted to them by their shaman — they were not able to conceive it visually. We are no different than they. The story speaks to how human beings create and discover their worlds.

There is so much we don't see or know. We can assume, in fact, that our known and agreed-upon world is only the tip of a reality that we barely grasp. Similar to the Fuegan people, we have a blind spot. We lack knowledge of providence, an understanding of nature and the earth that provides for us, and experience of our assured place in the abundant natural flow. This knowledge is not passed on to us and we do not pass it on to our children. Instead, we believe we must work hard for our gains, and guard over them to keep them. This is a great falsehood, a misconception that takes an extreme toll and places us in an economy of greed. This subtle greed permeates each single life as surely as it permeates our corporate, political, and social cultures. There is a solution; it requires commitment and courage; it requires that we forge beyond our comfortable little realities and out into the unknown, the unseen world. Doing this, we become the antidote for greed.

WHAT IS NEEDED NOW?

I'm very ill. Tremendous stress, poor diet, old emotional baggage, and genetics have combined, putting my health in serious jeopardy. My cholesterol is excessively high and, though I am only forty, I have angina and apparently some damage to my heart muscle. The medications are not effective and the surgical recommendations seem very poor options at best. I am told that I must curtail my activities from now on. I have never been so ill that I cannot work, but now I have to make a decision to close my gallery. I'm surviving only with the help of friends and family and by selling all my possessions. Now at the end of those resources, I'm frightened. "How will I manage to take care of my children, pay the bills, afford health care?"

I pray and meditate about how to proceed and always the answer I hear is the same, "Pray for what you need now." I am! For weeks I have been praying clearly and strongly for my needs — the money for food, my car payment, rent, medical help. Weeks of prayer, but nothing changes. There is little food left for my children, the car payment is due next week, my rent in two weeks.

My voice is hoarse with tension and exigency as I go once more into my morning supplications. The answer comes again, clearly and calmly, the same: "Dear one, pray for what you need now."

"I am!" I squeak dismally.

Again, "Pray for what you need now."

"*I am! I have been!*" At this point my frustrations and fears culminate. I feel like shrieking at God. I quiet myself. I stop to fully experience my feelings — I have a crushing sense of responsibility for my children and my debts. I feel trapped without options. I fear I am abandoned and alone in the universe, afraid there is no help out there. Am I dying? Will I be okay? I breathe raggedly, allowing myself to be aware of the extent of these feelings. As I settle into them, owning myself as I am at this moment, the voice of my prayers urges me again, "Pray for what you need now."

"I must be missing the point," I say after contemplation. "I think I have been doing this. What am I missing, overlooking, not getting? I've been praying for next month's rent, for my car payment, due in just two weeks..." I begin to feel desperate again.

"Shhh. Still yourself....Listen. Pray for what you need. Now."

"But I am." I pause. "I need my rent for next month, my car payment."

"Now."

"What? I..."

"Now."

I pause. Now. "You mean, now. Right this very *now* while we are talking?"

"Yes. In this now."

"This very minute only?"

"Yes."

"Well, I don't *need* anything right now, this very minute."

"Indeed."

A silence opens up. I fall headlong into it. A rush of understanding floods my being. I have the extraordinary sensation of having no need, being absolutely free of need. Throwing my head back I laugh aloud at the simplicity of it. My chest expands with the breath of it. My heart pumps fully with the ease of it. The moment expands and I weep at this freedom from crushing need. "How can I always feel so free?" I wonder.

"Add up all the moments you have no need. You will see that the moments in which you are free of need far outweigh the others."

The illumination begins to dawn across my mind more fully; it pours into my cells, informs my thoughts. I wait, open, receiving. It moves with my breath into my core. I see my need, I see my no-need. The times that I have absolutely no need are far greater. An enormous wave of gratitude engulfs me. Space begins to fill me — a rushing incoming tide of fullness, of providence.

As I integrate this understanding, another follows, "Examine what you have asked for."

Quickly I review: money for rent, money for food, money for the car payment.

"You have set the requirement of money. Do not limit how the Source will express this to you. Hold your requirements more lightly. Know they already exist for you. You live within a divinely provident universe. Speak your requirements softly and certainly, knowing they are already there for you. Simply call them forth, each in their own time. No sooner is required. All is in order for you, in this you may have certainty. Call forth your rightful requirements from the gratitude of this certainty."

Over the next three weeks I discipline myself to fully integrate this new understanding. I spend time in nature so I can observe undiluted providence in action, in pure expression. My requirements begin to be met in ways that are very humbling. At the post office, a stranger asks if I will consider trading my truck for his great little car and suddenly — no car payments! Neighborhood gardeners begin supplying me with an overflow of fresh food. The city tourism office inquires if we would like to rent rooms in the historic house we live in; this revenue begins to cover the house payment each month. A dear friend asks me to accompany her on a joint health quest at her expense and I begin to discover exciting new information and treatments for my health. I feel I am glimpsing the prosperity of an orderly and abundant universe.

Abundance can be had simply by consciously receiving what already has been given.

— Sufi saying

LIVING ON THE WIND

The period of my life encompassing the previous story was the inception of my journey into Divine Providence. As my health improved, I began to meditate about my next step regarding work. I assumed that I would put together a résumé and move into a new chapter of work. In my contemplation, however, a repeating injunction revolved in my thoughts: "Live on the wind." It was a mystery to me. There was certainly poetry in the intriguing phrase as well as a delicious hint of freedom, but I didn't have a clue what it meant. I mulled it over frequently, feeling that the root of its meaning lay in the passions of my childhood.

After some time I hit on it. It was a passage of scripture that suggested we didn't need to strive for our sustenance any more than the lilies of the field did. This was a scripture that I loved as a child for it expressed an idea I thought to be most amazingly true. It seemed so obvious to my young self that I wondered why most people didn't live by it. Why did everyone work frantically and worry so much about it? When I tried to point it out to people they looked at me like I was out of my mind. They explained to me that I didn't understand the adult world, it wasn't like that, they said — you had to work to get ahead. It was important; it was a serious and fearful business. Eventually I came to fear it was true.

As I remembered my childlike conviction, I began to experience an intense longing to know if it was true. I longed to deeply understand and be in harmony with the laws of Divine Providence. I began to yearn to reconcile my means of livelihood with the natural principles that govern prosperity. How could a human being have the quality of life referenced there? I longed to have my life become a reflection of the possibilities set forth in those simple scriptural statements. I contemplated the verses intently. I understood them this way:

* No matter how much effort I make for my physical requirements, I can never provide as splendidly as the lilies are clothed. The lilies don't try at all, they simply exist in a state of being.
* I am deeply loved and not meant to be any less splendidly provided for than they. My providence is planned for.
* It is not necessary or productive to have worry or doubt regarding my requirements.
* All that I require is contained within the kingdom of Being.
* Instead of striving for my needs, seek the kingdom; all within it is provided for me.
* The kingdom is within.
* It is God's pleasure to provide me with the kingdom.
* God is righteous — aligned with principles of justice. Providence is one of these principles.

Beyond the disbelief of my fears, I could feel the truth and the hope of these ideas rise up within me. The flint was struck. A glimmering spark was tendered in my soul. Then on a certain evening, I sat listening to the silent language of the stars in a small glade I frequented. There I made my covenant with all that I hold to be sacred. I committed to living on the wind, allowing myself to be supported by the Unseen. I stated my intention to leave behind the world of work as I had lived it and to learn it anew. I dedicated the resources of my life to the benefit and glorification of All. In this sacred moment I had a vision of commencement. I gained a simple view of my next steps and I agreed to move into them despite my fear. I left the grove knowing that I would change my life radically. I determined not to wait for the confidence and courage I needed, but to simply begin and ask my confidence and my courage to catch up.

In the next two months I sold my vehicle and my last possessions, settled what bills I could, purchased a plane ticket, and left Alaska. My two older children were now away at school and the youngest, sixteen, was with his dad. I was free to jump with abandon into the unknown. Everything fell into place so quickly that friends and family were startled by the suddenness of my move. In 1991 I left, trading my home of forty-one years for the uncertain experiment of living on the wind. With only three hundred dollars in my pocket I was afraid, but there was also a well of satisfaction in my heart. What I sought was the kingdom of sufficiency, the balance and order and birthright at the very core of our Being. The three years that followed were filled with wondrous lessons as I struggled to understand and surrender to the natural laws that govern prosperity within our world of Being.

The abundance of God is like a mighty ocean, so vast you cannot possibly exhaust it or cause a shortage for others. You can go to this inexhaustible ocean with a small cup and bring away only that small cup of bounty and blessing. Or...you can take a bucket and bring away a bucketful. It makes no difference to the ocean. Nor does it matter how often you go...abundance is always there.

— Henry Hamblin

8

Money, Money, Money

O*ften people attempt to live their lives backwards; they try to have more things, or more money, in order to do more of what they want, so they will be happier. The way that it actually works is the reverse. You must first be who you really are, then do what you love to do, in order to have what you want.*

— Margaret Young

From 1991 through 1993, I lived an experiment of abundance. It was an experiment of faith and hope, one of radically changing my ideas about my self-provision, a time of challenging my most closely held fears and mythologies about money. Leaving Alaska with only three hundred dollars, I landed in Seattle planning to start over and rebuild my health. I stashed my two boxes of possessions with a friend and flew to San Diego to meet with a natural health care pioneer, Dr. Bernard Jensen. Two important things happened on that trip. I met Dr. Ellen Jensen, his daughter-in-law and protégée, who figured prominently in the restoration of my health, and I fell in love with San Diego. I never did use my return ticket to Seattle.

During those three years I concentrated primarily on my health, never working more than part-time, and then only taking on work that fully suited my creativity, passion, and health requirements. I found it necessary to completely reexamine my beliefs and ideas about money. For example, I was aware that many of the world's great visionaries — whether entrepreneurs such as the Fords or Rockefellers, or humanists such as Desmond Tutu or Mother Teresa — commenced their dreams successfully without financial resources. In spite of these examples, I discovered that I deeply believed that money was the basis of most of my own needs, and that my dreams could not move forward without it. I could not write until I had money for a computer. It was not possible for me to have a certain job, or take a trip, without money for a car or money for gas. My son couldn't visit until I had money for airfare. It all seemed to be about money; my entire life, in fact, seemed horribly limited by lack of money. Though I knew better from my childhood experiences of self-sufficiency in frontier Alaska, the fears and misperceptions were deeply embedded in my psyche.

When I was young, we always had two freezers full of meat and lots of favors outstanding in the community. My father was often paid with fish, moose, and other game by local people that he flew to the good hunting spots. He also frequently flew supplies to people who lived a "subsistence" lifestyle. Money was not the currency with them, barter was; they would fix a piece of machinery or help wire a house. Remembering this, I began to examine my current ideas about money and look for freedom from my beliefs.

OUR MONETARY BELIEF SYSTEM

There are many ideas we have accepted about money, value, lack, work, and worth. These ideas form a belief system that creates the principles that we operate by regarding money. They vastly influence our relationships and dreams. As an exercise, I wrote down many of my personal beliefs as well as our cultural views about money and reviewed them alongside my experiences of money. Upon closer examination, I saw how commingled, confused, and conflicting this mix was.

- I have to work hard for money and if I don't put forth lots of effort I will be poor.
- People respect me more if I have money. I respect people more if they have money.
- I earned it the hard way, everyone else should too.
- It's not spiritual to have money; it's better to give than receive.
- It is wrong or weak to receive assistance from others.
- It's all about who you know.
- I can't trust people who ask for money.
- I should help people who are in need.
- People I give money to probably misuse it.
- Everybody should just get a job!
- When I have enough I will help others.
- Spiritual and humanitarian services should be free or at least darn cheap.
- No one should make that much money.
- People should be able to charge as much as they can.
- If I don't have enough money something bad will happen.
- People without money are losers, not interesting, charity cases, unhappy, don't have anything to offer.
- People without money are better off, happier, have simpler lives, don't have as many worries.
- I need a lot of money to be secure.
- There is never enough money.
- There is never too much money.
- There is not enough money to go around.
- Once I get money it's hard to keep it.
- I need to save enough to last me forever.
- Everything depends on money.
- I can't accomplish my dreams without money.
- It takes money to make money.
- Money is power.
- Money can't make you happy.
- I can't be happy without money.

It fascinated me to also go through the list substituting the word "money" with "power," or "love." Then for fun I tried the words "time" and "success." These five concepts — money, power, love, time, and success — are what we most commonly associate with wealth. As I looked closely at the underlying beliefs, I discovered many useless ideas, even lies. I began to question them all. What is the belief? Who says so? Does it serve me to operate from that belief? Who will be upset if I don't? Why do I care? What did I believe about it as a child? (We often knew better then.) To change our relationship to prosperity, we must first see what our current relationship to it is.

A PERSONAL ECONOMY

On Jewel's first tour of Europe we were in a different country nearly every day. Before going shopping I would get information about the local currency and exchange rate in each new country and then dutifully make the conversions into dollars, trying to understand the value of items we were purchasing. Pounds, lire, drachmas, pesos, centimes, guilders, francs, krona; Germany, Belgium, France, Spain, England, Italy, Norway, Sweden. Soon the currencies lost all meaning for me since I could not readily understand what anything was "worth." I stopped trying to keep track. Instead, I began asking myself different questions: Do I need this item? Do I love it enough to drag it around on tour with me? I entirely stopped asking, "How much is it?" though that is the first question we ask under normal circumstances. Suddenly, money had no value at all and the question of value shifted from cost to the items' value to me.

The value of money is fluid as well as relative. It grows and changes in one's life. We each have a personal economy. The framework of our personal economy is created by factors such as the region and culture we were reared in, financial circumstances of our youth, events such as the Great Depression, religious beliefs, or personality traits. These determine whether we dread tending to our money, fear it, or handle it with ease, whether we value thrift, generosity, luxury, where our comfort level is, and so forth.

It is important that we remember to place ourselves in our own economy. It is important to determine what our time is really worth and begin to value it. What is the value of our time? It's not how much we are making, but what we are worth to ourselves. We are the only ones who can spend time on our dreams. We may spend much of our time on chores, for instance, out of a false sense of economy, when our time would be far more productively spent developing a skill or project. Daily we bump up against the value of money in our individual economy. We may refuse to pay someone the thirty dollars to mow our lawn or clean our house because we "cannot afford it," yet we wish we had time to write or work with children, or take a class. We place "what we can afford" in the primary position in our economy. Meanwhile, our real life, our real self is indefinitely postponed. What we say in this decision is that we value money more than our own time and creativity. In doing this, we are devaluing our own dreams, demeaning our passion, overriding choice and freedom, and not putting ourselves into the equation of our generosity. And our dream suffers because the universe responds to the primary message: Leave me out of the abundance equation.

I know we can become so bound by the idea of what we cannot afford that we can hardly breathe, let alone take a class or pay someone else to clean our house or mow the lawn. But I also know that at the core it is never about the money. There is always a way for the determined person to understand their purpose and dream, and be guided to its fulfillment. There are moments in one's life when one has to stretch, to risk, to leap forward naked into the wind.

INVEST IN YOURSELF

One of the greatest thinkers of our time was Buckminster Fuller, scientist, writer, philosopher. He suggested that everyone quit their jobs and just go home. And stay there until they fully understood what is and is not necessary to do, what they are best suited for, most passionate to do, and fulfilled in. Only then did he recommend that we return to work, bringing those capacities and energies to the table, and even then doing only what is truly necessary. If we did this, he felt, we would have a vastly improved society.

Following high school I worked for two weeks at a car rental company at Anchorage International Airport. After just those two weeks of work, I felt dull and anxious and I was appalled at the prospects for my life: endless, mind-numbing work, minimum wage, one week vacation and some travel benefits after the first year. This staggered my mind. I quit. I committed to myself that my work from then on would be wonderful even if it paid me nothing, and I have never looked back.

Initially, I set a minimum wage for myself of twenty-five dollars an hour and determined that I would either get that wage — in work that suited my creativity — or make my hours an investment in myself. It was surprising how much people objected to this idea. Many argued emphatically with me, thinking me irresponsible, unrealistic, or crazy. However, I never lowered my minimum wage, and over the years I raised it to fifty dollars an hour. Following my divorce, I seemed to be qualified only for minimum wage jobs or welfare. Neither was a viable choice to me because they would not lead me out of my limited circumstances. People in my life harangued and pressured me to "just get a job." One person even sent in a McDonald's application for me!

Instead, I taught art and music classes. I led self-help and spiritual development groups. These were some of the ways I could meet my criteria. I developed a radio show, had a newspaper column, produced two record albums, developed an art glass business. There were many times that I worked for myself and received little pay. But it was a choice I made to have personal freedom, flexibility, and creative opportunity, which I value above money. Each work effort shaped my skills, and brought me important personal growth, leading me closer and closer to my most authentic self instead of farther away. Later, when I left Alaska and was "living on the wind," there were times when I got extraordinary jobs because of my unwillingness to work for less than my full value; on several occasions people invited me to make up my own job. Courage, moxie, and passion are far better stakes for one's future than cash.

If peace of mind is what you value, then value it monetarily as well. If writing, or nature, or volunteer work is vital to you be sure that it shows up in your personal economy. Value yourself, value whatever is your lifeblood, value your thoughts and dreams, your soul. Give them your power, your time and money, and energy. In business, it is necessary to invest a good share of the earnings back into the business so that it remains healthy and generative over time. In the same way, your investment in yourself will bring the highest gain.

In my own personal economy I bank on joy, fulfillment, and my values, on love, freedom, people, community, creativity, nature, spiritual consciousness, on my own soul. These are my riches. These are what form the foundation of my individual economy. Developing them seems always to bring financial satisfaction.

> Your prosperity consciousness is not dependent on money; your flow of money is dependent on your prosperity consciousness. As you can conceive of more, more will come into your life.
>
> — Louise Hay

HOW IT REALLY WORKS

Ten years ago a friend and I very much wanted to take a class on spiritual development. The cost for the half day was $65. He was affronted that a spiritual teacher would charge so much, feeling that it excluded too many people. He opted not to take the class. I felt that this was an exciting opportunity and, though I had extremely limited finances, I paid the tuition.

I have, at times, had to pay as much as $450 for just one hour of legal advice, or $125 for an hour of plumbing services. I felt that if I didn't pay well for what I actually value most — the right opportunity for spiritual growth, for instance — that I was creating a strange valu-ation for my personal currency. And a skewed message regarding my priorities.

When I first began in the music industry, I had a steep learning curve and an overwhelming task load. Many of those tasks were secretarial. The financial duties began to escalate as well, and neither are areas of expertise or interest for me; quite the opposite in fact. I had barely enough money to cover rent and food — this was early in Jewel's career, before there was much income. There was no money, but I was not the right person to take care of the filing, office organization, and bookkeeping. I made a decision to hire a part-time assistant/bookkeeper even though it appeared she would receive all of my meager earnings. Conventional wisdom seemed to dictate that it was foolish to pay someone money I didn't have if I could do the tasks myself.

However, I opted to trust that if I positioned myself so that my best abilities and my joy could serve the goal, this correct alignment would cause the money to expand to accommodate it. And, magi-cally, it did so. The woman I hired is still with the company and is one of our most valuable employees. She brought with her not only the support of her excellent skills but also her respect, trust, and delight in the intuitive and spiritual methods by which I work. This was invaluable to me at the time — she was one of the few people who understood and encouraged me. So the leap of faith had surprising payoffs to me.

MONEY, MONEY EVERYWHERE ...

In the desert city of Tucson, Arizona, the annual rainy season brings torrential downpours that flood the streets and arroyos. Millions of gallons of water rush through this town, but the city lives in drought conditions. Lacking rainwater catchment systems, water is piped from the Colorado River at great expense while water falls all around.

There is money all around us. While doing taxes this year, two friends of mine looked at their total cash outflow for the past three years, and they were shocked to discover that a million dollars had flowed through their hands. They were millionaires and didn't even realize it. Most of us would be surprised to see how much total money flows in and out of our life. One of the reasons so little stays with us is lack of catchment systems, or containers.

Our currency exists primarily in the virtual reality of cyber-space. It is systems oriented — a numerically based binary structure of valuation. As such, it responds on the physical level to structures and plans. It is made visible in tangible systems. Money needs containers. One of those containers is a good financial system. The system can be a simple one or a complex one, but for money to be sticky — to stick with us — it needs a grid to attach to. That system requires clarity, discipline, and order.

Our system reflects our beliefs and fears about money. The truth is that we have a lot of pain and fear surrounding our experience with money. Many of us want money but we don't want to deal with it; we want to pretend it is not necessary to pay attention to it. If we dread our accounts and keep them in chaos, if we hate the practical necessities of money, that constant avoidance will divert the flow around us. We are the most important container for our money. When we are clear, when we truly have room for money, for abundance, it will fill us, which is wonderful news.

To become "real," money needs to be grounded. Outside my window, as I write, stand several magnificent conifers. These ancient spruce are masterful containers. They know how to collect energy from the grid that is this planet. They stretch into the sky for its rich resources of sun, water, and pollinating wind, and they ground deep into the soil for support and nourishment. Accessing fully what both air and earth have to offer, they create the perfect container so they can spread out branches filled with a wealth of life, vitality, and abundant return into the system.

All too often we only have our heads in the clouds when it

comes to our finances. Money can be grounded by creating and tending to systems and containers for it, and by moving within to source our clarity and knowledge of providence.

When Jewel's first album became successful, money began to pour into our coffers. The mounting sales and touring augured even greater financial success to come. Many in the music industry criticized me for not capitalizing more fully on this. "Get more merchandise out there," they would say. "Do some endorsement deals. You are missing big opportunities; you could be raking in a lot of money."

I knew that quantum growth can capsize an endeavor. It was not time to make more money. It was time to pause, manage thoughtfully, and create larger containers. I formed a financial team with the expertise to handle this new level of abundance. I educated Jewel and myself to our new situation. Systems were put in place and a plan laid to assure her financial security and to allow for expansion. We were not planning for a rapacious gold rush career devised to make as much money as possible while we could. We were planning for a long-term career to serve artistic development and humanitarian goals. We revisited our goals and questioned what we wanted to do with our money. We established the channels it would move along, and by what means. And, as importantly, we paused to understand ourselves in relationship to this new abundance. A truly beautiful and expert system was created with very big buckets and we began to watch them fill with delight.

RADICAL GENEROSITY

My building contractor is a man who has made the courageous decision to work on only one job at a time. He believes that this is the way to provide the best service to the client and the most quality in his own life. There was a moment when he and his wife sat down and decided to understand their needs and ambitions in terms of their value for family and their honor and pride in work. They decided to forfeit the seemingly more profitable and secure method of juggling numerous jobs at once because it meant the clients were not well served and the longer hours brought him greater stress while taking him away from the family. They agreed that a simpler life financially was preferable for who they truly were. They determined not to give in to the fear that if they didn't have several jobs going at once he would soon be out of work. Because he loves his work, he chose to do it only at the level that allowed him to maintain the highest quality.

They made the leap to trust Spirit to provide the work. That was several years ago. He now says that not only does the next job always appear at the right time, but the quality of clients and jobs has vastly improved, bringing greater satisfaction into his work. I so greatly respect his values, choices, and what he lives that I am generous with him in bonuses and appreciation. Whenever possible in my own economy, I value people who make such choices by being generous with opportunities and/or financial reward. In addition, I feel I am supporting the development of a saner and far more abundant world.

I have felt it an important obligation, no matter my financial state, to practice a radical generosity in terms of what I will support joyfully, helping to birth it into our common experience. I want to support the development of services, talent, and expertise that are not typically valued in our culture. Because of this support, I have always gladly shared my abilities, encouragement, energy, and money with the ideas, people, and causes that strive to move us beyond our limitations and into our excellence. Though it varies from year to year, I challenge myself to disperse up to 60 percent of my income, after taxes, to benefit areas other than my own personal gain, primarily humanitarian endeavors. I am aware this constitutes a radical generosity, yet it seems my income expands so exponentially as a result of my commitment that my personal wealth continues to grow rapidly.

> Money is a lightning rod for what I call the lie, or the myth, of scarcity. It's not merely that we believe things are scarce, we have a mindset or a frame of reference that no matter what's happening, there is not enough. We are continually scrambling to get more of what we really don't need. We are reaching for this, wanting more of that.... If we can let go of the constant trying to get more, it frees up unbelievable amounts of energy to make a difference in our life with what is already right there in front of us.
>
> — Lynne Twist

A HUNGRY WORLD

What are we so hungry for? All of this striving for more, the feeling that there is not enough, that we must hoard our money, our love, our power, and time. All the while compressing ourselves into very tight corners, becoming enslaved by our financial goals. The clamoring ego, the body that feels vulnerable, are all so hungry to know what the Soul knows: There is enough. It is sufficient. It's going to be okay.

We can feed the hunger with any number of compelling addictions and distractions: possessions, food, sex, talk, relationships, television, work. But our hunger is not physical. It is the hunger to have purpose, the hunger to be filled with the wisdom of the Soul, to reconnect with our spiritual base, with one another, and with the earth that is our life. It is the hunger to possess peace and clarity and to abrogate our constant fear that there is not enough.

To return to Buckminster Fuller, he held that there was enough to go around. He believed that we had enough resources, for instance, to feed the whole planet right now, today. It is true. Our deficits are not about lack. They are about how we perceive and how we act on our perceptions. So much is possible when we realize what is available to us right now, when we see what we have. Stepping outside of the idea that "nothing can be done," we begin to see that much can happen incredibly differently, with great speed, and with preternatural ease.

BECKY'S HOUSE

One morning, a woman called a local San Diego talk radio show, with DJs Jeff and Jer. She spoke of an abusive situation she was in, without the means to get out of it. A female police officer called to offer help and a conversation developed about the need for a shelter for women in such situations. Jeff and Jer suggested that enough money might be raised to at least help "Becky" (not her real name) get a couple of months' rent. They suggested that anyone who wanted to give a few dollars could drop it off at a downtown location the following morning and the station would see that it was given to Becky. The following morning, in just an hour-and-a-half's time, $42,000 was dropped off by people on their way to work!

When Jeff and Jer shared the exciting news on the air that day it galvanized the audience. Almost immediately Becky had a new apartment, counseling, and support, and volunteers who helped her relocate, even moving her belongings. But the on-air conversation continued about a facility that could help others in similar situations. A city employee called to say that their office had land set aside for a shelter for abused women, but no resources to develop it. A contractor called in offering to oversee the construction, an architect offered to design it, and many people donated plumbing, electrical, and other labor for building it — all volunteering their services free of charge. Funds began to come together and in a matter of days Becky's House, as it came to be called, was well under way.

For years the City of San Diego had been trying to set up such a facility. Yet, in a very short time, generous individuals pooled their powerful and nearly boundless group resources, achieving what government agencies could not. Within seven months the ribbon was cut at the opening ceremony and Becky's House was a reality.

THERE IS ENOUGH

Switching through television channels one Sunday morning, I observed a dynamic black preacher interact with his congregation. It was a large group; thousands were in attendance. He called out, "How many of you need jobs? All of you stand up!" Hundreds of his parishioners stood.

"Now," he said, "how many of you own businesses that need employees?"

An even larger group stood up. "You see, it is all provided for us, if we only ask. I want all of you who are standing to leave before the sermon; we are going to do something about this right here and now. We have people that will take you into our conference rooms and help you find each other. God doesn't mean for these wonderful resources to go to waste. God makes everything ready but it's up to us to see what's in front of our face!"

Many people got jobs that day, even some who had been searching for months.

There is enough. Even in those passages in our life that seem to be barren, everything we need is there — all the resources, all the gifts. It is easier than we have come to believe. The power to demonstrate this is not franchised solely to the wealthy, or government, or the large corporations. That power is housed most fully, most limitlessly, within. And that power quite literally can move mountains.

Money has immense power, because we've said so, and now let's give it the power that the Universe, humanity, that the earth needs.

— Lynne Twist

9

THE Incoming Wave

> *T**he universe is constantly saying yes to us. It only says yes. It is our task to discover what within us it is saying yes to.*
>
> — *Lenedra J. Carroll*

I lay back on the pungent spring earth one morning, my mind drifting in the sun's warmth, when an understanding popped into my head. I was lazily ruminating on the saying "What goes around, comes around," rather idly wondering why that was and how it worked. A picture formed in my mind of a pebble hitting the surface of a pond. The familiar image lingered. At first it seemed I already understood the principle: our actions create ripples with far-reaching effects — not a new thought, certainly.

However, the persistence of the image captured my imagination and I began examining it for information beyond my usual understanding. That's when it got interesting. The mental picture telescoped in my view, revealing a magnified version of the wave. I watched the wave move out until it reached the edge of the pond and began to ripple back: *it rippled back along the path of the originating wave.* I was then able to understand that the quality of that originating wave determined the returning wave. My vision telescoped once more; I saw the original wave again and observed that, indeed, *the outgoing wave was actually creating the simultaneous incoming wave.* The rise and fall of the initial wave created a wave that traced back along the "under side"; the two waves, naturally, matched. In a rush I understood that, since all is light and frequency in our reality, it is the wavelength or frequency of what goes out that literally creates what comes in to us — they are a match!

An exciting part of the realization was that it not only applies to motion waves, *but also to thought waves.* I replayed some of my recent thoughts — watching them going out, observing what came back on the incoming wave. Time after time I saw that what came back from each thought matched the frequency of my originating thought wave — or group of waves. If the thought group was the frequency of fear, fearful results generated back to me. Loving thoughts generated the like. Muddy, unclear thoughts brought people and situations into my life that generated confusion.

Recently I had lunch with a man who headed a large multinational firm; we were engaged in a project together. He had read this section of my book addressing the incoming wave. "I wonder if you realize how true this is?" he said, referring to the wave information.

I replied that I was aware of its truth by the certainty I experienced in meditation, and because I began to apply the principle, proving it repeatedly in my experience. "But," I said, "if you mean from a scientific point of view, then no, I really have no idea."

He told me that he had studied wave theory for two years for his degree in civil engineering and he verified that it is indeed as I described. "I've never heard anyone express this concept so completely and simply," he said. "And the application to our individual human thought wave is a very intriguing one. It entirely affirms how waves behave and travel. Sound, air, heat, and water — these are the basic waves around us that greatly affect our lives. When people refer to frequency they are talking about waves, for frequency is, essentially, the measurable quality of waves."

He explained further, "To design things — bridges for instance — you have to understand how waves act and react. When you send out an impulse in a wave, like the pebble in your story, that pebble impulse creates a shock wave. From the surface, you see that shock wave as a ripple. But if you could see underneath water, you would see that a mirror image of that wave is effectively traveling back to the source.

"When you send a shock of sound at a wall or other medium," he continued, "that also comes back in a mirror image." He struck the edge of his water glass with a spoon and I watched the impact and the sound reverberate in the water. "This is measurable in sound, air, water, and heat; these all react under the same principles of wave theory — they each have a different specific gravity but they all react to the same basic principles that govern all waves.

"You saw this very accurately in your meditation," he said, leaning forward intently in his chair. "But what really interests me is the understanding you had about this applying to human wave theory. It's a burgeoning field of study, you know. This is really a very intriguing idea with exciting implications about how thought waves may indeed work."

PRIMARY TONE

The Universe *only* says yes to us. I am aware this is a radical idea and begs many questions. How can it possibly be that the Source only says — continually says — yes? It is an excellent question. We can certainly think of too many instances when we did not get what we so fervently desired.

Everything is in motion along a wave frequency. Human field theory is an established area of study and individual frequency is now measurable and is being studied on many levels by highly credible scientists. Each person has a measurable frequency, or wave, or prime tone. Let us take that idea and join it with the understanding I gained in meditation. It can be explained this way.

The outgoing wave has a primary tone. Who you are, what you do as an individual creates your primary tone, or wave. If fear is your primary tone it then reverberates out to your surroundings and the responsive universe says, "Yes, there is indeed a fearful world, let me bring it unto you." It recognizes your primary tone and grants it back to you. If love is your primary wave, then the Source says, "Yes, love is, love is indeed. It is provided unto you."

If desire sets your prime tone then the abundant source says, "Indeed, you are granted that." And you experience more desire, you always crave, always yearn and want because that is your primary tone. Desire begets desire.

This explains much. For instance, we desire peace, work for peace, and pray for peace unceasingly but until we begin to embody peace we will not have the peaceful world we so urgently want and need, for peace itself is not sufficiently a part of our outgoing primary wave tone, only the *desire* for peace is. The human group has a primary tone. It is comprised of the thoughts of the majority of its individuals. When enough individuals change their thoughts, so does the group wave tone change.

The primary tone articulates the wave. What you most embody sets your wave, your prime tone. That prime tone says, "This is what I want to experience of the vast banquet that is God." If you are filled with pain and fear, that tone says, "I want to experience fear and pain." It is served back to you in very short order as "Yes, here, it is yours." The dream, which is pliable, conforms to match the tone and that is how a life is formed.

CERTAINTY IN THE WAVE

When we are filled with fear and doubt, the frequency of our wave field becomes tattered; it stutters and falters inconsistently. That inconsistency creates inconsistent outcomes for us. The uncertainty translates outward and our reality — the dream — conforms to it. When we delve into our being, centering there, the peace and knowing available therein creates a coherent wave that then translates into our experience as certainty. *Certainty is very compelling to the universe.*

If we are uncertain of others, afraid of intimacy, holding back, tenuous, critical of our decisions and actions, this uncertainty will translate through our wave field and bring back the experience of it. What do we do when we feel uncertain, afraid, blocked? We know it affects the dream. But we also know it does not work to deny what we feel or project a false confidence. It is appropriate for the fears to be exposed, expressed; it is necessary if there is to be movement away from them. We can then create a container for the fears, mentally building a container and encapsulating the emotion or concern. Doing this prevents the uncertainty from traveling out into the prime tone. It contains it to our own arena for examination. Our attention grounds it, then questions can be asked and feelings expressed, without being controlled or denied.

Rather than deny your worry of what someone thinks of you, create a container for the feeling and have a dialogue with yourself about it. If you are afraid, for instance, about the outcome of a promotion, create a container and simply say to yourself, "I see that I am worrying about my promotion and I want to contain that concern for my own examination." Make a mental note to examine the situation in silence or with a friend.

This can be done at work as well; in fact I sometimes ask others to join me. It is not necessary to say more than, "Let's encapsulate the charged emotions we are all experiencing and the separate agendas we are stuck on. Let's recognize them for what they are but set them aside for the moment." I merely ask for containment. It is a highly effective technique with our mental dialogues as well as with children, marriage partners, and friends.

Using prayer or silence to steady ourselves brings an ease to the process. Instead of judging the feelings, we can allow them and know they are only passing storms. With the fear encapsulated by our awareness and actions, our frequency remains more certain, compelling the source to bring the solutions and experiences that will heal the fear.

It is your prime tone that sets the request. Change your prime tone and you change your incoming wave; your dream shifts to match the change. There is the automatic question, "What will you have your life be?" that you are always asking and answering — the answer and the question are the same. The need and the fulfillment of the need are the same. What are you asking for?

> Ask, and it will be given you; seek, and you will find; knock, and it will be opened to you. For every one who asks receives, and he who seeks finds, and to him who knocks it will be opened.
>
> — Matthew 7:7–8

GETTING THE QUESTION RIGHT

Understanding questions and the answers, and utilizing them creatively, can be surprisingly productive. My understandings and methods have grown organically out of the manner in which I live, breathe, and think — in the ways I break down ordinary circumstances. I am speaking of common circumstances that usually cause us to shrug and say, "Well, that's how things are and there's nothing that can be done about it."

When I find myself in a circumstance that is unique or troubling or stagnant, I ask myself questions that help assure a more graceful movement through it. It is a technique that came from a process I developed when I was eleven or twelve years old. At the time I often supposed someone was thinking, feeling, or acting in a certain way only to find out that something quite different was going on. I began to notice a high degree of fallibility existed any time I postulated about the highly idiosyncratic workings of another's world. For instance, I might think a grouchy teacher was displeased with my behavior only to find out they were having a dispute with the school principal. Again and again I observed this and realized there were a lot of options beyond what I first supposed.

This led me to develop a game I called "12 What Else." In the game, I asked myself to name twelve possibilities other than the one that occurred to me first. So in the case of a seemingly disapproving teacher, I might also guess that they were hungry, had a fight with their spouse, a family member had died, they didn't get enough sleep, or they were ill, depressed, had a headache, and so on. I began to apply the game to other circumstances — when I was stuck for a solution I would ask myself to think of twelve possibilities no matter how impractical. In fact I found it helpful to throw in some that were truly outrageous. When I needed a good idea for a report for school, I played 12 What Else for creative inspiration. If I was afraid to discuss something with my parents or a friend, I played 12 What Else to imagine different approaches and outcomes of the conversation.

As I grew older I began to understand that my initial impressions were all too often based on projections of what I *feared* someone might be doing or thinking, or what I *wanted* or *needed* them to do. I also observed that I typically thought of things more usual to *my own life* rather than circumstances having anything to do with theirs. Seeing this led me to sometimes add a step to the game. First I would think of twelve other things going on with them. After doing that exercise, I would ask why I cared and what was going on with me. For this part I played 12 Questions — a slightly different version. I might initially ask what was going on with me and answer I was afraid they didn't like me. Then I would ask another question, such as "Do I often think people don't like me?" The answer might be yes. Then the question "Why?" would take me to my home life perhaps, and an answer leading me to a deeper understanding about myself and eventually a question about how I could become less worried about what people thought. The answers to that would be 12 What Else again — I would come up with twelve ways to be free of this fear of other people. By asking twelve questions I would go further and further into important information for myself.

Becoming aware of my perspective and assumptions, I began to gain a freedom from my own fears and problems. And I gained increased independence from the opinions and expectations of others. Rather than being in reaction to others and victim of my own vaporous projections, I began to ask questions about what else was possible and more desirable. I played 12 What Else to answer that question. When I had twelve more desirable scenarios, I inevitably began to wonder how to create the one I preferred. Then I started to think of twelve ways I could achieve it.

ELEVATING THE QUESTION

I continue to play 12 What Else. I like to stay with a question, elevating it, asking one just beyond it. Then, looking at the horizon from there, I formulate another question. Going deeper and still deeper into the question creates tremendous movement in my process. When a question comes to me — from myself or another — I try not to accept it as rote. I play with it, noodle it around in my mind, understand it more broadly; I ask questions about the question to see if there are even better questions.

Recently, a supposedly sound investment of mine went south and my broker called to say I had lost a lot of money. A lot. Given the nature of the news, my broker was shocked at my reaction. "Hmm," I said. "I've never lost a huge amount of money before. I'm very curious to see what that is like."

I wasn't deep in denial or ready for the lockup; I knew that this was an embraceable part of my life, it would serve me. What is it like to lose a large amount of money? It's a pretty interesting question. Especially taken from the perspective that I had "dreamed" the experience into my life. Why? Another good question.

Oddly, I didn't feel I had "lost" anything. Why didn't I? Was the money "lost"? Lost where? Lost in what way? What was lost? From these questions I connected to the certainty that money is simply energy and energy is never lost — I knew that energy would return to me in the form of abundance. "When?" I wondered. "How?"

I kept my eyes open for intriguing answers.

I asked more questions. Naturally I asked, "What happened?" That answer revealed an important flaw in the communication and reporting with this particular broker. It required immediate correction and we requested detailed accountability. This was all excellent information; it revealed, in fact, that the situation was not as grim as I had first thought.

Then I asked what my *soul* felt was happening. Very interesting. I was able to reflect on numerous instances when I had "hunches" about this investment. Though I had mentioned them to the broker, I had overridden my intuition in favor of his "expertise." As I reviewed them, I saw that these hunches had proven to be true. I gained confidence in my intuitive tracking ability and determined to act on it in the future. Again, good question and outcome.

Next I asked, "What do I need to know?" which led me into another level of education about the world of investments. I asked what situation would be optimal for me and I determined I would like a percentage of financial recovery through innovative financial methods. By requiring my broker to get creative we made a substantial recovery through optimizing the loss in terms of taxes and so forth.

Throughout the entire process I never did lose my sense of adventure and wonderment. The questions I followed led me to an entirely positive experience of what commonly could be devastating. The game of 12 What Else led me to the answer to my original question, "What would it be like to lose a lot of money?" Like most things, there is much that can be done, gained, understood, experienced, and even enjoyed.

I recall once reading the response of the singer Bjork to her first encounter with a Los Angeles earthquake. She was on an upper floor of a high-rise hotel that swayed noticeably in the tremors. She held on to the bed whooping and hollering like a cowgirl and was disappointed when it stopped because she had always wondered what it would be like to be in a big earthquake. Even big shake-ups can be a fun ride.

Take a moment to identify the major events, each major turning point, in which you have experienced a profound change or lesson. In each you will be able to find the questions that faced you, the questions that you followed to a new plateau. Examine those times when you were stuck — they were likely times when you were asking mindless or boring questions, or no questions at all. Hold a question without fear or worry. Instead, hold it with excitement, curiosity, peacefulness. Hold your question with the certainty that there are excellent answers for it; it *can* be understood. Then have some fun with it, fiddle with it; keep seeking more and more interesting questions and answers. The answers will delight you. As children we absolutely understood the value of a question, but in maturing we sadly tend to lose our childlike curiosity and the ability to enjoy and master a question.

QUESTIONS AND ACTIONS

Circumstance after circumstance after circumstance, I have followed my questions. They have led me step-by-step to an experience that a vast majority of people in our culture crave: the experience of abundance, of being loved, of being able to be generous, of feeling within my being that I have more opportunity than I know what to do with. This experience is within everyone's potential. If we ask the right questions, the answers will inevitably lead us out of undesirable circumstances.

Choose your questions, rework them, challenge your common ideas and conventional wisdom, and find your way to the best questions — the ones that illuminate more elevated answers. Then, if you can get to the right questions, the next obvious step is to act on the answers you find. Action is necessary. It's certainly not always easy. Some answers require significant change and this takes courage. If you don't act on the answers, however, at best they are little more than an interesting mental exercise. At worst they become inner mandates, deep longings that go unfulfilled and block our energy over time. Action grounds the answers into material reality. The follow-through into action reaps the rewards of the process of questioning.

DIVINE PROVIDENCE

Following high school, my daughter, Jewel, had a series of dead-end jobs in quick succession that made her increasingly confused and fearful about her future. Seeing her whole life stretch out before her, solely her responsibility for the first time, she was filled with great uncertainty about what to do. Each meaningless job made her questions sharper and more urgent: "What do I want to do with my life?" "What do I want to be?" Her course of action was not at all clear and this filled her with fear and anxiety about her security and abilities.

At this time we lived in a lovely apartment on a hilltop in Poway, California. I was recovering from ill health and only worked part-time; this necessitated that we share expenses. I suggested that Jewel might reduce her worry by reducing her overhead. "Get a van and live in it — sketch, write, sing, take time to explore your questions, your fears, and dreams. Living simply, you could work only part-time, and it could even be by singing in local coffeehouses. Doing that you can easily make the little money needed." The idea was attractive but daunting to her.

She clung to the tenuous security of her most recent job until her boss settled the matter by developing an inappropriate attraction to her and making certain unacceptable requirements of her if she wanted to keep her job. She declined; he fired her. She came home in tears, distraught about the situation and about her future. Again I suggested the van and again she was overwhelmed about how it could work. My conviction concerning Jewel at this time was that she needed to choose her freedom, to have peace from financial demands for a time, to explore her creativity. I felt it was by moving outside of convention that she would discover her vocation and her passion.

A couple of years earlier I had come to fully understand the laws of Divine Prosperity. It was this lesson I wanted to share with her. I suggested that we both live in our vans. Many people have supposed, hearing our story in the press, that for Jewel and me this was an act of desperation; they imagine us on the streets, homeless.

While our resources were very limited, we did have choices. It wasn't the financial consideration that caused me to make the suggestion to Jewel. It was to *set ourselves free.* That was the choice. To be free and unfettered by the financial requirements that plagued us, free of all the mental chatter and fear. Free to be able to hear the voice of her soul.

It was a providential time for us. We loved the freedom of movement, the beautiful places we slept at night parked by the sea or on starlit cliffs. We often met at the beach to visit and plan. Parking side by side, we would throw open the sliding doors, boil a pot of water, and share tea and writings, ideas and questions. I began to hear new songs and poetry she was writing; I watched as she sharpened her focus on her own music.

It was a period of disconnection from the distractions and demands that are consuming in contemporary life. Jewel was able to focus on dreaming her new life. Free from outside pressures, she moved deeply into herself, discovering her values, fears, abilities, and her magic. Though our lives were very simple at this time, they were very provident. All that we required came forward with ease. We had taken steps that placed us in harmony with our deepest desires. We chose the freedom and passion that we craved to follow. We patterned ourselves after it and felt the peace of our freedom and the absolute providence of our simplicity. Doing this, being this, it is no wonder that the universe responded by matching our commitment, our peace, and our clear and passionate dreams.

We live in a vast and supremely responsive cosmos. Within this great Being we are held in divine providence, infinitely prosperous.

Lenedra J Carroll

10

Understanding THE Dream

"*D*reams, and mysticism," said
Arsene, "should be left to . . . liars. They are not for honest men."

"On the contrary," murmured Francois, "They are only for honest
men. Liars and mountebanks use them only for oppression and for
manipulation of the defenseless and the ignorant. Until honest men take
them for their own there can be no justice in the world, no faith, no
enlightenment. Without a dream, honesty, mercy, indignation and courage
must remain impotent."

— Taylor Caldwell

Here is the truth of it. You have dreamed your own life. All of
it, its abundance or lack, its joy, fear, sorrow, its good or bad — you
have dreamed it all. There are no exceptions. You are the omnis-
cient dreamer and the architect of your own domain. Your life literally portends itself, for you are both the dream and the dreamer.
There is nothing else.

There is nothing that is not your own dream. There is nothing
outside of your dream — no person, no circumstance, nothing.
There is no one that you are dependent on for your dream. No
one else is dreaming for you. You have full choice, full creative
license, complete power. Dreaming alone you create your reality.
It is your dream; you can dream a new one. Dreaming together we

created our world as we know it; dreaming together we can create a better one.

A lot of skeptic eyebrows raise here. What about people caught by prejudice and poverty, people imprisoned or ruled by tyrants, or those who are abused or disadvantaged physically? They too are dreaming. There are no exceptions. The evidence is available to review. Stories abound of people unwilling to accept apparent defeat or disadvantage. Instead they challenge themselves to go beyond them and against all odds their circumstances change, they overcome inconceivable difficulties. How do they do this? Why them and not others?

CONSCIOUS DREAMING

Aqeela Sherrills is such a person. Aqeela's world was two blocks wide by six blocks long. A very small box. Watts, Los Angeles, California. A war zone. Aqeela was a gang member, he had a reputation in the gang world, so if he strayed from his neighborhood he was a target for other gangs. His world was a small prison. By the time he left high school hundreds of his friends and former classmates had died in gang wars. But he got out of that dream and he brought an entire neighborhood out of that dream with him.

For Aqeela there was a moment when he wanted something else. That moment came when, in sixth grade, his best friend was killed by rival gang members. He realized then that he didn't want to get shot or die for the neighborhood; he began to want something more. Then there was a moment when he glimpsed another world. That moment came when he was recruited by a successful black businessman to sell candy outside the neighborhoods. Soon Aqeela had two lives — during school and late at night he was a gang member with a reputation; outside the neighborhood he was a top candy salesman. He was experiencing a new world, seeing himself in a new context, and it was changing him. He was learning about the philosophy of selling, about rejection and not taking it personally, about effort and discipline.

Aqeela began to dream of another world, one where there was no sound of gunfire and no neighborhood under siege. With his eye on this dream he graduated from high school against all the odds. He made it to college. A new life began to compel him until he thought of little else, and he conceived of a new dream for his people who were back in the old dream, the old neighborhood. After college he returned to Watts and, with his brother Duade, negotiated an amazing abiding truce between the rival gangs and between neighborhoods. They developed growth and training opportunities and jobs for kids there, and peace, safety, and connection for the entire community.

Aqeela is still there, dreaming. He is executive director of the Community Self-Determination Institute. Their mission is to ensure social wellness through positive thoughts and practice and to build the community through enhancement of individual self-esteem. They are very good at it.

April 9, 2002, will mark the tenth year of the gang peace treaty Aqeela and Duade accomplished in Watts. With limited resources, they continue doggedly making a vital difference to the young people in the area and solving some of the tougher issues that face our country. Aqeela feels the accomplishments in Watts can act as a model and catalyst for a peace movement throughout this country. This dream drives his vision-based organization that works to bring forth a new way of being, seeing, and doing that will affect politics, business, communities, and the entire social fabric of their lives.

Gandhi, Mother Teresa, Martin Luther King — and scores of people far less renowned, like Aqeela — all experienced doubts, fears, wounds, uncertainties. They took a stand for their new dream, however. They refused to accept the dreams they were raised with and they began dreaming, dreaming, dreaming others. In spite of the apparent futility, lack of funds or approval, or the opposition of others — in spite of all this they dreamed. They did not take their support from the outcome; they took their support from the compelling necessity of their dream. Conceiving the dream, connecting to the passion, imagining it, learning to live in it, becoming the dream, taking it forward day by day — these created their new world, and inevitably drew to them all the resources and opportunities needed.

CHANGING CONTEXT

Context is the set of conditions in which something exists or occurs. Context is pliable, fluid; it is the fabric of illusion. Mother Teresa, Martin Luther King, Gandhi, and Aqeela Sherrills all managed to shift their context. We all can. Our tendency, however, is to become attached to context, letting it define our perceptions and options. We see someone surrounded by a given context, at work for instance. How they dress, speak, their job title, our own judgments of them — all these form the context that determines how we perceive and relate to them. We see someone each day at work but at the gym or on the street we may not recognize them — they are outside of the context we are used to. We often relate to the context far more than the individual.

Aqeela's context was the environment of Watts, the gangs, and poverty. As long as he was defined by that context he was confined to it. Little by little he changed that context; he broadened it, expanding the horizon of the world available to him and changing how he defined himself. This naturally changed what was possible for him. He began making different choices; this altered the fabric of the dream that was his experience of life.

Context is a powerful factor in our existence. It defines our landscape and we relate earnestly to it even though it is fabricated, dreamed, learned. Context is a defining factor of our life and how we see ourselves, whether our story is contextualized by a slum environment or lack of education, by poor parenting, by affluence, loneliness, worry, or friendship. Context is about how we see ourselves; it is about our perceptions. They can be diminishing perceptions or expanding perceptions. We allow these perceptions to set how we respond, and what we think our capabilities and options are. This then determines the world we inhabit. We create a context for our personality and ego; we assign traits to ourselves and try to remain set in them. We dream up circumstances that provide the context for our surroundings, our relationships, all that we engage in.

In their book *The Cultural Creatives*, Paul H. Ray and Sherry Ruth Anderson refer to context as our "worldview":

> Your worldview is the context of everything you believe is *real* — God, the economy, technology, the planet, how things work, how you should work and play, your relationship with your beloved — and everything you value. For some, their worldview shifts first and their priorities come later. For others, it happens in reverse order. Most often, there is a mix of the two strategies, with values and worldview shifting alternately, influencing each other....
>
> Most of us change our worldview only once in our lifetime, if we do at all, because it changes virtually everything in our consciousness. When you make this shift, you change your sense of who you are and who you are related to, what you are willing to see and how you interpret it, your priorities for action and for the way you want to live. Regardless of whether you leave your home, change your job, or switch your career path, if your worldview changes, it changes everything.

Changing our worldview, or context, is not easy because context grips our focus, entrancing us. We become very attached to it, perhaps because it gives us identity and reputation and rules. These provide what seems to be order to our lives. We cling to these things, sometimes grasping so tightly they threaten to choke us. But context cannot be held fixed; it will always change. It is inevitable, *that is the nature of context*. The outer arena of context is an ever-changing world: we are married, we are divorced. We are popular, we are out of favor, we are employed and then we lose our job. Our appearance, opinions, friendships, tastes — all these change.

Our physical selves and surroundings, our emotions, our mental patterns and capacities — these are part of our context. They actually form a small, confining world that we relate far more to than, for instance, the expansive context of our soul, or the unlimited potential of our humanity. In the small context we suffer a loss of perspective, it's difficult to see clearly, the terrain shifts and moves under us. It is far better to choose to anchor to a larger context.

It is a wonderful exercise to ask yourself frequently in the course of the day, "What is my context in this situation or for this feeling? Am I involved in a very small and limited context or am I identified with an expansive one?" Is your context your work, or perhaps some pain from the past? Are you in the context of an old habit? There are so many experiences that are not sustaining yet they are very seductive because they constantly draw the ego into interplay with them. This consumes your energy and your focus. What is required is to notice when you are being engaged in the smaller context of your life and then challenge yourself to see your situation from a larger perspective — expand your horizon. A friend of mine once remarked, observing the landscape from an airplane at 30,000 feet, "It all looks so manageable from here." Get a little distance from your usual perspective or context and most things become much more manageable.

In Alaska during my twenties, I had unresolved issues with my parents. Anger and fear that could not really be resolved with them kept interfering with my ability to have a relationship with them as an adult. Within the limited context of a painful childhood memory I was stuck in a very unfulfilling interaction. One day I pondered this at length; I was tired of the repetitive and constrictive nature of our relationship, and I was looking for a creative application to bring change for me. In the course of my reflection, I hit on the rather obvious fact that they were not going to be with me forever. I realized that, whatever their problems or past treatment of me, they were inevitably going to grow old and die. I let myself fully comprehend this and it shifted my perspective on the relationships dramatically. To achieve this, however, I had to relinquish my attachment to my context of pain and fear. And I had to relinquish the context of my childhood expectations and needs and stop trying to fulfill that context.

In the context of my previous twenty-five years the problems always loomed at me, but in the context of the preciousness of the time remaining with them I was able to make my peace with the past and craft genuine, satisfying, and caring relationships with both of them. The gift of this was not only the fulfilling time I had with them but also the love and peace I felt when my father died some years later. I was free; I didn't have a load of unresolved feelings to interfere with my grief or appreciation.

People often ask me if Jewel has changed since she became rich and famous. Of course she has changed. It would be unnatural if she did not. We cannot keep from changing, and certainly our life experiences do change us, they provide defining context. What people are really asking with this question is whether she has "negatively" changed. The answer to that is no, because we are conscious of the forces of change at work in her life and careful to *choose* how the change occurs.

At the root of the concern is their unconscious awareness that celebrity is a powerful context, one that affects us, changes and defines us. But we can counter this: *we can affect our context, we can change it, we can define it*. We can *choose* our context. We are not simply destined to be the unconscious and passive victims of our confusing and illusionary circumstances, our context. We can be conscious dreamers of all the interrelated conditions in which we exist.

> Reality is merely an illusion, albeit a very persistent one.
> — Albert Einstein

THE ARCHITECTURE OF DREAMS

The teacher places me next to an easel and departs from the room. On the easel is a blank canvas; in front of me is a darkened stage. There are no brushes nor paints in sight; no one else is in the room. I seem to know what to do though I have no instructions. For a time I simply stare intently at the canvas. My mind is empty but I feel a growing fullness around me. A tension is mounting that begins to enliven the space. Suddenly an electric arcing energy leaps from my forehead to the canvas and simultaneously a picture appears on the canvas and in my mind. It is a swirling conjunction of spirals that possess a breathtaking beauty and meaning. I intuit this through my soul, not my mind. Concentrated mindlessness pervades my process.

I continue my focus on the canvas, arranging the swirls, giving them color, changing their patterns and shades with a gesture of will that issues from my forehead, throat, and heart. Sketching now, seemingly with my eyes, I refine the form before me. Suddenly breath sucks in and out of me and the object fully articulates on the canvas. It is a shimmering black kimono-type hooded robe with gorgeous embroidered spirals. A thought comes to me, "I need an expert to execute this sophisticated design." The moment I think this, a jolt strikes out from the power center at my solar plexus. In that instant another artist — a costume designer — appears abruptly at my elbow.

Startled, I jump in surprise, but my eyes do not leave the canvas. I say telepathically, "Here is a gown that needs to be created according to this drawing." The artist nods and moves away to his domain to carry it out. In the same manner — still sketching with my eyes in a way that involves my throat and heart — more forms take shape before me. Realizing they are crouching dancers, another burst occurs at my solar plexus and there in front of me on the stage are the dancers.

"I will need a choreographer," comes to my mind. Without pause, an artist who is a choreographer jolts to my side. I communicate what is needed, again without words, and the artist goes to her work. In this manner I visualize a cave setting; a set designer appears and begins his task. I hear music and a composer joins to create the music. Many other required artists come and go.

All the while, upon the canvas, the swirling pattern of the embroidery is worked and reworked, layers upon layers of color and form created by my focused intensity. Simultaneously the work was appearing before me as I was imagining and drawing it! On the stage, the dancers move in wondrous costumes, in lovely orchestration through beautifully spiraling light and shadow in a cave that beguiles with its mystery. The canvas fades, an auditorium has materialized, a dress rehearsal is in progress. I sit in a front row watching it unfold for the first time. The crouching dancers come together, move apart, come together in a hypnotic pattern. Only one figure is fully upright. In its black hooded kimono this central dancer moves, always facing the audience, revealing only occasional mysterious glimpses of brilliant embroidery.

I think of an audience and suddenly the auditorium is full, the lights darkened. There is no breath in the audience as the performance progresses and the music builds to the culmination. During the final climactic moments, the central robed dancer sweeps gracefully, dramatically. Arms outstretched, hooded head tilted just so, back turned to full view; the long folds of the garment at last reveal the powerful design on the back of the costume.

My mind explodes with understanding and implication. It is the eye of God, a swirling exploding nebula, a universe being born. It is the map of all creation, the Source of all things, the Holy Grail. It possesses a pervading radiance that revolves, filling the room. Imploding in my being, it is giving my life and taking my life.

Its exigent breath becomes my own, rushing like wind through my dry cells. I am a bursting star in an endless creation play.

Whirling now I seem to fall through a long tunnel and break suddenly into wakefulness on the couch in my home that sits across from the cemetery in Anchorage, Alaska. My heart is bursting, my breath comes in ragged gasps, my body is limp. It is some time before I can gather my awareness and when I do I am in thoughtless awe.

The totality of the experience is so complete that I have an eerie sensation that I have awakened into a dream, not from a dream. I cannot tell which is more real — this moment, or the one I just returned from. I now contain an understanding in a way I never imagined possible. I know the creative process; I see the necessity of it and the power of it in our lives. This understanding lies, not in my mind, but integrated into my own fabric by the graphic experience of this dream journey.

⚬

BURSTING STAR

The sun, the moon.
The stars, their prolific prodigy,
populate the domed domain.
Punctures of light
that rend the arc.
Heat of sun and cold of moon,
eclipsed union.
Bursting star
Bursting star
Bursting star
Bursting star
Bursting star

Lenedra J Carroll

AN ABIDING DREAM

Perhaps we do not need to discover our dream as much as we need to realize that we *are* a dream. We are both the dream and the dreamer. How could it be any other way? Our dream is playing out as our life — whether or not we are passive or conscious in it. Much of our current dream is by default, not by choice. It has been handed down to us by parents, or is sourced by our fears, sorrows, and vague longings. It is a valuable exercise for us to assess what we are creating for ourselves and decide if we choose it. Choosing what we will live to be our dream, choosing a life that is connected to our soul purpose — these are vital passages of our journey.

The only truly fulfilling life is one that comes forth from our soul. *This* is the nature of a truly abiding dream. Not a dream driven by our ego or our fear, or life experience, or intellectualization, but one coming from the very core of our soul. An abiding dream.

The dream, the action, will always be defined and limited by the underlying intent. If we implement a dream driven only by our ego needs, the dream will serve the ego. It will exist to satisfy our ego. We will never feel peaceful in such a dream. We can only have deep satisfaction when our dream is coming from the very core of our soul; that is an abiding dream.

When our dream is inspired by our fear, then it is fear that is the master of it; in an important way the dream exists to keep the fear alive within us. For example, if we desire a mate because we are insecure alone, we will dream a mate that will reflect that fear to us by perhaps clinging to us, or abandoning us, or being unavailable. The fear defines the dream. If we face the fear, struggling to gain our security from a deeper place, no longer willing to stay in the fear of being alone, this changes the dream dramatically. The mate we then dream into our lives reflects this new security. In that way every fear we can understand is a wondrous opportunity to clear ground for a new dream. What is repeating in your life that causes you fear and unhappiness? Seek it out. Ask it to reveal itself to you so that you can understand it better.

When it is fashion or fad that is the driving force, the dream is subject to these very tenuous, changing, unstable elements. The dream reflects that instability; it will be full of unstable, tenuous, and changeable people and circumstances. It will take great energy to keep such a dream on course and to sustain it over time.

If it is grief, insecurity, or anger that create the intent for the dream, the dream resembles these. If lack and need fill us, they will fill our dream. The dreamer is hostage to them and the dream limited by them. The less conscious or denying one is of one's underlying agendas, fears, and needs, the more likely it is that the dream will match them powerfully.

It comes back to context again. What are we identified with, what is our context? These then become what comprise our primary wave. When we are identified with the smaller context of our fear-based, security-seeking, ego-based needs and emotions, then our life and our creativity will reflect that smaller context. We are so much greater than our current life experience; we are also the promise of our life to come; we are beings with soul and larger purpose. Identifying with that expanded context changes not only our perspective, it changes our options and endeavors and it changes our lives.

Actions or plans based on the needs of the personality or subject to the tyranny of the ego are far less stable. They are also much more work to launch and maintain. Connecting deeply to our soul work, we engage our heart and passion and life purpose. A goal or project driven by these becomes our joy. We lose ourselves with ease into its implementation; an effortlessness and peace come into play. We then are far more available to experience the fullness of prosperity.

Your vision will become clear only when you look into your heart.... Who looks outside, dreams. Who looks inside, awakens.

— Carl Jung

11

Creative AND
Courageous Action

F ollowing my divorce I established an art glass gallery and studio and the business is growing steadily. Now that I'm earning my living as an artist I need to put a fee on my work that compensates me more accurately for my time. In this valuation process I begin to track the time I spend on various projects. After tallying the time involved in the many steps, I realize there is an unaccounted amount of time spent in the mental process. Mulling over, choosing, and changing ideas, anticipating problems, exploring subject, shape, color — working and reworking in the creative imagination.

In fact, I discover, the time spent in the imagination is usually as much as the time spent with the hands. I see that the thought process is crucial to the outcome of the work. It almost seems that they are imagined into being. Very interesting.

This makes me wonder how it works in the rest of my life — how my daily thoughts affect the outcome of my physical daily life. "In fact," I wonder, "what on earth am I thinking about all the time?"

So. I spend the next three days trying to see what I'm thinking. I make notes in my journal. It's not easy noticing every thought — one leads to another, mutating rapidly. Many thoughts are just pictures of information, others more like abstract feelings, but over the three days many pages are filled.

What I discover is this: Here it is! It's all here in my thoughts

— my whole life. Especially the past and the future. And it is *very* clear why my present is like it is. The fearful, boring, narrow aspects of my life are all laid out there in my fearful, narrow, boring thoughts. It's a total match!

As I read through the days of written thoughts certain patterns emerge. Thoughts that recur frequently are especially illuminating because they are more intense, less conscious, and many of them are quite limiting. Lots of worries and fears and mediocrity. There isn't much there that's innovative, playful, exciting, or even very uplifting. Exactly like my life.

Recently divorced, without job experience or skills, and struggling financially, I'm not able to have my children with me; they live with their father. This is a source of great anxiety and grief for me and it haunts my thoughts. I fearfully wonder when or how I will have a place for us. Now I can tell exactly when — it is repeated again and again in my notes — "When I can afford it I'm going to have a place for us to live." So it's obvious when I'll have a better place — when I can *afford* it.

That thought is defining my reality in a way I definitely dislike. There might be a lot of time between now and "affording it"; I don't want to wait. So I start applying the same thought process that I use in my artwork to create other options. I begin to think about other ways to have sufficient housing so I can have my children with me — house-sitting, elderly care, low-income housing, apartment management, roommates. I play with these ideas, choosing and refining, growing excited and hopeful. Very soon I have a far better situation. More and more I am applying this to other areas of my thoughts — to my fears, needs, perceptions. My life is beginning to improve dramatically.

We are thinking.
What are we thinking?

CREATIVE IMPLEMENTATION

Try keeping track of your thoughts; they will surprise you. Keep a log for a period of days and see what you are saying to yourself all the time. Another interesting way to do this is to choose a time during which you say everything out loud that you are thinking. I recommend that you choose a time when you are alone, unless you want others to assume you have gone mad. Unless you are on the streets of New York, in which case you may talk out loud and others may think you mad but will pay little attention. As you speak all of your thoughts you will be surprised how very like a madman you seem when you actually listen to all the drivel and nonsense and fear and fantasy and repetition you are going on about constantly.

Listening to your thoughts will bring a consciousness to them. Learning to think more creatively will change your life. My creativity has shaped my personality and my life. My father was an alcoholic and this consumed the energies of our family. In my parents' attempt to protect us from the substance abuse, the alcoholism was hidden, resulting in confusion and fear. They also had little energy for our emotional needs, and my sister and four brothers and I experienced many difficult and lonely years. My creativity, along with my deep faith in life and the solace of nature, were the means I used to cope, to heal and grow and, eventually, to radically change my life. It was my good fortune that I was raised in an environment where creativity and innovation were not only valued, they were necessary for survival.

Innovation and creative application, even eccentricity, were in fact very common in the frontier Alaska of my youth. There were many unusual characters in my childhood. I recall a man whose daily attire was worn and soiled tuxedos. His fingernails, filled with dirt, were nearly three inches long and curved like those of a Chinese sage. He was a gifted pianist who had fled the expectations of his family and the pressures of the classical concert circuit. One old-timer that we called "chicken man" lived with his beloved chickens in a tiny tree house that had plastic windows and a rope to haul supplies inside. There was another man who lived underground — you entered his subterranean dirt dwelling by opening and stepping down into an old refrigerator lying in his yard. Not all early settlers to Alaska were so eccentric, but they all were courageous, creative, and adventuresome people willing to leave convention behind and create anew. Their spirit of courage and innovation was an important example to me.

I loved music and art as a child, but there were few opportunities in school, so I pursued my own creative interests. I filled many notebooks with sketches, poetry, and stories to satisfy and develop my creativity. I thought a great deal about making my life my artwork. It was an idea planted at the time of my twelfth birthday by the unique Indian visitor who stayed with us, as related in the story "Make Space for Magic." This idea that my life is my own creative project has had much to do with my survival, growth, and my success.

The most interesting thing about art is that it can be done. An artist moves back and forth between the seen and unseen worlds, between the tangible and intangible, wresting a mere idea into physi-cal form — a book, or song, a poem, movie, play, painting, a life. Again and again the artist goes into the abstract world of ideas and comes back with concrete forms — becoming adept in the process. It is this familiarity and skill that have power: knowing how to ground a dream into this reality, to actualize it. They learn to imagine powerfully. Artists learn to allow ideas and beliefs to change, expand, contract. They become proficient at finding the right question to move their idea forward. They learn to reroute around apparent obstacles, finding options where none seemed to exist. They learn persistence and discipline. Artists have an ability to incubate ideas over time, waiting for the right moment. They know how to think creatively, uniquely if need be, to be inventive. The artist is able to surrender completely to creation, becoming aware of nothing else. Creativity is a dynamic energy, contracting and expanding. This vigor is available to the artist.

Frequently artists have admirable abilities to shift context; their creativity and discipline are great assets in the process. They are able to reroute, conceive anew, and overcome limitations, changing the context of their requirements and their projects until they are accomplished. They identify with a far broader range of options, emotions, and potential that form their context of living. They remain much more fluid in their perspective, identity, and context.

This is a most helpful group of skills to have. These tools, applied courageously to one's life, are the keys to the prison door. They are the keys to freedom. Throughout history tyrants have suppressed, exiled, and murdered artists because of their ability to question, think, vision, change, and create, and for their power to stimulate these qualities in others. These tools have a powerful ability to change lives and societies.

YOU ARE THE ARTIST OF YOUR OWN LIFE

There are few abilities as important and powerful as the creative process. The abilities of the creative person are absolutely key to prosperity; no one with a richly provident life lacks these tools. Without access to a creative process we are vastly diminished in our ability to experience the glory of life and we are also more prone to plodding, difficult, or confined lives. How many times does someone say, "Oh I'm not creative at all. I don't have a creative bone in my body. I'm no artist." Absolutely false. Without exception, every single human being has an innate creativity. In fact we are here, in part, to exercise that creativity.

We do not need to have ability or interest in "the arts" to develop and use this process; we need only begin to apply our innate creativity to the context of our emotions, our thoughts, and our circumstances. Becoming the artistic, creative force in our own life is one of the most important, productive, and fun commitments we can make. We do not need to be artists in the formal sense of one with "talent" in the arts. Not at all. Each one of us is already crafting our life, though perhaps unconsciously. Bringing a fuller measure of creativity and consciousness to that process is something we are all capable of. If we are to do more than survive, to become fully provident, we must bring these qualities into our day-to-day existence.

> The Artist's view of life is the only possible one and should be applied to everything, most of all to religion and morality. Cavaliers and Puritans are interesting for their costumes and not for their convictions.
>
> — Oscar Wilde

BEAR

I'm only five and I don't know what to do. Every night I'm afraid to go to sleep. Bear will get me. Bear comes in my sleep and chases and chases me. Each time Bear gets closer and closer as I run, until his huge jaw yawns around my little head. I smell his bad bear breath and feel his spit dripping on my scalp. Waking terrified, I lie sleepless, crying and listening to my fast-thumping heartbeat. This happens night after night until I can't stand it anymore.

I pray and pray to know what to do, how to get rid of Bear. I get an idea: in my next dream about Bear I am going to turn around and holler at him to leave me alone and get out of my dreams. That night I wake frightened and crying like usual. The next night Bear chases me again, and the next night too. But finally one night I remember in my dream to stop and stare him down and I holler at him angrily, "Get out of here, Bear, this is my dream. Go away and never come back!" I'm surprised because Bear stops and says he is my friend and to prove it he will give me a gift, he will be my helper. Then I wake up but I'm not scared, I'm excited. I did it!

Soon I start kindergarten and I like it a lot until something really bad happens. One of the big boys from the high school starts following me after class every afternoon. At first he just follows me and doesn't say anything. Then he starts to say things to me I don't understand and I feel scared. Then he starts to follow closer, each day a little closer behind me. He talks to me saying he's going to hurt me. He says that if I tell anybody he will kill my family. Now I'm so scared and every day I start to get sick to my stomach when it's time for class to end. I put my coat and boots on very slowly hoping he will go away, but he's always there, following me. I can hardly breathe and I feel like my heart will burst I'm so afraid. I don't know what to do. Then I remember Bear. He said he would be my friend so I ask him to help me. I decide I'm going to have to do the same thing again, face the boy and holler at him to get away. It is the only thing I can think to do. The next day after school I try to do it but I can't make my voice work. So I think, "Okay, tomorrow then." But that day I'm too scared again. Each day I try but I just can't do it.

After a few days, he is following so close that he shoves and pushes at me and I am crying and he's being really mean and I can't stand it anymore and I turn around to him and clench my fists by my side and poke my chin out and holler at him really mean and angry. I'm surprised at what I say: "Get away from me! I don't care what you do, you can kill me and everyone, I don't care. And I'm going to tell my biggest brother and he's a boxer and really tough and he'll come and find you and beat you up!" Suddenly the boy looks frightened, then he turns slowly and leaves. I never see him again. I feel so free, like I can fly. I'm glad Bear came in my dreams so I would know what to do.

COURAGEOUS IMPLEMENTATION

Courage is required to create dramatic change in one's life. Sometimes it is necessary to let go of all that you think is safety and comfort in order for providence to move into your life. Courage I have in plenty, but I gained it by acting courageously in spite of fear, and that is the essence of courage. My first memory of courage is the dream of Bear, facing him down. I then applied that to the young man who was threatening me in kindergarten. Even though I felt terrified I couldn't stand to go on any longer as things were.

It is first helpful to own and appreciate the fear instead of avoiding it. The fear is a flag, a gift really, showing us an area where — by overcoming it — we can gain considerable personal power. We lose focus and energy to every area of fear and pain that we give ourselves to. When we heal and move beyond our fears, we gain use of the energy required to hide or compensate for them.

We can then realize that while the fear is real it is also true that what we fear is like a mirage rising off the heat of a past or projected pain or experience. At the root of fear is usually a memory of the past or a projection into the future. Even when the fear is before us it is still our own perceptions and actions that determine the outcome. Our perspective and beliefs about it give us our range of choices and determine how we respond in the situation and whether we remain victim to fear.

To gain courage we must act — especially when we are deeply afraid. It is courageous when you change a habit, take a new direction, are deeply truthful and compassionate with yourself or another, when you act true to your values. It was an act of courage when I determined to get on my feet after divorce, to take charge of my health, and when I began to follow the voice of my soul rather than outside advice. Again and again I learned that when I took action I was able to move beyond my fear and became free of it. And even more, I brought home the gifts, the trophies and victories of fear. Repeating this process frequently, my courage has grown and I have developed a discipline and strength, a pride and self-trust that now form a powerful platform for my dreams. I highly recommend the courageous journey into fear. There really is nothing to lose. Welcome all your fears. Know them intimately. This will free you to live an abundant life.

THE GUEST HOUSE

This being human is a guest house
Every morning a new arrival —
A joy, a depression, a meanness —
Some momentary awareness comes
          as an unexpected visitor.
Welcome and entertain them all
Even if they are a crowd of sorrows
Who violently sweep your house
          empty of its comforts.
Still, treat each guest honorably
He may be cleaning you out for some new delight.
The dark thought, the shame, the malice —
Meet them at the door laughing and invite them in.
Be grateful for whoever comes
Because each has been sent as a guide from beyond.
                                        — Rumi

12

THE Soul's Intent

The seagulls screech vituperatively at each other. Our two Volkswagen vans, parked side by side, reflect the sun's glare from the water's surface; a languid ocean breeze lazily shifts puffs of sand near us as Jewel and I sip tea. Just a few hours ago I received an urgent message from her asking if we could talk and now we sit at our usual meeting place, on a lovely stretch of beach in San Diego, as she shares her impatience and frustration about her future.

"I'm eighteen years old; why can't I tell what I want to do? I hate not knowing! All my friends have summer jobs and college plans — I feel so aimless and anxious. I'm doing everything I can think of but nothing is working. Why can't I figure it out?" Her voice is tight with concern.

After she vents her fear and frustration, we sit quietly and I contemplate her question. In these months following high school she has indeed been feeling lost and consumed with worry about her future. Many times she has come to me asking for help with a wide variety of ideas. Will I help her arrange an art exhibit for her sculptures or drawings? Will I help her look into singing on cruise ships? She considers college and a career teaching grade school music. Will I help her put together a demo tape of her songs and try to get some music industry people to listen to it?

Each time my answer is the same: "When you are very sure what it is you want to do, then I will certainly help. Until then keep your prayers and your focus on connecting deeply with what you feel to be your soul's purpose at this time." This only serves to frustrate her further, but it is my sense that Jewel must connect with her soul to understand her next actions. The recent weeks of living in her van have been good for her in many ways, but she does not feel closer to decisions about how to proceed with her life.

"Jewel, I think you are nearer to a breakthrough than it feels to you," I affirm with an anodyne tone. "There is probably a fear blocking your connection to yourself. I have an idea that may help. Sit quietly, hear the water, feel the sun heating your skin, and experience the salt breath in your lungs; dig your hands into the sand. Close your eyes and know that this is the absolutely right place for you to be in this moment of your life. Then let all the sounds and sensations soften as you slip into the place where all is held in knowingness.

"Imagine yourself seated in an empty auditorium. There is a stage in front of you; it is cloaked with a red velvet curtain. You cannot see behind it. Allow yourself to become more and more curious and excited about what might be on the other side of that curtain. Then, as mischievously as a child, run down the aisle, lift the curtain, and peek behind it."

Leaving her to her meditation, I walk along the shore contemplating the meaning of the images that I spontaneously gave her. During our conversation, I had silently and quickly sourced that silent center of knowledge that we are all connected to. The image of a stage seems tailored for her contemplation and I ponder this. I know the exercise will serve to distract her fear and concentrate her attention. When I return she is writing furiously in her journal.

She looks up as I sit by her and says with elation, "I know what I want to do — and I know what I am afraid of!"

"This is exciting, Jewel. Tell me. What is it?"

"First," she says, "the fear is this — what I really want to do is so amazing that I couldn't bear it if I'm not able to do it."

"You mean you are afraid of failing?"

"Not exactly, it's more that it's so wondrous and so absolutely me that there isn't anything else I can imagine wanting to do. If I couldn't do it I wouldn't care if I lived. So I was afraid to even know about it."

"Well, what is it?" I say, laughing. "Hurry, tell me!"

"I want to sing," she exults. "I want to sing my own songs. And I want to sing to millions of people."

The gulls continue to keen, the sun to warm our crowns, the waves to shush themselves on the shore, but the air seems to have a peculiar quality.

The moment encases us in portent. We both resonate to a future that palpitates around us. Our hearts acknowledge that a soul chord has been struck.

Jewel breaks our silence: "Now will you help me make a demo tape of my songs?"

"There's something you need to do first," I tell her. "I want you to reflect on why you want to do this. Write your reasons down. All the good reasons, and 'bad' reasons, the secret ones, the embarrassing reasons. Contemplate those that come from your ego, your fears, your pain; the ones that seem insignificant and the ones that seem most important and deeply connected to your soul. All of them.

"Be in dialogue with yourself about all the underlying reasons you feel compelled or attracted to this dream. Why do you want to do it? What do you want to accomplish? What do you want out of it, and why? What can you sense that you are hiding from yourself? Be deeply honest. Write it all down and we'll discuss it." I leave her and go into my van to make iced tea.

She sets about the task, creating her carefully contemplated list. After a time she brings it to me. We sip tea and talk.

"The first thing I wrote down was 'money,'" she says. "I saw that it is so related to my fear — fear about feeling vulnerable in the world. I thought 'Why do I want money?' and I saw that mostly I wanted enough money for food and gas and to take care of my health. I realize that my desire for money is really a desire for security. Also I thought about the things that money could accomplish to help others.

"I wrote 'fame.' I was a little embarrassed about this because I realized what I really meant was that I wanted everyone to like me! I'm such a kid!" She laughed. "Mostly I saw that fame scared me. I was afraid of it because of the loss of privacy and stalkers and things like that. But I also thought that maybe with fame a person could do something for the world."

Going over her list, Jewel has many revelations as she becomes better acquainted with fears and feelings within her. To my eye, a pattern begins to emerge in her list; I am able to discern an underlying theme.

She speaks to this theme. "There is one reason, though, that means the most to me. It's so close to my heart that it is hard for me to talk about," she says, emotion filling her voice. "I want to help give people a sense of hope, especially kids my age; to try to help heal the despair that people feel. I want to sing to help make a difference in the world. This is what I just have to try to do; I have to. It feels like it's what I'm here for."

We sit in silence for a time in the heat of the day, grateful for the shade of our vans, and for our process together. She breaks the silence with a question.

"Why did you have me do this — write all this down?"

"The vision you had, Jewel, of singing your own songs for millions of people — it's such a huge dream, one that you haven't contemplated before. I know that in the process of fulfilling such a dream you will have to birth qualities in yourself that do not exist yet. I know that this dream will challenge you, excite you, tire you, discourage you, change you. You will be criticized and exalted, and buffeted by many conflicting energies. It is not a localized dream, like teaching music for instance, that places you in relation to a smaller community. It is a dream that places you in relationship with the world; you will feel the force of this. That world will project itself forcefully on you. To live this without losing what you hold dear about yourself, this dream must be one connected to your soul and to your sense of purpose.

"At times you will feel so afraid, exhausted, and overwhelmed by the demands, needs, and the agendas of others that you will wonder why on earth you are doing this. There must be a very good answer to that question or your fear, fatigue, and ego needs will beg answers that are destructive to your higher nature. You must have a real answer to why you are doing it — one that keeps you connected to your most authentic self. One that can realign you to your values and serve to remind you of who you most essentially are."

We contemplate and discuss these ideas and then Jewel asks, "Will you help me develop my career? I feel that I need your support and abilities, and your knowledge of me."

I am thoughtful for a time and then reply, "For this to be right there must be two elements present. First, the career must be so fully 'you' that the process is more one of my assisting in the unfolding of your soul, the development of who you truly are. The second is that it must fit with what is timely in my own life.

"Your dream is aligned to your soul's desire to make a difference and I can easily assist in that. My own passion is to be a difference, to embody the difference in my being — to live it — and to make the understanding of this opportunity available to people. Your desire to 'make' a difference and mine to 'be' the difference are facets of the same aim. They constitute the basis for a wonderful partnership — one we can enter into to accomplish our humanist goals, creating a global humanitarian platform in the world."

We stare out to sea idly watching a barge on the horizon that is harvesting seaweed, feeling the fabric of our lives weaving together on a journey toward separate and conjoined destinies. The moment had a peculiar quality of pellucidity and of certainty to it.

GENERATIVE MEANS

Jewel and I took time in that moment to speak our hearts to each other and to the beauty that is the Source. We shared our desires and our commitment and sent our intentions scudding out over the waves that rolled toward us, establishing our covenant to take our blessings out into the world.

This was a seminal moment for us. At the time, in the spring of 1993, we had little money and lived in our vans; but just five months later, Jewel had a record deal. Two and a half years later she had a multi-platinum record. Within five years of that day on the beach, I ran a global company with multimillion-dollar revenues — a company poised to become a powerful influence for humanist principles in the world. The principles of generative prosperity were at work in our lives.

By generative prosperity, I am referring to prosperity that generates and sustains itself through the application of natural principles. In the natural systems of this earth that supports us, prosperity involves influx and outflow, income and outgo — a rhythm and balance between these over time. Hoarding is not a defining principle of such systems; hoarding is nongenerative. To be fully self-generative and sustaining in one's prosperity requires knowledge of the true source of our prosperity and the understanding that all is already prepared for us.

During my time living "on the wind," I learned that generosity is one of the foremost principles of achieving a prosperity that generates further prosperity. I had been through a period of examining my ability to receive and my personal ideas about money, exuviating many ideas that limited providence in my life. I examined my desire for security, my wants and needs, learning to be very precise in the dreaming of my life. I had achieved great growth, reaching a place of trust and peace; I experienced many miracles of support and abundance.

I was determined to expand this support into all areas of my life. As Jewel and I both experienced health problems that required medical care, and lacking insurance or funds for it, I wondered why the support was so minimal. What else did I need to understand and perhaps change in myself to live and be cared for as are the lilies of the field?

> God has put a secret art into the forces of Nature so as to enable it to fashion itself out of chaos into a perfect world system.
>
> — Immanuel Kant

THE ABUNDANT WEB

A vision came to me during a time of contemplation about the very basic level of support I experienced in my experiment to be cared for as the lilies are. I was shown a layered web that covered the earth. Differing life forms were fixed within different webs. I observed that the "web" of animals was loosely woven, as was that of plants and other natural forms. Within these webs I could observe an exchange of elements and energy between the separate life-forms as well as from web to web.

The human weave, however, was exceedingly tight, so tight that little could pass through. The vital nourishment and energies were a mere trickle, as was the exchange between the human "web" and those of other life-forms. And even between humans, the exchange was minimal.

The voice of my understanding explained, "You see, there is a limitation to your experiment that is not created by you alone. You are part of a system, the human one, that does not know itself to be part of the larger system. You know yourself to be part of the small system, but struggle to relate yourself with the vast system within which you reside. Without a vibrant exchange with that larger system you cannot be fully provident in any way, not in health, or resources, or energy. Within this great system the human is designed to provide important support to the human 'web.' This conduit between humans is largely blocked by fear."

As I viewed this system of webs, I reflected on my own experience, remembering that people were very fearful of being of any assistance to me in my experiment of living on the wind. Most were afraid they might be taken advantage of, even by giving a job referral. People often didn't know when it was right to give and when not; they were unsure of what kind of assistance would be wise. They didn't know what, or who, to trust. They hoarded their contacts, their love, all of their resources. I observed that people were often afraid that if they helped there might be no end. Some feared they might end up broke as well. Most were unwilling even to share their unused items with others. I recalled one Saturday driving through a neighborhood, passing house after house with open garage doors. The garages were stuffed to overflowing with spare televisions, clothing, decorations, and tools that would never be used. They were not items I needed but I knew many who did. I realized how much we hoard our resources.

The voice of wisdom, following my thought process and remembrances, brought me back to the vision, explaining, "Human beings are intended to be one of the chief conduits of abundance into one another's lives, but you are so densely woven in this regard that little can work through you and thus there is a trickle into your systems instead of an abundant flow. As a group you currently experience a very low quality of flow."

"So the quality of flow affects the quantity?" I asked. "Does it follow, then, that if it trickles in by the spoonful, but I dish it out with a shovel, that I will have a more abundant life?"

"Indeed this is profoundly true," came the reply.

"But won't I end up broke and unable to care for myself? I know of many well-meaning people that this has happened to..."

As I asked, the answer came into my heart, "That is because they did not realize that they could — they *must* in fact — include *their own* requirements in their generosity. To practice fully the principle of generosity, you must include yourself in your expression of generosity. Place yourself in the equation. You cannot place yourself outside of the system, the abundance. It is a simple adjustment. Go forth now and see."

I did. I challenged my generous nature to expand; I counted my many resources and began to share outrageously. I had an older second car that I kept for the times when my own needed repair or in case there came a time when I needed to sell it to have some cash. On the highway one day, I saw a young Mexican-American couple struggling to push their broken-down car off to the side of the road. I assisted them into the nearby gas station. She was visibly pregnant with, I learned, their first child. The mechanic said that the repairs would be more than the car was worth; the couple was distraught, he would lose his job without the car. I asked the couple to wait for me. I drove home, returning with my second car, which I signed over to them. The happy scene was gratifying but it went further. Two weeks later the brakes went out on my own car. Having no money for repairs, I asked the mechanic if I could make payments. He replied, "You know, I saw what you did for that couple in here a while back. It got me to thinking maybe I owed one to somebody, so this one's on me."

We have all experienced these ripples back to us, we need only to magnify their occurrence with our creativity. When we give, we simply make room for more to come in. When we become deeply, authentically generous, it signals to our abundant universe that there is a conduit open to receive and to distribute. We become part of the vital natural system.

As a net is made up of a series of ties, so everything in this world is connected by a series of ties. If anyone thinks that the mesh of a net is an independent, isolated thing he is mistaken. It is called a net because it is made up of a series of interconnected meshes, and each mesh has its place and responsibility in relation to other meshes.

— Buddha

13

A Higher Ground FOR Humanity

We believe the blessings of our lives are for the benefit of humanity.

— Lenedra J. Carroll, Jewel Kilcher

GENERATIVE PROSPERITY

In the summer of 1986 I was at Pilchuck School, an international school for glass artists in Washington State. I was a teaching assistant in the copper electroform class and a student creating art prints on glass plates and lost-wax glass figures. News came to us of a garbage barge drifting up and down the eastern seaboard of the United States looking for a home. It was piled high with refuse from New York's overflowing landfills. Naturally, there weren't many takers. It was an ironic picture and, at the same time, a sobering one. The nationally reported incident was part of an ongoing wake-up call. The realization was beginning to sink in that our unconscious relationship to our planet was not a sustainable one. Important questions were being asked about use of all our natural resources as well as the disposal of our mountains of refuse and toxic waste.

The dialogue about sustainability is a vital one. Beyond environmental issues, the topic of sustainability is important. It applies to our own personal resources: our finances, relationships, employees, our life energy. These are areas as much in need of reform — and easier to impact than the global picture. And there, in the individual arena, we can also influence the global one.

Are our personal lives sustainable? Sustainability implies that the resource is efficiently used, is renewable, properly valued, and replenished wisely. Are our businesses in harmony with natural systems? Are our employees able to renew themselves? Are our personal finances sustainable or are we burdened by debt? Do our relationships and our jobs consume far more energy than they return to us? Individually we are nonrenewable resources. Do we tend to our personal resources responsibly? These are great issues for us to be grappling with and bringing change to.

What is beyond sustainability? What can we integrate into that idea to take it further, perhaps making it even more applicable to each of us? The idea that opens the dialogue further for me is the one I call "generative prosperity." It is primarily the thought that we frequently can do more than sustain or conserve. We can generate. This is an expansive idea as opposed to a retentive one.

A stagnant body of water develops deleterious bacteria and organisms that foul it and make it unusable. Moving water aerates itself, cleans itself, supports and feeds other life, and joins the cycle of water that ultimately feeds the whole planet. One is a small, closed system. The other is vastly connected and generative. With generative prosperity one experiences the sort of growth that comes from participating in passing along the energy. How can we be part of this? There are many answers. I like to start with values that, when applied to the business of living, are generative.

GENEROSITY, GRATITUDE, GRACE

The pebble in the pond illustrates how generosity generates more abundance. It's a simple principle that is profoundly accurate. To have a more abundant life, a more abundant world, generosity must be a defining wavelength of our society. Generosity of spirit, of resources, of action — all these find their life in the generosity of our thoughts that then reflects as our generous interaction. We all have a responsibility to participate in creating this plentitude.

Gratitude is another generator. Complete, humble gratitude at the inception of a desire or action signals recognition that the abundance is already there, is made ready for us. The responsive universe acknowledges this without fail. Gratitude throughout all processes of our lives soothes all outgoing and incoming waves, calms them and brings an ease. Gratitude is a magnificent rudder that steers us more surely. Learning the secrets of the grateful heart is one of the most beneficial things that Jewel and I have applied on our journey together.

Grace is earned by heeding the longings of the soul. "Grace," Jewel once wrote, "is the refinement of the soul through time." The continued forward movement of the soul expression in our lives begins to lend a grace that has charisma, an ability to attract or magnetize Divine Providence to it. It is well worth contemplating, yearning for, and valuing as a quality to embody.

Generosity, gratitude, and grace expressed through the outgoing wave are amazing manifestations of incoming waves of prosperity. It is the genuine gratitude of our thoughts, the generosity of our hearts, and the implicit grace of the limitless intelligence of the universe that have literally created the enormous resources that fill our lives. We feel a responsibility to share these. So many opportunities come to us, far more than we could ever act on. It's the same with money; while we take care to plan for our futures, and we enjoy many material luxuries, it is hard to conceive of being able to spend all the money ourselves. I don't believe that all those monies and opportunities are really ours — in actuality, they have someone else's name on them. The opportunities or resources come to me because of my ability and commitment to be a channel for resources. I think of myself as a conduit; part of the fun of my job is finding those for whom I have incubated opportunity and discovering people or organizations that will receive their endowments through me. This is something that I am prayerful about; it occurs with a great deal of divine serendipity.

HUMANIST PRINCIPLES

It was to serve this purpose that I founded our humanitarian organization, Higher Ground for Humanity (HGH). You recall that Jewel and I sat on a San Diego beach one warm spring day in 1993 and united in our idea to use her interest in a career in music to serve our real goal of building a large humanitarian platform in the world. HGH grew out of that desire. Jewel and I consider ourselves foremost to be humanists. The dictionary defines a humanist as one who cares about the condition of humanity, a person having strong interests in human welfare, values, and dignity. We think of Higher Ground for Humanity as a humanist organization.

It is a charitable organization with a nontax status, but I do not think of it as a nonprofit organization. Nonprofit is an idea that can sometimes foster a lack of accountability and sound business practice. The system of "nonprofit" frequently focuses on what is lacking; never enough money, time, or volunteers. Always needing, never full, it can be a need-based system — the need of the organization and the need of those it serves — neediness crying loudly and constantly for attention. This lack can result in frantic fundraising and competition among charitable organizations. Instead of nonprofit, I think of HGH as a profitsharing or providence-sharing organization. Our prosperity and that of others is redistributed in the world through Higher Ground for Humanity.

I require HGH to be generative, to practice conscious stewardship, and to operate with sound business principles. We are committed to being self-sustaining, and profitable; to this end we often develop ideas, programs, or products that generate proceeds.

All proceeds, as well as the resources donated by Jewel and me or by others, are dispersed to serve humanist goals.

We have supported a holistic health clinic in New Delhi, India, assisted a number of humanitarian organizations to get started, and supported many youth programs. In Nigeria we helped develop a civil liberties program. We assisted in the development of an environmental education program in schools throughout Chile. We are developing a grant program for alternative health aid and establishing natural clinics in Puerto Rico and Costa Rica.

In addition we are developing two separate workshops. One is a series devoted to improving health through holistic methods. The second is workshops for individuals and companies to deeply explore the principle of abundance in all aspects of their lives.

HGH endorses programs and organizations that promote humanitarian values and that operate on the basis of higher principles. We support global community and individual action to inspire positive change. Our areas of interest are youth issues, the arts, environment, alternative health care, and development of the human spirit. We accomplish our goals through education, research, innovative partnering, and program development. Primarily, we support our own programs, creating alliances with others working on similar goals. Application is generally made to us by invitation only.

> Our mission is to promote human excellence by pioneering what it means to be a human being in the highest sense, inspiring new possibilities for humanity. Our aim is to join with others in the world community in assisting to create peace and generative prosperity for all peoples.
>
> — Higher Ground for Humanity Mission Statement

WATER, WATER EVERYWHERE

The rainforest steams up around me. Even the turgid Amazon River's glistering cascade cannot cover the cacophony of animal sounds surrounding me in the gloaming jungle cover. The smell of plants rises up in the fecund air, bringing the drift of a bounteous and ancient pharmacopoeia. It is July of 1995; I am deep in the remote Amazon of Peru, the guest of a wonderful shaman whose love of God and understanding of nature and mankind is a blessing to his people and to us. Nature here is so immediate, so pure and undiluted that it is hard to remember pollution even exists on the planet.

We are here for a meeting of leaders from tribes indigenous to the area. Many of them have walked for days to greet us. We join with them in ceremony and exchange of culture and vision. It is a rich and wondrous time as the love and knowledge of the Divine is expressed, wisdom and prophecies shared, prayers given, concerns voiced. During a break my friend Jaqueline lifts her water bottle for a drink. Suddenly, one of the tribal leaders grabs her arm and says urgently, "Don't!"

Surprised, she stops, arm in midair, and looks at him inquiringly. "Don't drink bottled water!" he repeats. "You can afford to buy water, but we cannot. If your people keep drinking bottled water, the problem will not be stopped."

His urgent statement makes me realize that as we drift complacently into the habit of buying water, we barely realize the scope of the problem. There are millions who cannot afford to buy water and suffer the result. He tells us that there, in the pristine Amazon, clean water is a tremendous problem for people. Downriver from cities and industry, these remote areas ironically become the catchment systems for the refuse of civilization.

The moment lingered with me. Each time I drank bottled water I remembered and wondered. One evening a couple of years later I watched television in my comfortable study. Light from the fireplace and candles coddled me in reflected security; the world and its problems were far removed. I was on a journey through Africa, following the melodious voice of a British television commentator. There were curiosities, beauty, and travel hardships all spiced up with quirky humor to be enjoyed from the comfort of my couch. The camera caught a young African bystander who came unexpectedly forward and questioned the show's host. "Do you drink all of that today?" he asked, indicating the liter-and-a-half bottle of water the host was drinking from. "Yes, and more" was the reply.

The look of shock on the adolescent's face prompted a spontaneous question to him, "How much do you drink in a day?"

"None," he replied.

The camera and the show moved on but I did not. I turned off the television, realizing that here was a reality so compelling that I had to sit with it, delve into it. "How many people do not drink water every day?" I wondered. "And why?"

I began to pay attention to water, think about water, ask about water. I discovered that more than 10 million deaths each year are caused by diseases borne by water — that's more than from cancer, AIDS, and diabetes combined. I learned that 1 billion cases of water-related illnesses are occurring at any given moment in the world. Eighty percent of all illnesses and half of all children's deaths in developing countries are caused by water-related illnesses. There are 60 million cases of stunted growth and physical deformity associated with drinking contaminated water. I learned entire communities and even major geographical areas were rendered nonfunctional, nonproductive. I was stunned — I could barely conceive of the loss of human resources that this single issue was causing humanity.

Reared in an environment where one could drink out of any natural source without concern, the enormity of this staggered me. What had happened to our planet's water? What could be done?

More important, what could I do? I suggested to Jewel that we make clean water the environmental focus of Higher Ground for Humanity. I began to conceive a program that would begin first to bring relief to those suffering from lack of water and diseases caused by contaminated water.

14

THE Clearwater Project

*T*he lack of clean drinking water
has become the number one health epidemic in the world.
— *The World Health Organization*

In 1999 we launched The Clearwater Project. Since that time
we have demonstrated that, though it is a big problem, it is one with
simple and affordable solutions. On four continents we have
worked to provide safe drinking water to thousands of people. We
have installed treatment systems in schools and villages, provided
the means to pump clean water up from the ground, and piped
naturally clean water down from high mountain streams to communities below.

We have forged alliances with technology, education, and
installation partners, implementing solutions across the planet. We
have a program with exacting criteria, high standards, measurable
results, with successful follow-up and educational components.
And we have a program that is able to move quickly to save lives
and vastly improve the quality of life for millions who do not have
the simple necessity of water. We require a high level of local
community responsibility and involvement. We are succeeding,
too, in working across political, religious, cultural, and economic
boundaries.

We are solving serious water problems and paying attention to long-term sustainability, thus beginning to bring wellness to thousands of people. These are people now able to be productive who were previously unavailable because of serious illness. In addition, countless hours are also available that were formerly spent acquiring water. The families, communities, their countries, and our global community gain this productive time and these invaluable human resources. In this way the projects are generative — they create resources.

In the process we have met extraordinary people committed to similar goals. Some of them, like our vital associates at WaterPartners and WaterHealth International, have been working at high personal cost with very minimal resources for many years because of their dedication to the crisis regarding water. Borrowing from their years of experience and success, we have been able to move quickly into methods that produce positive results.

SISOGUICHI, MEXICO

For twenty years Jorge Morales has been taking bottles of safe water out to the end of a 250-mile road leading from Chihuahua, Mexico. There stands an ancient church-run boarding school that is the heart of the sparse 300-year-old village called Sisoguichi. The school serves the community by offering housing, food, and an education to more than one hundred Tarahumara Indian girls who bear the familiar symptoms of waterborne disease. A small infirmary, yards away, is necessary primarily to treat the painful intestinal ailments, chronic dysentery, and resulting malnutrition. It is because of the high rate of disease and his love of these native peoples that Jorge took the long monthly trips to the village to supply them with what relief he could. As a water engineer and former university professor living in Chihuahua, he had seen firsthand the immense suffering that waterborne diseases cause among the Tarahumara.

It was Jorge who first brought the Clearwater Team to

Sisoguichi in the fall of 1999. After assessing the situation and creating a plan, we returned a few months later to install a water system for the Tarahumara in the boarding school. Since installing the treatment system — which purifies water using ultraviolet light — Jorge has traveled back to Sisoguichi and each time finds that the clean water has improved the lives of its residents and its community.

AMONG THE MASAI IN SUKENIA, TANZANIA

The sun-dried air continued to suck all moisture from the earth. Drought was a way of life for as many years as most Masai could remember. Long ago, a well had been provided by the British but it had not worked for twenty years. Help had been sought many times, and promises made and broken. The people were forced to walk incredible distances to take water from holes dug deep into dry riverbeds that leaked small amounts of water to the surface. This water was often unhealthy water and always the amount was insufficient to sustain the lives of their people and their precious cattle. Their elders went out to a place sacred to them and held prayer and ceremony to consult with Spirit on behalf of their tribes. They returned with a vision of a group of people from the United States. "They will be good people, ones we can trust, and they will keep their word. They will help us get water," they told the villagers.

It was our privilege to be that group of people. In Sukenia, our team met a large community of three thousand proud Masai herdsmen and women eager to get to work. They were deeply committed to the project and met every requirement with enthusiasm. They gave us a number of their cattle and goats to help with the costs; we are now the proud owners of a small herd in Sukenia. Though these animals represented a minimal financial amount to us, they are their most valued resource and constituted a very large gesture of partnership.

They agreed to assign their warriors to guard the well as they guard their cattle. Raids are prevalent in this region, and this was another important commitment on their part. They also committed to opening a bank account in a distant village and pledged an amount of money from the sale of cows and goats each year for the long-term maintenance of the equipment. They provided labor for their well. The Clearwater staff and community of Masai men and women worked long days, side by side, digging trenches for pipe, erecting a tower for the storage tanks, repairing the well, and reinforcing the water trough with fresh concrete. A week of hard work and soon there was a full system ready, with an array of solar panels assembled by hand and mounted on posts facing the sun. It was deeply important to the Masai that it was the sun that took the water from them through drought and the sun that returned water to them through the solar panels.

The moment finally arrived when the pump was switched on. There was a long pause. Nothing. Hearts began to sink. Had we gambled incorrectly? Was there no water in the well after all these years? Then the solar power surged through the system and deep in the earth the pump could be heard purring to life. All eyes turned to the trough and the outlet pipe. Seconds later a great shout went up as water gushed to the surface. Our team cheered and the Masai led their animals forward to drink.

Then, in great concern, they rushed to fix a tiny drip that might leak less than a cup in a day. In that moment — seeing the look of wonder and reverence, the gratitude and deep understanding on the noble faces of the Masai — our team realized that though we knew the situation in the world and cared about it passionately, we did not really understand and value the resource of water nor hold the wisdom about it as they did. It was an important lesson and gift to us.

The Masai are proud of their culture, their ancient lifestyle. They are thoughtful and wise about change. They have experienced great loss: loss of their lands, loss of a vital way of life — one they know to be sustaining to their people and their world. Their population has declined. Many groups, from journalists to governments and religions, have taken advantage of them. They are now cautious and reserved about opening their ceremonies and lives to outsiders and cameras. This was a caution that we respected, but during the Clearwater Project, they opened their hearts and their world freely. They taught us their jumping dances, shared their thoughts, culture, and kinship, and invited us to have free range with our cameras.

"Tell the story of the Masai. Use our story to tell others about water, to help others," they said. This amazing group of people, with thoughts and traditions so different from our own, taught us about water, about community, and the depth and range of the human spirit.

LEMPIRA, HONDURAS

Seventy-five percent of the population of Honduras does not have access to safe drinking water. Chronic dysentery and cholera outbreaks are common. In the poorest region of this impoverished country lie the villages of Gualcea, El Sitio, Santa Rita, and San Antonia. In these communities things were desperate. Each day most women walked six hours round-trip to the Rio Mocal, a small dirty river contaminated by sediment and sewage from the city of La Virtud, upstream. Water is heavy and they could only manage to carry enough for their basic daily needs. Though the water was contaminated, they had no other available source. They were forced to make the impossible choice between the inevitable illnesses and even death caused by the water or to do without water.

When the Clearwater Project and WaterPartners visited the communities in July 2000, the people were hopeful, organized, and willing. They were ready to work hard to construct the project. They provided all the labor, they dedicated the equivalent of a day's wages each month into a fund for maintenance and repair of the project. They elected local water commissioners to oversee operation and maintenance, and they agreed to build fences and plant trees as part of a watershed protection program. With our team, they installed a six-mile gravity flow water system to bring water from a safe spring high in the mountains above. They also agreed to share the system with surrounding villages and to help educate and organize those communities about how to build and fund a water system. This combined effort created a simple low-tech, low-cost system that provides safe water to four communities.

Children there are now healthy enough to go to school. Mothers — whose days had previously been consumed by getting water — now have time to care for their families and communities. They have time and water for gardening to supplement their meager food sources. Many are beginning to pursue income-generating activities. A celebration was held in the village when the water flowed clean from the new site. During this, one man thanked a member of our team, pumping his hand emphatically. "Thank you, thank you," he repeated again and again. "You have given the gift of life to my village. If only you had come last year, then my own son would still be alive, but now at least the polluted water will not take more of our children."

A WORLD UNITING

You can well imagine the satisfaction Jewel and I have felt in being associated with a program that has such an important positive effect on human life. But with so much that can be accomplished by group effort, Jewel and I are thrilled at the growing participation in this project. It no longer feels like our project — it has grown far beyond the capabilities of any two people. Children are working with Clearwater as class projects. Organizations are adopting sites in urgent need of safe water. People are volunteering their skills as administrators, directors, videographers, organizers, camp workers, engineers, water experts, fund-raisers, educators, or laborers. Individuals are joining Higher Ground for Humanity to support the programs and this is creating a vast and powerful community of like-minded individuals working effectively to bring about needed change. Donations small and large come in from many countries —

from individuals, companies, churches, organizations, and governments. Doors are opened to us; the way is smoothed again and again. All of this help and more is welcome and needed. Something wonderful is happening. Individuals are joining together in the world to generate the healing and to be the peace that we all so much desire.

Generative prosperity is the principle of abundant creative expression. It is a natural principle that maintains that we are all expressing one spirit within an openly provident system. When a person, group, or country tries to stop the flow, hoard or capture it, they block the natural flow of generative prosperity. Then, although the abundance exists, the flowing input and distribution are cut off. The system becomes stagnant. It becomes ineffective in supporting the varied life force and the system as a whole begins to decline.

The principle of generative prosperity acknowledges that there is a source of the abundance that surrounds us. It allows that we are receivers, generators, and stewards of that providence. It advocates awareness and participation with the observable natural principles. And it celebrates the experience of sharing and redistributing the bounty that continually surrounds us.

Millions of hearts yearn to make a difference.
Every one of us has the potential to be something powerful,
a beautiful candle with the capacity to
illuminate an entire world.
Global transformation begins at the
level of the individual life.
Each of us, being what we want our world to be.
The opportunity is in our daily interactions.
Each moment a choice to align to our highest values.
To be more selective in our thoughts.
To make different choices in our conversations.
To elevate our actions.
Something wonderful happens,
unfolding every moment
in graceful and powerful ways. A natural force,
with the capacity to transform.
An unstoppable force that dwells in all of us.
It is the power of the individual life.
One by one we are hearing the voice of our soul,
sharing its wisdom, inspiring us to be the more
that we can be, to become our highest possibility.
A soul on fire that can set the world ablaze.
We can be the better world we wish for:
Be the healing, be authentic, be honoring, be peace.
Just one and a half percent of the people in the
world simply being more peaceful in their own lives
create a community one hundred million strong.
One hundred million people
living what they value and dream for the world.
Something wonderful is happening.
Be the difference that makes a difference.

— Higher Ground for Humanity script,
Be the Difference video

15

THE World We Have Imagined

H e was nine. It was his job to fill the coal bucket when it was empty. He always took too long and got in trouble every time. It was explained to him, sharply, "You need to be more responsible." So, the next time he vowed to hurry and win the elusive praise. But as he explained later, he found a lump of coal that looked like a space ship and he wondered where the space beings were. So he started searching, but you have to be very thorough and patient if you want to find space relatives. Soon his name was being hollered impatiently from the cabin.

He said later that he felt sad to get in trouble again, and he felt sad to hurry all the time and maybe even miss out on space people. And also he worried about what "responsible" was.

She told him not to give up playing and dreaming and that she thought he was already a very responsible young man. He said he thought so too, actually, and she said, "Good, believe yourself on that."

But that wasn't the end of it.

When he was thirteen, he called her and said he had just found out he had ulcers. He was afraid. He didn't want ulcers. He wanted help figuring out what he was so stressed about. They talked a long time. It came down to this:

"Grown-ups say I need to be a certain way — like them. Jobs, responsibility, college, vacations, relationships. And all the things that get you those. But this is what I see: they aren't happy. Sometimes they are, but most of the time they just aren't thinking about it so they can get by. They are doing what they think they should. They grouch at their kids and fight with each other. They are worn out by their jobs that not many of them like. They live for a few weeks of vacation, or they think they are their jobs. And the way they all argue that their way is right in politics or religion or whatever.... Well, they act like they have answers but most seem confused and lonely and anxious to me.

"I don't think I want what they have. When I was little I couldn't wait to grow up, but now I feel afraid to grow up. I hardly know any grown-ups with lives that are very fun or satisfying."

"I'm afraid that if I do what they say," he said, *"I'll turn out like them."*

She told him these are good questions. They are "trying to stay awake" questions. "It's easy to nod off and find that it all got away from you. Keep asking. And know that you can carve out the kind of life you want for yourself. Just keep at it, enjoying the process, until it feels right. Be responsible, also, to yourself. Keep listening to yourself and asking your questions. You will know."

❧ ❧

THE WORLD YOU IMAGINED

When my son called me on those occasions to share his concern about responsibility, I knew he had an outlook that deserved validation and questions that needed to be properly understood. When you were a child, when you couldn't wait to grow up, what was the world that you dreamed of and so looked forward to? I remember how confusing and frightening it was when I began to fear that the world was not the supportive and magical place I thought. Over and over again, from parents, teachers, church leaders, and the media,

I heard the same advice: "It's a hard world out there. Get realistic. You'll need a thick skin." At first I was incredulous, then aghast, then deeply frightened.

I recall a teacher who angrily told Jewel and her fifth grade class, "You kids don't know how good you have it. Wait until you're grown up and have to pay taxes. You'll have to work all the time just to make ends meet and you'll wish you were fifth graders again."

Jewel came home from school that day terrified about how she would ever be able to afford taxes on her allowance. That teacher was projecting her own fear, despair, and conditioning onto her young students.

Do you recall what you believed was possible as a child — the hope you had for the world, and for your life? Do you recall when you started getting talked out of it, retrained? "Silly daydreams, unrealistic ideas, get real," we were told. "People can't get along. There's nothing you can really do to change things. Be realistic, it's human nature. You have to really work hard."

This happens for some at a very early age. For many, it is around the age of eleven or twelve that the mists separating childhood from the so-called "real" world begin to be dispersed. It is a confusing and frightening time. Often grievous loss is suffered — the loss of much of our hope, innocence, and dreams, a forfeiture of creativity and imagination. For some it is the end of playfulness and outrageous joy. There is an inner struggle — something in us knows we are right, something struggles not to give in, not to give up. Many of us deal with our shock and fear by vowing to do something about it when we grow up — aching to make a difference in the world.

THE DIFFERENCE

Over the past several years I have met thousands of people who want to make a difference. I have been so impressed with their abilities, their leadership, energy, and passion and, in nearly all cases, their open hearts and good intent. These are people working very hard, often in extremely difficult circumstances and under great strain. I have been deeply touched by their stories, their commitment and determination, and their results.

I am also concerned about a pattern I have observed. These people work unceasingly and most are deeply fatigued. They usually have a high degree of stress and a deep sense of worry about the present state of the world and the future of our planet. They often feel alone and enormously responsible. They sacrifice their health and personal lives. They are concerned about how they will be able to carry on. And though they feel they must try to make a difference, they often despair about whether anything really does.

There are thousands of our young people in this group as well. Hundreds of thousands. With their beautiful hope, their boundless enthusiasm and energy, and their astonishing abilities, they are involving themselves on local and national levels in heartening numbers. They don't want to be part of the problem or to become like so many numbed and cynical adults they know. But they also are fatigued. In addition, they fear that somehow, in the stream of their increasingly adult lives, they might lose the qualities they hold most dear: their sensitivity and innocence, optimism, passion, their faith in life. I know that as young people, the adults of my generation were like that. We were sensitive, hopeful, and passionate about things that mattered, and engaged in taking or planning positive action. Now a high number of us are cynical and jaded. Or, at best, too tired and too busy for elevated ideas or even good deeds. Those involved in helping create change are often worn out and overwhelmed. Our children have determined not to become like us, but the chances are too high that this may happen to them.

new/good ideas + old methods = the same old results

Even important new ideas or humanitarian work, when carried out in the same old way, can only lead to the same old results. Observing myself, my organization, and others who are attempting to make a difference, I often see the common method: doing, doing, doing. I see nonstop effort, working endlessly at visioning, planning, strategizing, fund-raising. I see us not taking time to heal our wounds, or deal with our fear and despair; we are networking and traveling constantly, often living without basic support, eating poorly, sleeping little, stressing and worrying.

These are erosive factors. They create brittle results. They are based in the fear that it may be too late; there is too much to do; there is not enough time, money, or people to do it. These methods will wear us down and tire us out and this will affect our energy, our judgment and integrity, our passion and sensitivity. And our effectiveness. Over the long term, non-self-sustaining methods can have no other result. They cannot sustain a high quality result. The cost in human resources — our own or those who work for us — will be high. Eventually, the costs will be too high — areas of our life will suffer: our health, work, relationships, finances, environment.

We can assess how far advanced we are in this erosion by looking at the areas of our life in chaos. Have our important relationships suffered? Are we frequently emotionally charged, mentally fatigued, spiritually bankrupt? Are we often ill? Our life may be out of control yet we keep on going...and doing.

DOING. DOING. DOING.

Doing! That word should sound a little alarm in our head. If action was the key, it would have all happened by now. There have been countless doers who have been fearless, gifted, and successful in many ways. And yet, our overall situation in the world can be argued to have worsened generation to generation. There have been enough doers to pull it off if doing was the only part that mattered. There *must* be more.

THE "MORE" THAT IS POSSIBLE

There is something that we must combine with our action, with our doing. It is our being. We are human beings. How did we get that name? It expresses our most fundamental nature. We have become so focused on the world of doing that we have lost sight of it. I suggest the necessary world changes will never happen without the "being" part. I even go so far as to suggest that we could all start "being" and give up the doing entirely — just pack up all that effort and go home and play — and have a better chance at extraordinary results. The doing part can be pretty fun, though, and personally satisfying, even important if it's done with a sense of joy and being. I can't really imagine stopping all the action, but I can imagine being it. By "being" I mean living. If we are working for peace, we can *become* peace. If we are striving for love, we can *become* love. If it's kindness, we can become impeccably kind. The challenge is to examine the ways our lives are not peaceful, or loving, or any other thing — then determine to become it, really grappling with the difficulty and the opportunity of it.

> The opportunity of our times is for each one of us to understand, at a very personal level, that we can have a profound impact on the world in which we live. The greatest possibilities for global transformation exist in the fabric of our individual lives. If we can learn to become our prayers and hopes, expressing them in our daily interactions, then together we can create a more peaceful and loving world.
>
> *Lenedra J Carroll*

WHAT DO WE VALUE?

What do we each value most? I ask this question of people around the world — people of many different races, ages, religions, and politics. The answers are the same. Throughout the world the similarity of the things we value is one of our strongest commonalities. Time and again, people from all cultures list the following among the things they value most: peace, freedom, family, love, environment, quality of life, their spiritual beliefs, parenting, financial sufficiency, service to others, fulfilling work, education, beauty, kindness, goodness, authenticity, honesty, wisdom, hope. These are what we value, and yet our worlds may seem so different. Why? We would do well to ask which values we are living. Are we, perhaps, living our ego values by bickering and gossiping? Is intense judgment of ourselves and others the value we express most? If we value family most highly but have no time or spirit to give them, what are we really valuing?

It's not the world that is the problem — it isn't just Bosnia, for instance, that is troubled by great dissension — it is our individual lives that are not aligned with our highest values and that is what creates our world. We have created things to be the way they are of our own free will. Our human world absolutely reflects us. God gets blamed for the state our world is in, but that's actually a major cop-out on our part. It's time to get out of denial about that. We *are* responsible for the horror in the world — as it exists in each one of us. It won't get undone until we each create something else in our thoughts, words, and actions. *We are the fulfillment of the world we dream of.*

> You must *be* the change you desire in the world.
> — Gandhi

When one human commits to be what they value, anchoring those critically needed qualities into their own personal life, it is felt in their world and this makes a great difference. Children raised by parents who deeply live their goodness and wisdom can source those qualities. Organizations run by individuals absolutely committed to being harmony, peace, and stewardship have those qualities throughout. Good works done by those who deeply *are* their good works have far-reaching results — think of Gandhi or Mother Teresa, for instance. Think also of the ordinary people you know who live elevated values. We each have friends, coworkers, schoolteachers, neighbors, church leaders, and acquaintances who are living higher values. We all can. We can do so to an amazing degree, and as we do, our own lives change and begin to reflect the peace, harmony, freedom, and abundance that we choose to place in our being. Our work, friendships, family — all begin to change; our lives and our world are transformed.

Developing Jewel's career has created the opportunity for our organization to inspire and support this level of change. It is why we established Higher Ground for Humanity with the vision to facilitate the ongoing discovery of what it means to be a human being in the highest sense and how to live it.

REJOICE!

Send forth your expressed longing
lest the banked embers
become gray dust,
losing form to ashes.

The clouds move
and take their shadows
Hope riots at the gates
Go out in greeting!
Go out!
Release your joy!
Rejoice!
For all that you have hoped for
and prayed for
All that you have ever dreamed
        is coming to pass.

Be led at last to the secret heart
of that in which you live
and breathe and have your being.
Something wonderful is happening.

Lenedra J Carroll

THE
Architecture
OF THE
Workplace

WHY, IN OUR BUSINESS RELATIONS, ARE WE DOING THINGS IN
THE SAME CONSTRICTIVE WAYS, PRODUCING THE SAME PRE-
DICTABLE, UNSATISFACTORY, AND EVEN DESTRUCTIVE RESULTS?
I HAVE FOUND THAT BY ALTERING MY PERCEPTIONS, PIONEER-
ING CREATIVE METHODS, AND ADHERING TO VALUES, THOSE OLD
PATTERNS CAN BE BROKEN IN THE WORKPLACE. THIS ALLOWS
BUSINESS NOT ONLY TO BE TRANSFORMED BUT TO BECOME A
TRANSFORMING FORCE IN OUR LIVES.

Old Business, New Business

For most of us, the largest portion of our day is spent in our workplace. For many, as much as half of our waking hours are related to work. If our work does not contain our joy, does not embody our deepest sense of purpose, does not offer us the opportunity to express our most authentic selves; if through work we cannot develop an increasingly respectable self as well as more meaningful relationships with others — if we cannot do these things, then much of our life is truly wasted.

It is an unacceptable truth that all too often our work has nothing at all to do with who we are. In fact, work frequently seems to require that we hide or protect ourselves and disguise our real interests and responses. It can pit us against our coworkers, place us at odds with our own sense of integrity, and separate us from our spiritual selves. It is my experience that this chasm between our work self and our more authentic self creates deep-seated feelings of despair and futility. It is at the root of the question, "Isn't there more to life?"

ALTERING PERCEPTIONS

Something deep inside of us yearns to know what it means to be a human being in the highest sense. What really matters in life and how does that relate to our working hours? What is possible in a life that is a full expression of our soul? Can we satisfy our desire to be part of something bigger, to make a difference? We sense that we can be more, that we can make a significant contribution, yet there is a feeling of restriction, a draining of energy in a major portion of our lives and we are at a loss about how to do more than survive.

We can do far more than survive, though we may not know how. We are deeply habitualized to certain actions and reactions and find it hard to conceive of other things to say or do. It is an area where our creativity is most needed. Harnessing that creativity, allowing ourselves to step outside of our normal patterns and seek another view entirely, we can enter a new realm of satisfaction in the workplace.

YOU'LL NEVER WORK IN THIS TOWN AGAIN

I am in the office of an industry mogul. A few days ago he side-stepped the reason for the meeting. "Oh, let's just spend a little time getting to know each other better," he said vaguely. Before coming today I make an inquiry or two and discover that he, of course, has a very intense agenda. He is, in fact, inviting me in for a little deadly combat. He has something he wants and it isn't something I can do. Knowing his reputation, he isn't going to take no for an answer.

I seek some pre-meeting advice from our record label and the response isn't encouraging: "You can't say no to this guy without major consequences. He'll cause you serious trouble and damage Jewel's career if he doesn't get what he wants. And he's someone with the power to do it. Just do what he wants, it'll cost you less in the long run." Often our label will say no for us in politically difficult situations, but with this guy they aren't in a position to anger him. They need him too much.

The mogul's office is as black as a cave. Gleaming black granite floors, black fabric walls, black desk, black chairs and bookcases, black accessories. The black curtains are drawn and the black lamps with their black shades seem only to cast shadows. This is one serious dream I've entered, I think to myself. What fun! What are the chances of new light being shed on anything in this room?

He enters the office and welcomes me. He's wearing black!

The man is tall and powerfully built. His hands and head are oversized. His watery eyes seem to size me up — mother/manager, easy prey.

"Sit down, sit down," he booms heartily, gesturing to the couch. "I am so sorry — I forgot I have a call to make. If you don't mind. No need to move. It will only take a moment."

He picks up the phone, calling some unlucky artist's manager and proceeds with one of the most vicious, blackmailing exchanges I've had the chance to witness. His eyes bulge, the veins in his neck protrude as he threatens the manager with the demise of his artist's career. The mogul's voice alternately lowers threateningly then rises in rage, lowering and rising, in hypnotic rhythm. Then, amazingly, he finishes the conversation by hollering, "If your artist doesn't do what I say, neither of you will ever work in this town again!"

I'm astonished to hear him actually shout that old cliché, and then he hangs up! He turns his attention to me with a smile feigning candid concern and friendly ease. "I'm so sorry... couldn't be helped. Thank you for waiting," he says in his fruitiest tone.

I move from the couch to a chair in front of his desk. The black chair sighs as I sit. He again apologizes for keeping me.

I laugh. "You did that entirely for my benefit!"

He acts shocked, innocent.

I look at him calmly, "Have you ever had to blackmail me?"

"What?" he sputters. "Blackmail? Really..."

"Now come on," I say, "that's just what was happening on that phone call — we can speak frankly. You've never had to blackmail me and you never will. It's just not necessary to work that way. You've never had to blackmail me because I've worked hard to have a respectful, cooperative, and mutually profitable relationship with you. I think we've succeeded in this."

There is no aggression in my tone. There is nothing in me that feels combative. I am deeply calm when I speak. "I know that you asked me here because you want 'X.' You know an artist can't give that under these circumstances without economic consequences. I'm not going to be asking you to take actions that will be detrimental to the health of your business and I don't think you want me to take actions that would be detrimental to the development of my artist's career. That would be shortsighted on both our parts."

I continue, "I've been thinking that if you can attach 'Y' to 'X' and change 'X' in a couple of small ways that I don't think matter to you, then it's workable for me and probably gives you what you need."

I pause. He's considering what I said so I continue: "It's not a bad solution. But it's not the best solution possible. What annoys me a little is that if our relationship was not only a cooperative one but also a creative one, a lot more would be possible. We are both creative people. You've had many more years in the industry than I have. If our relationship was creatively based you'd have the freedom to come up with a much better idea than I did. So it annoys me to be limited to simply cooperating."

We are quiet. In the dimness I see him pondering. Then he laughs.

"You're right," he says, "I can think of a better way." He suggests another solution that is indeed a better one. It gives me an idea.

"We are planning another related event," I say. "We could add it to the mix, making our deal very innovative."

Now we're cooking, doing what we enjoy, what we're good at. Within a few minutes we have a great solution that excites us both. At this point I turn to him and say, "That only took us a total of seventeen minutes. You planned an hour for what you anticipated would be an extended arm twisting."

I grin. "Let's get some tea in here and relax for the rest of the time, hide away a bit. I remember when we first met a couple of years ago we had a surprising conversation in which you mentioned your spiritual interests. I've wondered about that, and I'll bet you haven't had a chance to discuss them at work since then, knowing what your life is like."

So I sip tea and he has his coffee — black. He throws open the black curtains and a magnificent view of the entire city floods in. We chat about our values, our lives, our work. We discuss the difficulty of integrating values into the workplace. He speaks of feeling cut off from himself. He speaks of his faith and his spiritual views and his desire to make a difference.

More and more, over the years, our mutual desire to make a difference forms the core of our business relations. He continues, in other dealings, to work out his confusion about power, his fear of losing control; but our relationship is now one that is both cooperative and creative, and is built on our highest individual values.

⁂

Business has become, in the last half century, the most powerful institution on the planet. The dominant institution in any society needs to take responsibility for the whole, as the church did in the days of the Holy Roman Empire. Business has to adopt a tradition it has never had throughout the entire history of capitalism: to share responsibility for the whole. Every decision that is made, every action that is taken, must be viewed in light of that kind of responsibility.

— Willis Harman

MAVERICK METHODS

Why, in our business relations, are we doing things in the same constricting ways, producing the same predictable, unsatisfactory, and even destructive results? No wonder many dread work. Much of our interaction in the workplace proceeds in mundane and even disturbing ways. A majority of us are deeply tired of the futility and irritation of these interactions, yet are enslaved by deeply habitualized methods, lacking a sense of choice regarding interaction or result.

There is a saying that defines "madness" as repeating the same thing again and again while expecting the results to be different. By that definition we are all, arguably, stark raving mad. Applying this to business, we can say that, at the very least, things will certainly remain the same as long as we employ the same methodologies.

To avoid the madness of the same predictable, undesirable outcome and to change the face of business will require us to employ maverick methods. By pioneering visionary and holistic methods, we can break the old patterns. Then, with new methods and new patterns, business will not only be transformed; it will become a transforming force in our lives.

Knowing where to begin is difficult, yet even the simplest of techniques can yield far better results. Slowing our thoughts down enough to notice our experience, choosing our words and tone purposefully, asking ourselves to be thoughtful, remaining even and nonreactive — all these allow business to be conducted in the power of stillness. Letting conversation slow down allows for greater precision. The greatest amount of misfiring of communicative and creative energy occurs when conversations speed up, particularly in those that are pithy and contentious. Slowing our thoughts down allows us to tap into the source; it allows stillness to inform our conversation and actions.

APPLYING MAVERICK METHODS

Recently we experienced a difficult negotiation regarding a concert appearance. The tour promoters, who were having financial trouble, were trying to get out of our contract by saying we were in default. Instead of contacting our offices with their concerns, they had their lawyer contact our lawyer, making threats. This was unusual for first-round dialogue. Their methods, as well as the accusations, were a tad irritating. They had not bothered to check their information and were simply venting in an inflammatory way that disturbed the smooth operation of both our aims. I was frustrated by the time required to sort things out with the lawyers.

I called the promoter to express my surprise, concern, and irritation, suggesting that we both research the situation and speak in two days. I let him know that I expected the two of us to move quickly to keep the situation from becoming something we would regret. I intentionally avoided any statements, opinions, or further dialogue in that initial conversation for several reasons. I was very irritated and needed to examine my responses to see what might be petty ego defense on my part. I wanted to allow my pique to settle and become more productive.

Also, at that moment, I didn't have all the information; I was unclear where the true problems lay and had no solutions. I like to have as much clarity as possible before beginning dialogue. Over the next two days my team worked to bring the complex matter into a summary of bullet points outlining the promoter's concerns, our position, questions, potential next steps, contractual issues, and evidence of what had actually transpired.

I completed a self-assessment and personal dialogue, taking a frank and humorous look at my own reactions and feelings about it. I spent twenty minutes in meditation before calling him, which allowed me to speak from a quiet and centered place. When we talked I was calm but firm. I asked that we handle any future problems differently. I outlined the situation from my summary, gave my view and suggestions, and asked him to share his information, questions, and ideas. It was my assessment that they were trying to create sufficient dissatisfactions to claim breach of contract and reduce their financial obligation to us. I spoke to this in a very bald manner, making it clear that I had little respect for such tactics and that I was absolutely immovable regarding the contract. I insisted that we create a joint view of the matter that served the furthering of both of our goals. As a result, a grave contractual dispute was averted in a fairly short time and important precedents were set for the duration of our relationship.

THE CALL TO CHANGE

Conflicts occur nearly every day in the workplace, as do opportunities for the solutions to overcome them. A coworker gossips about us. Management makes unrealistic requests. Someone is served with a lawsuit. We feel misunderstood or overlooked. And on and on. Our responses reflect a spectrum of emotion: retaliatory, passive, fearful, defensive, or victimized. If, however, we could elevate our responses in such circumstances, the outcome would also be elevated. There is always a way to elevate — to bring authentic but grounded feelings and solutions into — a situation. It requires a bit of practice, but the skill is not so daunting to acquire. In fact, simply remembering not to respond in a typical or rote manner will almost immediately change the outcome. We can bring a new interest, effort, and inspiration to every situation.

In order to change the face of things to come, we must change our relationship to power, anger, greed, and fear. Looking closely at my episode with the promoter is an excellent way to examine our relationship to these. There was definitely a power play made when the other company contacted our lawyers and made threats. This was intended to intimidate us for their gain. The next obvious steps could have been retaliation and dispute. It is an old, old game and business has been driven by such games long enough. When we continue with these worn approaches, business is conducted from fear or from exploiting someone else's fear, but acting consciously from our values puts us in a new playing field.

> Nothing is more powerful than an individual acting out of his conscience, thus helping to bring the collective conscience to life.
>
> — Norman Cousins

HARBINGERS OF CHANGE

Around the world a broad spectrum of companies — from small entrepreneurs to multinational corporations and business associations, from non-governmental organizations (NGOs) to government bodies — are collaborating to transform business. They are the harbingers of a more conscious, creative, and prosperous workplace, pioneering new methods for sustainable development and addressing social, political, and environmental needs.

- Ford Motor Company has assembled an international work team that is demonstrating how their global workforce can construct a lifestyle that positively integrates their home life, work life, and their community service. The company who brought the assembly-line mentality into our culture is now committing to the health of its employees.

- The Venkataswamy family in Madurai, India, started a twelve-bed eye clinic with the daunting mission of bringing sight to the blind and enlightenment to the soul of the poor of India, and to do so without grants or fundraising. Today, their five-hospital business performs more than 180,000 operations each year by world-class physicians. The endeavor is profitable even though 70 percent of the clients are non-paying. Their innovative hospital management combined with pioneering surgical procedures and technologies serve as a model to reform clinics in many countries.

- The Xerox Corporation is implementing a plan to reclaim its used products and refurbish them, eliminating waste. Over a five-year period Xerox found that the program saved an astounding $200 million in parts, inventory, and labor.

- In Holland, the flower industry created solutions for the industry's release of pesticides, herbicides, and fertilizers into soil and groundwater by creating closed-loop green-house systems. This greatly lowers the need for chemicals, and those that are still required are recycled within their closed-loop water circulation systems.

※ The American Society of Civil Engineers has revised its Code of Ethics to require compliance with principles of sustainable development and they are developing guidelines and materials to help the principles be applied.

※ In Texas, the Applied Sustainability Company brings groups of fifteen to twenty companies together in each of their regions to benefit from the fact that one company's waste is often valuable material for another company. Sharing resources has substantially reduced waste and costs for these companies.

※ The Hannah Anderson catalog of children's clothing encourages customers to return used children's clothing by offering a 20 percent discount on future orders. The company then sends the clothing to the poor in a program called "Hannadowns."

> You have powers you never dreamed of. You can do things you never thought you could do. There are no limitations in what you can do except the limitations of your own mind.
>
> — Darwin P. Kingsley

Companies are beginning to ignite with the possibilities for business to *give back* to the planet instead of focusing solely on how to profit from what they take. Innovative and concerned people are challenging the workplace to change to accommodate these possibilities for generative use of both human and environmental resources. In my company, we too are working in unique ways to serve similar goals.

BE THE DIFFERENCE

I remember a conversation I had with Jewel in 1993. We envisioned a global platform for making and being the difference. It is gratifying to look back eight years later and see how much has been fulfilled. For Jewel it has been through her music, writing, touring, appearances, and charitable work.

I have done this through artistic endeavors and through the creation of Mani Management Group (Mani, or MMG). *Mani* is a Sanskrit word meaning "the wish-fulfilling jewel at the center of the lotus." It is an international company that develops, manages, and funds a variety of business ventures. Mani includes entertainment and publishing ventures, a merchandise company, a multimedia production company, humanitarian organizations, and other business ventures. Jewel's career is managed by Mani from my company, Mani Artist Management, which represents several authors, screenwriters, and performers.

A common theme throughout all the Mani businesses is that of combining commerce with humanitarian goals. For instance, in Mani Artist Management, I only manage artists who are impassioned to be and to make a difference in their arena. They are artists who value the unique methods and principles that typify my management style.

MMG is a team-based organization operating with many common goals. This commonality gives us an unusually harmonious flow of operation. Throughout the company we have found ways to be innovative in our methods and create a healthy environment.

We have a somewhat unusual health plan that allows workers to choose alternative health care. In addition, special programs are offered as health options. For example, most team members have participated in a unique cellular and colon cleansing program overseen by a health care professional. The program reaped surprising health improvements for everyone involved.

Team members also are supported to attend classes or functions that serve their individual goals for personal or spiritual growth.

They are given opportunities to take time off for personal change, to take retreats. One woman was given two weeks off when both of her parents died in close succession. This allowed her time to come to terms with some of the deep issues that such passages bring up. Rather than staying at work with impaired efficiency, as usually happens at such times, she took the break and returned far better able to cope with the process of grieving as well as work. Several new team members have been put on salary with the injunction not to come to work until I felt they were sufficiently rested. For one employee, this amounted to ninety days off with pay. When he did come to work, he completed a six-month project in thirty days. His time off proved to be well worth my investment.

Thirty minutes are set aside each day for company-wide silence at three o'clock. We have a number of "virtual" employees in several states who join us in silence at that time. Occasionally we will be in meetings with outside parties and, when appropriate, we break for the company meditation. We are surprised how often the other parties ask if they can join us. Jewel or I may be on an airplane or in another country but we always try to link up to the company in this way.

It was my passion to create a unique company willing to fully live its principles, to be them. We have a company program called Be the Difference That Makes the Difference; it serves to assist all of us at Mani to discover the power of "being" and maximize the impact each individual can have on their life and world.

Each of the Mani companies are not only commercial enterprises but are considered humanitarian organizations as well; humanitarian values are woven into the goals and operations of the organizations. We monitor our impact on earth and human resources carefully and channel profits from the companies into humanitarian projects.

Some of the more abstract qualities of Mani are best summed up in a letter sent to me by one of my top executives. In part, she wrote:

I just returned from a week of meetings in Los Angeles and I had to tell you how grateful I am for the incredible work environment we have. I had forgotten how drab the "corporate" world is...not that the offices weren't nice — they were actually among the finest L.A. has to offer — but the color, the energy, and the feeling was drab. The people felt colorless, they seemed tired and listless and disengaged from their work. It was such a contrast to the work environment we have. Our world is so full of joy and conscious endeavor and purpose.

After more than twenty years in corporate America, I find myself only now in a place where the work environment is not only safe and highly productive, and where my abilities are fully appreciated and utilized, but even more, I realize that here my soul is seen, and valued, and nurtured. I feel so blessed to be part of what helps this company "be" what it is.

Mani Management Group is only one of thousands of companies around the world who are striving to bridge new ways of being into the workplace. As the numbers of people involved in this movement grow, we can begin to transform even at the global level of government, finance, and environment. Once again we see that it is through the individual commitment and efforts to change — in each negotiation or private exchange — that we can impact our national, local, or individual communities in ways that forever alter what has been.

17

Journey through Fear

May the atmosphere we breathe
breathe fearlessness into us:
Fearlessness on earth
and fearlessness in heaven!
May fearlessness guard us
behind and before.
May fearlessness surround us
above and below!
— The Vedas
(translated by Raimundo Panniker)

I know how overwhelming life can be. Years ago, I had a business experience that threatened to engulf me, capsizing my fragile vessel in serious legal waters. I was a young businesswoman unskilled in the "system," unprepared for federal auditors, the FBI, and the local district attorney's office to intimately enter my life. I became front- page news. But the adage "any press is good press" had not yet entered my lexicon. Looking back with compassion, I see the importance of the event and how it changed who I am.

In 1984, broke and recently divorced, I started a stained- and etched-glass business. I designed and created decorative glass for private homes, builders, and local businesses, and soon added an art glass gallery. In a move to further expand the business, we conceived of employing developmentally disadvantaged adults. Hiring special needs employees, I worked with them to create a line of Alaskan gift items, corporate gifts, and artful dinnerware. They were wonderful employees and imaginative artists; their "outside the box" thinking resulted in spontaneous and delightful designs that were very popular in my gallery.

During the process of working with their service agency I learned that this group was entirely dependent on federal and state funds for most aspects of their survival. I determined to create the gift and award line as a separate employee-owned business, with the profits providing financial independence for the disadvantaged employees. Since this had not been done before, we began to create a new model with the encouragement of several national foundations. We presented a business plan and received a large grant from HUD, the federal Department of Housing and Urban Development. It was a happy day when the check arrived for a quarter of a million dollars for the first phase of setting up the business.

This federal grant was administered by a local city office. Our project was a shining example of entrepreneurial humanitarianism in the local community. Everyone was pleased: HUD had created the first grant of this kind, the city had its first such HUD grant, and I had the first grant I had ever received. Here is what I have since learned about first experiences: if it's everyone's first time, no one knows what they are doing.

The contract was signed but the promised rules and regulations did not appear. Though everyone was nice, and friendly, there were never answers to my questions about how the grant was to be accounted. I had been running a small mom-and-pop enterprise, and had little business experience or education. In fact, I kept my business receipts in brown paper bags and at year's end I handed them over to a bookkeeper with my simple ledger for taxes. Understandably, I was a little nervous about what I didn't know. But the feeling of goodwill on all sides tempered the fear, and everyone's advice was "Don't worry," so I continued with the plan.

Eventually it began to feel as confusing as a virgin's wedding night, lots of groping and bumbling in the dark. The second installment of the original grant was due and a new grant had been approved; I became concerned about proceeding in such confusion. I called a member of the committee who was an accountant and asked for two things: I wanted him to review my ledger so I could determine how they required it to be kept, and I wanted a meeting of the city's grant committee to help sort everything out. He looked over my ledger and felt it was rather rudimentary; he said he would arrange for help to set it up properly. He also requested the committee meeting. At the meeting no one seemed to clarify anything at all, as an audit was required at the end of the grant cycle anyway. I suggested to the committee that an audit would serve to answer our questions and insure that all was properly set up for the second grant. They agreed and we arranged for the federal audit.

Things heated up fast. When the audit results came in I got a few demerits and was requested to make some changes, but the local committee was in serious trouble. Their contract with me had been drawn up improperly enough that it could be considered illegal. There were so many other infractions in their administration of the grant that HUD threatened to revoke all funding to them. This meant the loss of millions of dollars and numerous jobs.

One of the local auditors, a man with a lot of integrity, later told me what happened next. In the panic to justify and hold on to their jobs, they decided to create a plan to show their ability to correct current problems and administer the funds. Part of that plan was to take a hard line with me. They suggested in hushed and serious tones that there might be a misappropriation of funds on my part, or commingling of funds. To divert attention from themselves and show they were serious administrators, they drop-kicked me to the FBI.

I had always had all my monies in one account. In my small struggling business there was never enough money to differentiate, so all the money was in one pot. If you add federal funds, such as a HUD grant, to that pot it is called commingling of funds. It is a federal offense and that was news to me.

The ensuing drama overwhelmed me. I was thoroughly investigated — I recall stepping from the shower with a towel wrapped around me to see an agent peeping in my window. I was examined, interviewed, badgered; friends and associates were hounded for information. A local failing newspaper picked up the case and made me front-page news in an attempt to boost their sales as I had some local renown. At a critical stage of shifting the business focus from my studio and gallery to the new manufacturing business, I no longer had the choice to revert to the former business. Without funds to continue, I had to shut the business down.

I was frightened. No, I was terrified. I didn't know where to begin or where to turn; I didn't know what kind of help — legal or otherwise — I needed. I immediately returned every cent of grant money still outstanding in my account, but other than that I didn't understand the situation, or how to proceed. I wanted to pull the covers up over my head and hope it would go away. It all seemed so much bigger than me. But there was no place to get away from myself, so I was forced to take action. I borrowed money from family to retain attorneys, hoping they would take things in hand. I didn't know how to use or talk to an attorney, I didn't know what they did or didn't do; I had never had cause to require one.

Living in a state of nervous shock, I wasn't eating or sleeping well. I was worried sick about how I would take care of my children in all of this. I didn't know where the money would come from for our support and the mounting legal bills. The extreme stress mounted, combined with a poor genetic inheritance, and eventually resulted in serious heart problems at age forty. I suffered a minor heart attack and, with a cholesterol level over 750, doctors considered me a high risk for another.

All around me, voices spoke urgently of situations and action needed. The voices of my doctors suggested radical and baffling solutions. The confusing and strident voices of lawyers, district attorneys, FBI agents, government officers, newspapers — all were filled with their own agenda-laden versions of who I was and what I had done and what I should do. Everything seemed out of my control.

In desperation, I resorted to the only method I knew. I went into the forest and asked God to make it clear to me who I was, and what I had done. I wanted to know how to face this, what action to take. I wanted to know what to do with my feelings of failure and my guilt about that failure. And I wanted to know what, within me, dreamed a situation in which I became president of the local chapter of the Joan of Arc club.

In the quiet of the evening forest a sense of peace came over me. In that peace was confirmation of my good intent, my innocence, and my noble effort. This was followed by a gentle but probing review of my fears, patterns, weaknesses, and blind spots. I saw the many warnings I had ignored because I was fearful about what to do. My fear of confronting situations head-on because of feelings of inadequacy had played an important role. Confusion and fear about money caused me to minimize the attention that the monetary systems needed. My emotional need to be praised and liked made me emphasize the flattery and overlook the faults. I preferred to stay in the excitement of vision and was not sufficiently grounded in concrete action. I was too often vague and indirect in my communication.

The list was long, but it was the information I needed so that I would not end up in such a situation again. After this review I sat in silence for a long time. As darkness fell around me I realized I was shivering with cold, but still I sat, staring and drained. The wind picked up, rustling through the trees, and slowly an energy began to rise up in me. For the first time I felt the white heat of anger at the injustice that had been visited on me as I allowed myself to finally realize the extent to which I had been used to cover the errors of others. I realized fully that they had pointed the finger at me simply as a diversion to cover their own backs. I shouted with fury into the wind and vowed I would not be taken down by it.

It was with this energy that I came out of the woods. I re-entered my world with the gift of knowing myself *fully* in the situation. I began to gather my resources, educating myself and investigating what had happened. I turned the situation from one of ignorance to one of determination and then to one of wisdom. I would not simply give myself over to the flow of something that seemed larger than me. This was the turning point. I took charge where I could do so. In the end I was probably the only person involved who had a clear sense of all that had transpired and my own part in it. Everyone else remained caught up in the blaming and justifying, trapped in bondage to their guilt and fear.

Eventually even the FBI and the district attorney's office came to believe an injustice had been done. They helped find a solution that put an end to the situation. I was free at last. I refused suggestions that I take legal action against other parties involved — I wanted my life's energy available for what lay ahead.

My old life was finished. I met fears and changed patterns that had plagued me most of my life. I left behind much of the person I was for forty years. I had learned I was strong. In fact, I realized I was bedrock to the core of myself. I had learned I could trust myself deeply. I turned my attention to my health and my future. I knew I would return to business, but I knew I would never do it the same way again.

> How do geese know when to fly to the sun? Who tells them the seasons? How do we, humans, know when it is time to move on? As with the migrant birds, so surely with us, there is a voice within, if only we would listen to it, that tells us so certainly when to go forth into the unknown.
>
> — Elisabeth Kübler-Ross

In the previous story are many of the seeds of my current business operations. Because of this experience I began to educate myself about business, reading and taking courses. I questioned my values and my methods. I learned to maintain a deep commitment to the truth about myself, to my passion, and the values that guide me.

Today I move my businesses forward from a place of stillness and teach others to do the same. I pioneer the understanding and integration of new principles for operation and bring a powerful intuition and innovation into my guidance of the company. From the silence I bring forward the creative vision necessary for business development. But this time around, I am surrounded by people far more adept at daily operations than I am. This time I have very talented advisors, and masterful financial officers and systems; I insist on sound business practices and principles that are grounded in universal values and humanitarian interests. It is my intention to change the nature of business by beginning at the heart of my own domain.

ANGER, A FORCE FOR CHANGE

The anger that welled up in me during the turning point of the litigation experience was the fulcrum for change; that kind of anger is transformative. Anger is generally considered to be destructive, and anger certainly appears to be running amuck and wreaking havoc in our families and schools, as well as our global relationships. Because of this we fear anger, we often under- or overexpose our angry feelings, missing a valuable opportunity.

Anger is a powerful force for creativity. We have all noticed that when we are angry we can get a lot done. We might, for instance, clean our entire house from top to bottom without even being aware of the labor. Or, tapping into the anger of "Boy, I'll show them!" we find that a project or goal can be completed brilliantly and with ease. Generally we believe that anger requires a target, that there must be a situation or person that we project it at. It does not need a target; it is merely energy.

The goal is to utilize that energy masterfully rather than letting it master or consume us. What is necessary is to elevate anger by allowing ourself to be in the moment in which the emotion is experienced. Not to interpret, judge, or act but simply to be. Be with it, be in it, be it. Let the emotion be expressed as a beingness rather than one that must be mitigated, transformed, contained, feared, acted out, diverted, or projected. All of these have to do with judgment. Beingness acknowledges the fires of the emotion and its connection to our divinity. Beingness — being with it, being it, allowing it to consume our being, letting it be what the physical body and the emotional body, what the whole self fully experiences — allows anger to burn hot and fast and to give way to creativity.

Tracking the emotion back to its essential impulse, it is the desire to be able to express fully. That is what we seldom do with one another. It is the deep desire not to be reigned in by constantly editing, examining, controlling. When taking the step to access the freedom to fully experience our anger, we might experience some unevenness, a wider swing of emotion, more irritation. That is simply the stage of learning to play the instrument, running the scales, experiencing our capacity within.

It is good to stay with that desire to express more fully and freely, embracing the passion it unleashes within us, noticing how alive we feel. We will discover it is a compelling energy that flows back to us, changing and feeding our lives. We can allow ourselves, from time to time, to step right into the center and rout out that power that is vested in us. In it are the seeds of what we know can come to be — for each of us singly and for the world that surrounds us.

Fear-based anger is destructive, yes. But anger that is the passion of forward motion, the passion of a dynamic evolving self, that essence of anger is a fire that is brilliant and compelling. We know that what we call "righteous" anger is anger that brings alignment. It is anger that has no fear attached to it, no needs and agendas. That energy of anger is nothing short of the most creative power that we have vested within us. We view anger from the narrowest of perspectives, but anger, and the energy of it, is the energy of the sun. Blasting! Transformative! It throws off energy that generates life, connected to the impulse of birth, of change, and creativity.

Our life, our government, our purpose, our planet — these all cry out for this constructive force for change. Imagine the strength we can wield against the rampant injustice, great or small, that permeates our personal and business arenas.

> Power! Did you ever hear of men being asked whether other souls should have power or not? It is born in them. You may dam up the fountain of water, and make a stagnant marsh, or you may let it run free and do its work; but you cannot say whether it shall be there; it is there. And it will act, if not openly for good, then covertly for evil; but it will act.
>
> — Olive Schreiner

POWER, A FORCE FOR GOOD

Everyone has an arena of influence, of power. The most immediate, of course, is oneself. This is the arena in which we can have the greatest effect. Then, to lesser degrees, our family, work, or community feel our influence. We fear power yet we also crave it. We are often loath to take up our power, to be empowered, whether for ourselves or for a cause, yet we are quite frightened and mistrustful about relinquishing our power. In our confusion about this, we often engage others in fruitless power struggles.

The world languishes in the shadow of those who are not afraid to wield power for their personal gain. They do not hesitate to seize control of the environment, of human resources, or financial systems. They posture and threaten to discourage anyone from challenging them. So effective are they that we believe we are powerless. It is a myth, an illusion. We have as much power vested in us; it simply remains dormant, lacking the passion of purpose, of joy, of anger to ignite it.

Those who abuse power to further their greed do not outnumber us but they are more aggressive and fearless, they are passionate about their game, quick to rally, slow to retreat, more certain, and much better at bluffing. The forces for good need and deserve to have servants with the same qualities. Perhaps the most prevalent and damaging "evil" is the failure to powerfully cast one's lot with the numbers of people engaged in the right use of power.

We all know the seduction of power from our own willful attempts to impose our agendas on others. We know, too, from our frequent observations of people with increasing amounts of power. Power has a great temptation in it. The greater the scope of one's interplay with people, the bigger the temptation to use the power for personal gain. This is easy to observe in global politics and religion and global business. It is all too apparent in our own individual lives and countries as well.

We need to grapple with power. The unhealthy, fear-based relationship to power has brought chaos on our planet for long enough. We need to come to peace with power. We need more leaders willing to pioneer new relationships to power, willing to discipline ego, and willing to face — with grace, wisdom, and humility — all of the many questions and temptations that arise.

There is a dialogue we can each have with ourselves, asking, How do I use my power? Do I use it to get what I want or to manipulate others? Do I use it to get taken care of? Do I use sex as power? Do I intimidate others with silence? Is money my power, or beauty? How can I channel my power more creatively, more fearlessly, and for greater good? The more we fully examine the limitations of our beliefs about power, the more we can impact the evolution of humankind in an important way. By understanding and changing how we perceive and interact with power, we enable ourselves to become powerful and to influence our common good.

18

Facilitating Transformation

R ecently a friend asked me how someone like me manages to work in the entertainment industry. "It's so lacking in integrity and decent values," he said. "It's full of sharks. How do you do it?"

I laughed and told him, "There are no sharks."

"Either you are pulling my leg, or you are horribly naive. I've been in this industry for thirty years and I know it's full of sharks," he replied incredulously.

That's certainly how we all think of the entertainment industry — sharky waters. I remember the first time I saw one of those bad boys headed for me with ill intent. He wanted our participation in his event no matter what contracts we had to break and regardless of the cost to us or to others. He was condescending and threatening. He tried some fairly heavy intimidation and hinted that there was much to lose if we declined. It felt very real; I experienced a fight or flight response. However, I had already come to realize that such things are often different than they seem. Our reality is merely a lot of simulated projections.

So I decided to take a look behind the perceptions: the perceptions that I was at risk, that he could harm me, that I had something to lose. Even the perception that he was a shark at all. "How is this situation different than I have been conditioned to think about it and react to it?" I wondered. For some time following, when dealing with the "type," I stepped back and observed throughout the interaction, noticing, pondering, puzzling.

≈ DISCOVERING THE ILLUSION ≈

I may be in a little trouble here. The negotiation has become a tad ugly. I have the sharkiest shark of them all circling for the kill. His small close-set eyes are beady. His nose is a sharp narrow ridge on a hatchetlike face. Full of threat and venom, his jaw seems ready to crush my little cranium. As he saws back and forth with his will and his threats, saying he'll ruin Jewel's career, that she'll never work again, I take a moment to dive down, down into the depth of the source of my peace. From there I pause to breathe and observe. What else is at play here? What can be seen from here that is less apparent on the surface? He circles back around, coming full face and at that moment I look right into his eyes and a recognition nearly floors me.

I get it! He's wearing a shark costume!

As with any mask, the eyes give it away. Behind the shark posturing, under the costume, is simply a man — a guy in a shark getup. The realization is such a good one that it's hard not to throw my head back and laugh right here.

I'm looking at him and saying in my head, "Amazing. An absolutely amazing costume. My hat is off to you. Where on earth did you get such a magnificent outfit? You made it? Inconceivable. It's perfection, well done."

While he's laying out what I need to do for him "or else," I'm thinking, "I know that costume; we all do, whether we ever put it on or not. It's just another choice available in the costume shop. We all know how to get a shark outfit; we know the power of it, the allure of making the kill. We know the cost of it, the weight of it, how hot it is in there and confining. It pinches in vital places!"

His face is quite red and he's worked up a case for himself, but instead of fear or combat, I'm feeling some humor, compassion, and enthusiasm and I know I'm on to something because those three qualities bring an incredible ease into any situation.

He goes on a bit more while I feel out what seems a productive direction. I'm excited because I know precisely what this whole incident has to do with me. It has everything to do with why I'm here on the planet at all — to pioneer new ways to be. So I'm wondering what else can be done here besides the same old stuff we all keep doing that is absolutely proven to have the same old results. I go deep into myself in the small moment available. It doesn't take much to go there, mostly presence of mind.

Suddenly I get clear: a) I can't do what he wants; b) there's a connection here, find out what it is; c) have fun doing it; and d) don't relate to the costume, relate to the human being behind it.

So I wait for a pause and I say, in an easy way, "We don't have to go there."

"What? Go where?"

"We don't have to go through all the threatening and posturing." I say this humorously and raise an eyebrow. The direct take is often best.

"I can't do what you are asking and I know that you are very aware of why. Right now our time is short — I have another meeting and you have a conference soon. Yet there's certainly a great deal of energy here and it seems to me there's a connection worth pursuing." His face shows me that he's puzzling about where I'm headed. "Obviously the connection isn't the idea we've been discussing. Let's take a little time to think about what it might be — there are probably any number of things we can do together. I have a hunch we'll have a very productive relationship over the years." His body is relaxing more in his chair and it feels like he is open to my direction, so I continue: "I'm still in town for a few days; let's meet again. We can share information on our future plans and needs and see where our agendas meet."

We do. Two days later we have lunch. I tell him what we care about, what we're building; he tells me what he needs, where he's headed. We learn a great deal more about each other, and we find something pretty interesting to do together. After that we work together on several projects but he never suits up as a shark again. At one point he confides to me that it's a great relief to work with me because the cards are always on the table, things move quickly, we have fun, and we often end up making a contribution to things that matter. He says he doesn't get to do that often.

THE COSTUME

Imagine you are going to a costume party. It is one you are very excited about. You put a lot of thought into your costume. You decide to go as a brunette with blue eyes. Tall. Attractive and exotic. Colorful. Superb outfit, really great hair. Original, with flair, very artistic.

At the party, you get a lot of compliments on your costume, people like it. They call you an artist, which you like. But they all feel the hairdo isn't quite right and eventually you change it. You respond to their identities too and everyone begins to feel very comfortable in their costumes. The party goes on and on and it all seems so real. You certainly feel very artistic in your costume, and it helps you know how to act with others, which is handy. Everyone is having fun being what they have chosen to come as. Gradually you, and everyone else, begin to forget that it is only a costume. You think the costume is who you are.

Lenedra J Carroll

ALTER THE GAME

Each morning we get up and dress for work, not realizing that we automatically put on a costume each day. Our ambitions, agendas, fears, hopes, wounds, opinions — all these combine to form belief systems that create learned behaviors. They become automatic over time. They create a virtual costume that describes for us a role we then play with little thought. Choosing to recognize this, and committing to thinking and acting differently, allows us to go beyond our current limitations in the workplace.

We can hold less tightly to how we think things are done, shake that loose in ourselves, by remembering it is all simply an inherited or fabricated costume. It's costume as context. Like any costume, we can alter it or set it aside entirely. People with the ability to consciously access a vast range of choices of expression have far more successful and fun lives. It is possible to enjoy this free range of characterization while staying true to our core values and self.

Now, when I encounter the sharks, I don't take the bait. I have no shark reality and therefore no participation in it — no exaggerated response. This is due to the fact that I am not in interaction with their costume. I don't respond to their threats, posturing, manipulation, flattery, or other similar methods. Their tone, their force of will, choice of words, facial expressions — all costume, costume, costume. I don't react to any of the trappings of their costume. It dramatically alters the game.

RELATE TO THE SOUL

I relate to the soul that wears it. At the level of the soul we are both merely two beings in costume. He has his and I have mine; they are very different but they are simply costumes. It is common for there to be scripts and agendas attached to the costumes. They need not be of great dramatic concern.

How does it change the interaction when I no longer relate to the costume? Locked in the same old game we know the rules, how to get the upper hand, how to build a strategy to outmaneuver. We know the techniques: threaten, rage, out-strategize, one-up, resist, bluff, lie, pretend, flatter, cover up, blackmail. Beneath the costume we are simply two humans with human feelings and needs — two souls having a life — there is no game and the rules are off, the footing is equal. It's a relief to all involved; it shifts the context and allows a new situation to develop.

GENUINE EXCHANGE

This more elevated relationship can't be postured, pretended, or strategized. When the relationship is to the soul, that relationship is based in authenticity, a far more genuine exchange.

In a genuine exchange one comes from a less complex place of being. Rather than wearing the costume or engaging in the games and strategy, there is the opportunity to move away from posturing, suspicion, and judgment. Directness, honesty, and a simplicity of action and thought become the order of the engagement.

By the nature of its genuineness, a different outcome is assured. The outcome begins creating itself from this more real place. It doesn't matter, then, whether the agendas ever get served; sometimes they do, sometimes they don't. In my experience more often they do. But when a genuine human exchange occurs business is no longer detached from our lives.

BEYOND WIN-WIN

I am not talking about creating win-win situations. I am suggesting developing a style in which winning is not paramount — one in which the winning outcome is not the goal but where the goal is to have a brilliantly successful process. The successful outcome will follow — it is a by-product of thoughtful, soulful action.

This way of working is not a strategy; it cannot be plotted and planned ahead. It springs from a commitment and it then occurs spontaneously in the moment. One can prepare, yes, but all thoughts and ideas about the situation must be held loosely. It is imperative to be fully in the present and open to what is seen, known, intuited, and acted on in that moment. It is in that moment that the more that is possible will reveal itself.

I'm suggesting that we do more than create win-win scenarios. I'm advocating changing the focus from winning to being. When we access our thoughts and actions from that limitless Source, the core of our existence, we can absolutely trust the results. They are some-times surprising, but always productive, and very right.

> Probably above all, they [business leaders] will need integrity and personal mastery — an ability to remain centered, especially in times of crises, with a sense of inner peace and an uncompromising commitment to living the values they espouse.
>
> — Jane Nelson

WORK, WORK, WORK

A prominent natural health doctor from India visited me for a period of months. At the end of her stay she said that her most surprising observation was how hard Americans work. She had arrived with the idea that we were wealthy and therefore somewhat idle, but she was shocked to see that we work so very hard for our wealth and keep on working after we achieve it. Judging by our affluence as a nation, the incessant industry seems to be paying off. But is it really what brings the success; is it the best way to achieve our goals? Thomas Merton challenges the idea that the frenzy is fruitful:

> There is a pervasive form of contemporary violence... [and that is] activism and overwork. The rush and pressure of modern life are a form, perhaps the most common form, of its innate violence.
>
> To allow oneself to be carried away by a multitude of conflicting concerns, to surrender to too many demands, to

commit oneself to too many projects, to want to help every-one in everything, is to succumb to violence.

The frenzy of our activism neutralizes our work for peace. It destroys our own inner capacity for peace. It destroys the fruitfulness of our own work, because it kills the root of inner wisdom that makes work fruitful.

WORK STILLER, NOT HARDER

In the late fall of 1994, the cover of *Newsweek* magazine ran a photo of Harvard president Neil Rudenstine with the headline: "Exhausted!" He had collapsed from overwork, requiring a three-month rest before he could return to his duties. This is not an isolated case. Our belief that time, productivity, and activity are the elements that lead to suc-cessful outcomes is causing an epidemic of fatigue and health issues related to it. It is the American work ethic, grounded in the dream that anyone in this country can become prosperous if they just apply themselves hard enough. And so we strain and toil to an amazing degree. Perhaps we should call business "busyness" because we believe our success is directly related to how busy we are.

One of the most transformative actions we can take is to change the pace of our work habits. We are familiar with the expression, "Work smarter, not harder." Perhaps we would do well to change it to "Work stiller, not harder." To do so we may need to examine what we are so afraid of, what do we think we will lose if we cease?

Another visionary who is rethinking this matter is Wayne Muller. In his wonderful book, *Sabbath: Restoring the Sacred Rhythm of Rest,* he tells of his own frenzied journey to a hospital bed that very nearly cost him his life. Following the experience he began to take a close look at rest, or the lack of it, in our lives. He was shocked by what he saw:

> I have sat on dozens of boards and commissions with
> many fine, compassionate, and generous people who
> are so tired, overwhelmed, and overworked that they

have neither the time nor the capacity to listen to
the deeper voices that speak to the essence of the
problems before them. Presented with the intricate
and delicate issues of poverty, public health, community well-being, and crime, our impulse, born of
weariness, is to rush headlong toward doing anything
that will make the problem go away. Maybe then we
can finally go home and get some rest. But without
the essential nutrients of rest, wisdom, and delight
embedded in the problem-solving process itself, the
solution we patch together is likely to be an obstacle
to genuine relief. Born of desperation, it often contains enough fundamental inaccuracy to guarantee
an equally perplexing problem will emerge as soon as
it is put into place. In the soil of the quick fix is the
seed of a new problem, because our quiet wisdom is
unavailable. . . .

Life has become a maelstrom in which speed and
accomplishment, consumption, and productivity have
become the most valued human commodities. In the
trance of overwork, we take everything for granted. We
consume things, people, and information. We do not
have time to savor this life, nor to care deeply and gently for ourselves, our loved ones, or our world; rather,
with increasingly dizzying haste, we use them all up and
throw them away. . . .

As it all piles endlessly upon itself, the whole experience of being alive begins to melt into one enormous
obligation. It becomes the standard greeting everywhere: *I am so busy.*

We say this to one another with no small degree
of pride, as if our exhaustion were a trophy, our ability to
withstand stress a mark of real character. The busier
we are, the more important we seem to ourselves and,
we imagine, to others.

The Chinese pictograph for the word *busy* is composed of two characters: *heart* and *killing.*

EFFORTLESSNESS

Constant effort does not yield the best results. Two studies of athletic performance validate this. In one study a group of Soviet athletes was brought together and divided into four groups. One group spent their time training for their sport. Group two was asked to train only 25 percent of the time and spend the other 75 percent *visualizing* the precise movements and outcomes that they wanted in their performance. The third group spent half of their time in training and half in visualizing, and the fourth spent 75 percent in training and 25 percent in visualization. At the 1980 Winter Games in Lake Placid, New York, the group that excelled was the group that spent the highest amount of time in visualization. The lowest improvement was among those who spent all of their time training. In each case, the group with the higher visualization periods did better than the other groups.[1]

Another study netted similar results for Australian psychologist Alan Richardson. He tested three groups of basketball players on their ability to make free throws. He instructed one group to spend twenty minutes each day practicing free throws and a second group to spend the same amount of time visualizing that they were throwing perfectly. In the third group, which he instructed to neither practice nor visualize, there was no improvement. However in the group that only visualized their shooting he discovered that the rate of improvement was nearly the same (23 percent) as the group that practiced (24 percent). The visualizations — a meditative exercise — netted high results with less effort.

---

1. Michael Talbot, *The Holographic Universe* (New York: HarperCollins, 1991). This study and the next are described in Michael Talbot's book.

As these studies illustrate, it is not necessary to work nearly as hard as we are conditioned to believe, though it is quite difficult to break the habit. To get at this chronic problem in the Mani Management Group, I have instituted a thirty-minute period of stillness in the afternoon of each workday. This time is for rest, prayer, meditation, inspirational reading, or walking on the beach. It interrupts the afternoon windup with breath. It slows the pulse, heart rate, and adrenal reactions and fully refreshes the teams. We find that it improves our communications and brings an element of effortlessness into our actions.

The tide rises and then retreats. Between tides there is a pause. It is the same with breath: in, pause, out, pause. Neither the tide nor the breath can stay in or out. But holding our breath is what happens when we go from phone call to phone call, task to task without pause. Even with this encouragement, we are constantly challenged to break the pattern at Mani. Some team members have reported it useful to try to stop and pause a few seconds before going on to the next call or task. Others give themselves frequent mental reminders that if they work less, they will get more done. As they track this, they observe the truth of it unfold repeatedly. We are learning that working too hard costs the company money, results, and human resources. It robs us of the transformative tool of effortlessness.

> There is much to be done; therefore we must proceed slowly.
>
> — Buddha

STILLNESS AND WORK

Frequently I will begin a meeting by asking for a few minutes of quiet time to gather our thoughts. I simply say something like, "We've all just come whirling in from a lot of business. I don't know about you, but I could really use a few minutes of quiet to gather my thoughts and get more present for this meeting." I've done it with television and record executives, heads of global companies, religious leaders, and indigenous peoples. I've never had anyone be offended. Usually they comment afterward that it was surprisingly helpful. It has the effect of smoothing and focusing the energies and bringing cohesion to agendas. It's great for cutting through ego. On one occasion, after I had started several of our meetings this way, one dot-com company leader said, "You didn't start with silence today, and I really missed it. It's a great way to start a meeting."

As we become more still in our work, understanding and clarity enrich it in invaluable ways. Stillness is where the generative factor is and where the economic factor is greatly boosted. Artificial complexity eats vast amounts of our energy and other resources. With stillness, economy of resources is vastly improved, because simplicity is engaged and unnecessary complexity is diminished.

Solitude, respite, silence, rest, stillness, Sabbath. These correlate far more to the bottom line than we have understood. The courageous exploration of this in our work life is very profitable. I know in my businesses the thirty-minute mandatory respite in the afternoon has netted us more ease in our methods, higher productivity, more efficiency of communication, refreshment for our minds and bodies, and — for those who practice it — communion with our individual and group soul and purpose. These are rewards we cannot afford to forfeit.

19

THE Question OF Time

*T*he "home" of the mind, as of all things, is the implicate order. At this level, which is the fundamental plenum for the entire manifest universe, there is no linear time. The implicate domain is atemporal; moments are not strung together serially like beads on a string.

— *Larry Dossey*

WHAT TIME IS IT?

"I'm afraid I have bad news about that demo tape, Jewel," I tell her playfully. "I'm not going to help you make it." We are walking along a favorite stretch of beach; the low sun casts a golden hue on the foam at the water's edge. It swirls around our toes. For months now she has been requesting my help to create a tape of her songs to pitch to record labels. Each time I asked her to focus instead on deciding what she most wants to do. Now that she knows she wants to pursue a career in music she is asking again about making the demo.

Splashing in the sea froth at my feet I say, "Let's not do it that way! Making a demo tape and knocking on doors, trying to get others to listen, pitching you loud enough for someone to hear...all of that is part of an old way of working that has nothing to do with us. We don't need to participate in any of it. No one needs to really. There's an entirely different way to work in business. It utilizes the principles of the outgoing wave."

"What do you mean?" Jewel said, "I don't know what you're talking about!"

We stop at a favorite meditation rock and sit facing into the sunset. "What is needed instead, Jewel, is for you to know what time it is. Asking the question, 'What time is it now?' is a great way to determine what the next step is.

"If it was truly demo time, the demo resources would be more apparent. But when we examine our resources, there aren't any for it — no money or people, no situations, or energy even, that would create it. Instead of forcing a demo simply because everyone says you have to have one, let's ask what time it is."

"Okay," she said, "What time *is* it?" She was flipping sand into the air with her toes, partially intrigued and partially annoyed, anxious to take action.

"It's not time for you to get someone else to hear your songs and give opinions about you. It's time for you to get your own feel for yourself as a singer-songwriter. You don't feel like a writer or singer; you're very uncertain about it, you've only written about a dozen songs. You don't know if you can keep writing, you aren't certain where they come from. You don't know if larger audiences will like your songs or if a fan base will start to grow. There is no place in you where you can own all of this yet — this idea about yourself and your work, your talent, your audience. And you will need this self-knowledge to create from and take your dream forward. When we ask what time it is, the answer is that it's time for you to have that experience — the one of performing and relating to the group that would become your audience, experimenting with your material, feeling yourself in the role."

The orange orb of sun dipping into the water interrupts our conversation and we sit quietly, our skin taking on a rosy sheen. I think briefly how grateful I am for Jewel's trust and her willingness to innovate.

"When it's time for a demo tape we'll know why and how. Right now it's clearly time for a small venue where you can perform your songs and interact with an audience."

We resume our walk along the molten water's edge. A golden retriever leaves its owner and bounds over to Jewel, begging her to throw the stick in its mouth. She wrenches it away and heaves it far out over the waves. The dog lunges enthusiastically into the sunlit surf.

After watching the dog she turns to me and asks, "How do I get a venue, should I call a bunch of coffeehouses or theaters? How do I talk them into letting me perform? When I get a show set up, how do I get an audience? Should I make a lot of flyers and advertise for a show?"

"That's more of the same straining to make something happen. Feel the energy that accompanies those ideas...you seem anxious and revved up just thinking about it."

"Well, what do I do? I have to do something or nothing will happen." Impatience marks her voice.

I laugh. "Taking steps just because you can, because you want to, because everyone says you should...it doesn't work — or rather, it's a lot of work to make it work.

"You need to do what you love. Sit in your favorite coffeehouses and on the beach, write and sing and meet people. Hang with the local musicians you are meeting. Daydream a lot; flesh out your dream. Have fun with the idea."

"I already have," she grumbles. "That's all I've been doing for weeks and weeks. Nothing's happened."

"That was before you were so clear about what you want to do, Jewel. That clarity will absolutely affect the results. You'll talk to people differently, notice things you didn't before. Hold your idea strongly in your Being, speak it in your prayers, imagine yourself in this new future you are conceiving of. You'll be amazed how easily, how naturally it comes to you. Trust the time it takes and enjoy the time. It will come when you are ready. The next step will make itself obvious. Don't take it until you see it clearly."

Two weeks later Jewel calls elated. "I have a gig!" she shouts. "I was singing with Poltz on one of his shows at the InnerChange coffeehouse and the owner heard me. She wanted to know whose songs I sang and I told her mine. She asked if I had enough original material for a show so I told her I did. Then she offered me Thursday nights! I worked out the money with her and everything!"

It is a thrill to hear the passion and the wonder in her voice.

TIMELINESS

When one allows everything to take a rightful place in the time flow, one comes into harmony with the natural, seamless, and amazingly effortless rhythm that is the natural order of all that is. Ease and even magic can happen, kismet, serendipity, good luck — all of these have space to occur when we strengthen and clarify our outgoing wave and hold it loosely in the time flow. For Jewel's career, I had spent time clarifying her interests and goals, discussing her fears, strengths, liabilities, and then creating a very detailed five-year probability plan. I call it a probability plan because I feel projections depend on probabilities and probabilities shift in the flow of time and need to be revisited. They can and should, however, be intuited from the outset and revised with new input.

An important goal I had for her career time line was to allow it an organic development, giving her time to adjust in her psyche, to understand herself and her creativity, to know her fans. She didn't, at this point, feel at all certain of her creative ability, she didn't yet think of herself as a singer-songwriter and had little solo experience of her ability to capture an audience. Jewel needed time to discover these things and grow in confidence regarding them. As a nineteen-year-old in a crucial phase of development, a more accelerated plan would place her personal and creative growth in jeopardy. It was not something I could allow — not as a manager, nor as her mother.

For that early plan I also established goals for record sales. My first projection was 100,000 in the first eighteen months following recording, 500,000 within two years, and 1 million following closely, with 10 million as the final goal. Jewel could not relate to these goals because she couldn't imagine how they could be met. She felt pressured by them. She was not able to imagine, in any concrete way, being bigger than her gigs at the InnerChange coffeehouse. Sales interested her far less than her music and the fans, so she focused on what time it was for her — time to develop her creativity and relationship with her audience. As her manager, it was time to understand and plan the long-term career she desired.

A goal of this plan was to create a situation in which she was sought after by numerous record labels, which would increase the ability for her as an untried artist to get a more advantageous record deal. In addition I laid out a time line that showed the type of career we wanted to forge, based on other well-established artists with similar careers. I established goals and time lines for her development as a writer and actress. All of these goals guided the career but timeliness drove it.

> Spiritual power molds physical and material conditions, but spiritual power is never in a hurry. . . . Never try to force the door and to go into any condition by force; just wait and you will conserve all the power which will be necessary for you to accomplish your work at the given time. If things do not happen as you want them to happen, know that a better way is being found. Trust, and never forget that the true way is the way of love. Flowers do not force their way with great strife. Flowers open to perfection slowly in the sun. . . . Everything happens at the right moment. . . .
>
> — White Eagle

DEMO TIME

Jewel got her gig quickly, easily — Nancy Porter, an enthusiastic supporter of music in San Diego, heard her jam with another musician at Nancy's coffeehouse, the InnerChange, and immediately offered her a gig. Jewel's popularity among young people grew rapidly; within six weeks there was standing room only at the coffeehouse. Then, without any effort on our part, one of the major record labels, Virgin Records, caught her show and approached her for a meeting. By the time we could meet with them, Atlantic Records also requested a meeting and we went to Los Angeles for two meetings without making even one phone call or inquiry to entreat other interest on our behalf. I maintain that this ease was due to our clarity and certainty. I have seen it proven again and again.

At that first meeting with Virgin Records, they were so taken with her that the meeting went long and we had to call Atlantic to say we were delayed. Then, on the way to them, we got lost numerous times. It was the end of the day, and Jewel was very nervous that we were keeping the president of Atlantic Records waiting.

We pulled into the parking garage at Atlantic in Jewel's Volkswagen bus just as the woman we were to meet was getting into her car to leave. As we apologized, she interrupted and said the president had to leave to pick up his son at day care. Jewel was crestfallen.

But the woman then added, "Well, it turned out to be great. The president said that he actually hates those little scenes where a group gathers in his office around a nervous artist who struggles awkwardly through some songs and then everyone looks at him to see what he thinks." She was almost breathless as she continued, "He suggested that what we do instead was have Jewel go into a studio at Atlantic's expense and make a demo tape so we can hear how she sounds, and then meet again and talk. He said you can keep the demo with no strings attached and even use it to shop for a deal at other labels!"

Apparently it was demo time. We now had a need that a demo tape would fill expediently — we could use it to give to other labels who were becoming interested in Jewel. Word spread in the close-knit music business, other labels approached us, and soon six record labels were courting Jewel. From there the job was, again, to stay focused on what time it was. It was time to hold to our own clear understanding of our goals, her abilities and needs, and her career trajectory as we had outlined it. It was not time to get all caught up in the needs and ideas of record labels or the fear that we might lose an opportunity and so on.

It was time to get educated about the process we found ourselves entering into and time, as always, to ask the right questions. My question was, "What constitutes a truly great deal for a beginning artist — an impossibly great deal even?" Typically a beginner can't get the royalties and agreements in a contract that a successful artist can so an artist will try to renegotiate their deal later, after they have successful songs. In our case, by understanding what would comprise an outrageously good contract and holding that goal, not hurrying into a relationship with any label, being confident that there was time and probability, we were able to get a deal so favorable that it left us with nothing further to ask for after her success.

Within three years of signing the contract we achieved all of our goals, ending that first cycle of her career with sales of 10 million records and a profound humility and gratitude for the grace in the process. Knowing what time it was led us to that enviable position.

> Isaac Stern, the celebrated violinist, was once asked why the music played by other violinists didn't sound as good as the same notes played by him. His reply: "But it isn't the notes that are important! It's the intervals between the notes."

CONCAVE TIME

She hears her big brothers discussing the race. They are in track and field at school and one of them won the tournament so he is going to the big state meet. The conversation is all about the four-minute mile. For a long, long time, everyone thinks the record can never be broken. But then, unbelievably, a guy named Bannister does! And then amazingly soon someone beats that new record! And seconds continue to get shaved off by other record breakers little by little, year by year.

Where will it end, she wonders? Will they keep at it determined second by determined second? Then inch along by the relentless tenth of a second? Forging competitively and inevitably ahead to a zero point? Is it possible? Then what? The possibilities boggle her. Will they fall into a time funnel that narrows and narrows to no time? Is there "minus time"? Maybe someone could run it in less than no time at all. Or is "no time" a sort of time barrier like there is a sound barrier? If they break the time barrier what will happen? Will time cave in and the runner disappear like with a time machine? Is anyone afraid of this? Maybe professional athletes are a type of fearless explorer.

It's a lovely and yummy thing to think about. She imagines a shrine to the missing athletes who disappear into the time barrier. Where might they go? Will the world be affected, like if you go into the future in a time machine and change it and then that changes the past? Will anyone come back from there? If nothing seems to happen at all, how will we know if nothing really did or not? We could be changed and not notice maybe. These are some of her wonderings.

NO TIME, ALL TIME

There is no time. Not really. This is profoundly true but difficult to fully grasp. Quantum science has fascinating explanations of this for those who are interested. Time is a construct. A human construct. Not all humans live so tightly bound in it as Westernized cultures do. Many cultures live in time with the seasons, the sun and moon rhythms, broader measures. They do not break things down into the millisecond.

Breaking time down to its most minute increments has the effect of getting our face so close to it we no longer can operate within the big picture. Remember the story of the blind men who were trying to understand an elephant by touch? One, feeling the trunk, declared it to be long and pliable. The men at the elephant's knee, or tail, or side had extremely different ideas of what the elephant was. Focusing only on one limited view, we form ideas that we then live by to our limitation.

The four-minute mile was a record long believed to be unbreakable. In fact it was thought to be humanly impossible. Athletes and coaches declared it impossible; physiologists thought the mind and the body would not be able to endure the strain. Most people agreed, but Roger Bannister did not. He was not deterred from his belief that he could break the record. He said, "It all starts with desire; the drive to be the best. Fueled by my faith in my training, I will overcome all obstacles. I am brave! I am not afraid to face anyone on the track. I believe this is not a dream. It is my *reality*."

On March 6, 1954, Bannister accomplished what was hailed as one of the greatest feats in history. He ran the mile in 3 minutes, 59.4 seconds. He showed it to be possible and just forty-six days later another athlete broke his record. Since that time a small group of superb athletes has continued to break that time barrier, setting new records.

Time is a barrier indeed. As we live within its confining territory at greatly accelerated speeds, we create for ourselves a reality that vaults forward. We continue inventing faster and faster machines, more timesaving devices, more precise clocks, counting every moment, placing an ever-higher value on time. It begins to feel that we are careening through space with little time even for thought. Indeed it is true. Our thoughts race as does our pulse. Adrenaline floods us as though we were in flight from danger. Time, a tool we constructed to serve us, now rules our day. Time is money and there is never enough. We constantly try to "make" time for more activities, more work, more meetings. But making time is a much more accurate idea than we pause to consider.

There are many things that "make" more time. Music makes time — it can alter our awareness of time and induce states of seeming timelessness. Intense focus such as exercise or intent work or play are known to do the same. Inner stillness makes time and can even end time. Love creates a timelessness, as does joy. These are all known to affect the physiology in ways that alter the consciousness of time. In slowing down, we do not lose productivity, as we fear. Instead, we are able to hear our thoughts and the voice of our soul. Effortlessness is accessed that reduces our friction within the so-called time frame.

DISMANTLING TIME

My eldest son, Shane, had an unusual experience regarding time. For many of his young and teenage years he had a frequent visitor to his dreams, a man called Bashi-Kâ. This mysterious man would have night chats with Shane about intriguing issues. During the time Shane was in Europe at college, he played with the idea of time as it related to his homework. He tried to reduce the amount of time needed for homework by changing his assumptions about it. Rather than assuming that long hours were needed — the prevalent idea at the school — he decided not to make it about time at all. Instead he focused on the benefit he wanted from the study, and relaxed into studying until he felt he had received that benefit. He soon was able to complete his work so effortlessly that he no longer needed every minute to complete assignments; he now had every weekend to travel and many evenings to socialize. And his grades improved to nearly all As. It was such a dramatic change that it caused him to wonder about the nature of time.

This questioning seemed to trigger an extended series of dreams with Bashi-Kâ. He was unaware of many of them until his roommates began to tell him he was sleep talking. One roommate found Shane's nighttime mumbling annoying and began to sleep on the living room couch. But the other was intrigued and took notes. He reported that Shane was having conversations with someone called Bashi-Kâ about the nature of life. The roommate wrote many things down and found it all rather fun and often deeply thought provoking.

Then one morning Shane's friend woke him urgently, pointing with wide eyes to the nightstand. There was Shane's watch on the nightstand, completely dismantled with all the miniscule little screws and workings lined up in tidy rows. On his notepad next to the array was scrawled a poem in Shane's hand:

Time is of the essence
Both chapter and page
Meant to be thought
Not kept in a cage.

With no watchmaker tools available both boys were at a loss about how it had occurred or how to get it back together. After the initial wonderment, they began to recall the night's dream and sleep talking. It seems that Bashi-Kâ had been instructing Shane on the nature of time.

THE FINISH TIME

While I was writing this chapter, my deadline for delivery of the final manuscript was looming at me. Taking my commitment to the publisher seriously, I began to feel pressure and anxiety about whether I would be able to finish on time. I fidgeted and fussed and wrestled with the writing, growing more anxious and less productive at an alarming rate. I recognized the irony, of course — I was writing about freeing ourselves of the confines of the calendar and clock-oriented time structure while feeling totally bound by it. I challenged myself to apply the principles to my writing.

First I brought myself into the present *where there was no deadline.* The deadline was in the future, but in the present moment there was only protected space for writing. I determined to focus on writing instead of getting finished, remembering there was no time and there was all the time I needed. I held that place and felt immediate relief.

Then I hit on an idea that intrigued me. I read that studies have shown that many people with multiple personalities heal much faster than normal (bones and cuts heal quicker) and that those people often report they have a personality assigned to be in charge of their healing twenty-four hours a day, visualizing, praying, learning about health. I decided to try assigning a "part" of me to work on my book during my sleep. I passed a noticeable night — each time I woke I remembered dreams about my writing. On waking in the morning I recalled several paragraphs that I was working on just before awakening. I went immediately to my computer and typed them in. Those paragraphs, without edit, follow in the section titled "Holding Time." Over the next eight hours I wrote seventeen pages that flowed effortlessly, requiring very little reworking.

In one of my dreams I was instructed to connect with the reality in which my book was already finished and to hold that idea as I was writing. This changed how I related to the project. I had the energy and relief of completion instead of the pressure and dread of the work ahead. Doing this while keeping my awareness on how elastic and expandable time is, staying in the moment, and working in my dreams brought the book in on time with far greater ease; I even had time to play with friends, exercise, and take lovely walks on the beach.

Learn that eternity is now, the future is now. There is no past or present or future as separate periods of time — all are within the soul's embrace now. It is your reaction to the now which is your future.

— Anonymous

HOLDING TIME

There is a distinction between fearfully avoiding a moment and creating a pause. When waiting indecisively in confusion and fear, we are looking and acting outside of ourselves, dependent on others' ideas and outside resources. But by purposefully allowing a pause, we use *the time gained* to clarify and strengthen our position. Allowing our clock-driven sense of time to dictate our action and nonaction jams up the works, compresses the moment, bringing in stress and limitation. As we step away from this addiction to time, we can know the true nature of each moment.

A great power is found in this ability to hold, to contain the energy. You can feel an energy building around an enterprise, a project, a dream and an enthusiasm and excitement for the project. It is then most tempting to press the go button and begin to take steps to move it along a fast track, or engage others to become involved. Yet that is the precise moment when it is best to be quiet, to contain the energy, holding our own counsel. We can watch while staying steady in our thoughts and visioning. The idea and plan grow clearer, steadier, and their wave frequency begins to emit that clarity and strength. This builds an energy that is attractive. It is magnetic. It begins to attract the required resources. Broadcasting the idea too soon, taking action prematurely, can disperse the energy.

SPLITTING ATOMS

Take a mental look at the picture of an atomic bomb detonation. We have seen, and been fascinated by, these pictures. I know what intrigues me about them; it's watching the energy pattern. The atom bomb does not scatter its initial force; it has an extremely concentrated ground blast that sends out waves of tremendous force. Then a powerful column thrusts upward and a platform mushrooms out but does not disperse broadly. Then another column moves upward, again forming a platform or mushroom cloud on top.

The early stages of a dream are like that initial impact or detonation. If the first impetus is concentrated and held until precisely the right moment, it will produce a strong physical column and then the platform will form.

Holding the energy can begin to feel like sitting on a bucking horse — it takes skill to hold on. We want to take action. We think that if we are not in action then nothing is happening. We believe we have to *make* it happen. We feel anxious that the opportunity will be lost or others will beat us to the idea, or we are so excited we simply cannot wait. Moving ahead for these reasons is like getting a plane off the ground with only enough fuel to get halfway to the destination. The primary wave tone of the project is unsteady, fear based, unclear. The progression of the work will reflect it. It will take far more effort to complete it; there will be more stress.

During the "holding phase" we refine our project, asking questions, growing in understanding of what it is, why it is, and how it will be. We can distinguish its correct relationship to us and the world it will take form in. This clarity builds a power into the project. By repeatedly asking what it is time for, we take only the action appropriate for the moment and avoid scattering our energy. We can monitor the energy. If it has gone flat we may have fallen into uncertainty, waiting in fear. But if it is still building and we continue to hold, we will come to know when to engage the glorious man-made illusion of time. We will then be in harmony with the greater rhythms of the universe, which allows the outcome to serve both our immediate goals and the greater goals of the soul.

THE TIME IS NOW

Between here and there, between then and now, there is no time and space. There is no time; there is no distance. There is only this extremely pliable moment now. And now. And now. During the time that I was ill and had no money for house and car payments, I was told to pray for what I needed now. I was being asked to come into that one dynamic moment, the only truly vital moment. Either side of this moment is the past or future — both are subject to the intense friction of time and space.

Time is a convenient illusion; created to navigate this plane of

existence and the agreements built in here. It is a structure to organize around; we can certainly use it to our advantage. However, it has
become a context that we are impossibly bound by. We can loosen our
attachment or even step out of time altogether when it serves. We
can hold both ideas simultaneously. Understanding that a certain
reality exists somewhere down the river, we can intend it to be so. At
the same time, we can know that there is no distance from here to
there, no time between that time and this time we are in. Becoming
now-based and relinquishing our obsession with time we reduce the
stress and friction that wears away at us in our ever-accelerating lives,
costing us dearly in our health, energy, and quality of life.

There is an Immediate Intelligence. And by "immediate" I do
not mean fast paced. It is a Timeless Intelligence that emerges in the
moment; in it is all wisdom, all knowledge and love. It is now-based.
It is present moment–based. And it has access to all eventual outcomes and therefore knows a wisdom that is at once courageous and
still. Courage has in it the connotation of action. Stillness brings
with it the idea of sitting in receivership, though not passively. These
two qualities emerge in that Immediate Intelligence available to us
as we slow our bodies, slow our thoughts and minds. As we ease away
from our constant focus and addiction to time, we discover there is
a vast and eternal universe to experience.

> There were times when I could not afford to sacrifice the
> bloom of the present moment to any work, whether of head
> or hands. Sometimes, in a summer morning, having taken
> my customary bath, I sat in my sunny doorway from sunrise
> till noon, rapt in a reverie, amidst the pines and hickories
> and sumacs, in undisturbed solitude and stillness, while the
> birds sang around. I grew in those seasons like corn in the
> light, and they were far better than any work of the hands
> would have been. They were not time subtracted from my
> life, but so much over and above my usual allowance.
>
> — Henry David Thoreau

20

A Reason to Be

T his is the true joy in life, the being used for a purpose recognized by yourself as a mighty one; the being a force of nature instead of a feverish clod of grievance complaining that the world will not devote itself to making you happy.

— George Bernard Shaw

One of the greatest difficulties for people surrounding work is the consistent and pernicious belief that they are working for money. That is not to say that anyone should be required to work without pay. But it is valuable to understand that of far greater importance than the money received is the sense of having a reason for being. Having a purpose is far more what the body, the soul, the will, the psyche need and want and derive from the work engagement. If that is taken away in the workplace, if the purposeful sense of being there evaporates — due either to circumstances in one's own dream or a shift in the landscape of the work environs — it will affect performance because it will affect the willingness to give, to contribute.

From time to time we all wonder why we are doing what we are doing, if it is worth it. These are important and consistent human questions that come from the level of our soul. At such times we need an authentic and clear answer to be able to continue in our activities in good emotional, spiritual, mental, and physical health. To truly serve, purpose must be connected to our unique authenticity. That is why money cannot serve as our purpose. It can be a goal, but not a purpose. Purpose must be connected to and driven from our souls, which hold the vision of our life purpose. That is why indigenous cultures build the seeking of vision into the fabric of their lives. It is the seeking of the soul's vision or plan for an individual or a group. We can glimpse that vision and be guided by it. Vision connects us to our passion and passion often exposes our purpose.

RAISON D'ETRE

We yearn for that one right purpose in our life, for in purpose is clarity and joy. Gaining that understanding need not be a complicated process. An easy exercise is to revisit the passions of our childhood. In them are often the seeds of a life purpose. The story titled "The Rabbit and the Chicken" from chapter 1 illustrates a childhood focus for me that sourced my life purpose: to know what it means, in the highest sense, to be a human being.

Following the delight of the heart is another method. Take that class that interests you, pick up the skill, volunteer for the project that you have been wishing you had time for. These are often simple interests that don't seem like a grand life purpose. Let them become what they will. Following what compels you often leads to surprising places. Bringing yourself to those things that generate the greatest delight allows you to create the most sustainability in your forward motion. Drop very deeply into your being, identify what it is that thrills you, that delights you, what you can envision that would cause your soul to sing. Then bring that forth, identify the critical path for it, and set it in motion.

The most simple and potent way to discover passion and purpose is to dialogue with your soul. Talk to your soul, honor it, welcome its presence in your life. Value it and come to understand its values. And take time to seek vision through prayer, silence, retreat, and journal writing. This retreat need not even take you fully out of your life. It can be a long weekend, or every lunch hour over a period of time. One woman dedicated a month to establishing this connection. She continued with her job but set aside every evening for being in silence; she read inspirational material, meditated and prayed, and kept a dream journal. She did not watch television or talk on the phone. At the end of the month she had a new plan for her life.

Taking the vision into timely action is the next obvious step. Without action you have conceived and designed a wondrous castle in the sky. Possessing an understanding of our vision, what is left to us is to access the exuberance and enthusiasm, the willingness to grab hold of that passion with discipline and do whatever it takes to serve that passion.

MOVE

Whether it's a turtle who drags herself
Slowly to the sandlot, where she digs
The sandy nest she was born to dig

And lay leathery eggs in, or whether it's salmon
Rocketing upstream
Towards pools that call Bring your eggs here,

And nowhere else in the world, whether it is
     turtle-green
Ugliness and awkwardness, or the seething
Grace and gild of silky salmon, we

Are envious, our wishes speak out right here,
Thirsty for a destiny like theirs,
An absolute right choice

(continued)

To end all choices. Is it memory,
We ask, is it a smell
They remember,

Or just what is it — some kind of blueprint
That makes them move, hot grain by grain,
Cold cascade above icy cascade,

Slipping through
Water's fingers
A hundred miles

Inland from the easy, shiny sea?
And we also —
In the company of our tribe

Or perhaps alone, like the turtle
On her wrinkled feet with the tapping nails —
We also are going to travel, we say let's be

Oblivious to all, save
That we travel, and we say
When we reach the place we'll know

We are in the right spot, somehow, like a breath
Entering a singer's chest, that shapes itself
For the song that is to follow.

— Alicia Ostriker

A COMPANY VISION AND PURPOSE

There are many ways to define purpose. Some would call it a vision or mission; others may refer to it as soul urgings, while others think of it as a moral compass. Whatever the term, it brings peace and clarity and guidance to the work life by understanding one's reasons and parameters for being and doing.

A sense of purpose can be integrated into work in numerous ways. Many of the stories in this book — the shark story and accounts of various business negotiations — illustrate how I have done this. I have also done it by creating a vision and purpose for my companies and operating from a set of values that reflect them. Early in the process of business development, I wrote a code for myself, values to guide me in dealing within the music industry. As the company grew I formalized these as a company covenant and a set of beliefs and operating principles. The covenant serves to define our vision, our mission. It includes a number of ideas each employee agrees to abide by. I used the form of a covenant to bring attention to the importance of commitment to the ideas. Combined, the covenant and beliefs form a foundation, a company code — a statement of who we are and why and how we are engaged in business together and in the world.

Following my desire not to exclude the spiritual nature from the workplace, I integrated terms such as "spiritual" and "divine." These are values that I believe facilitate our projects and interactions. I included them to provide guidelines but not to create or enforce a spiritual environment. Spiritual beliefs are highly individual — within the company we have a great diversity in this area. It is not a requirement for employees to have a definable spiritual ideology, only that they agree to abide by the company's guidelines in their working interactions.

Mani Mission and Covenant

It is our mission to be a powerful global force for positive financial, social, political, and spiritual change.

It is our vision and experience that the greatest business success occurs when humanitarian, spiritual, and environmental principles are practiced along with sound business operation. It is our aim to demonstrate this model in the world.

We intend to understand what it means to be human beings, in the highest sense, and to integrate this understanding into our being. It is our covenant to:

Serve Humanity We dedicate our resources and endeavors to be of service. We believe that the blessings of our lives are for the benefit of humanity.

Embody Spiritual Principles We agree to incorporate spiritual virtues such as integrity, peace, humility, love, generosity, compassion, authenticity, and faith into all our actions.

Embrace Diversity and Support Unity We honor diverse beliefs and cultures, each part being vital to the integrity of the whole.

Practice Sacred Stewardship We agree to carefully assess the true costs and contributions of our endeavors and establish balanced exchanges. We are accountable to the whole.

Promote Generative Prosperity Our prosperity is an expression of Divine abundance. We receive it in alignment with natural laws. We revel in it and share it with joy.

Mani Beliefs

Self-Responsibility We believe that the organization's aims of global influence, humanitarian service, integrity, and profitability are served when individuals are self-accountable and self-generative, bringing their excellence to the support of the organization.

Expanded Human Potential We believe it is the responsibility of each team member to transform the workplace by moving beyond limiting behaviors to pioneer processes and actions that expand the individual's capabilities and the organization's accomplishments.

Conscious Prosperity We believe it is possible to be financially prosperous while practicing spiritual principles and serving humanitarian goals. We believe that prosperity must be grounded in stewardship and balanced exchange.

Balanced Implementation We believe all life requires a rhythm of rest and action. We believe that quiet contemplation, meditation, and prayer are important tools to access stillness and the deep well of creativity to help accomplish our goals.

Relationship with the Divine We believe an intimate relationship with the Divine is central to joyous and sustainable creativity and responsible productivity.

Be the Difference We believe it is the challenge and opportunity of our times to translate our values, beliefs, hopes, and ideals into concrete actions.

OPERATING PRINCIPLES

In addition to our covenant and beliefs, we have developed operating principles that augment the beliefs. These continue to evolve as we grow in our understanding of our group purpose. To give an example of how they work, I am including copy from the operating principles regarding self-responsibility:

Belief

We believe that the organization's aims of global influence, humanitarian service, integrity, and profitability are served when individuals are self-accountable and self-generative, bringing their excellence to the support of the organization.

Purpose

The purpose of this belief is to build an efficient and creative organization that attracts and retains individuals who are self-managing and self-sourcing; and to have a company that is effective in pioneering and developing new methods of operation, profit making, distribution, and contribution to the global business community.

Principles

As a group, we are committed to clear and concise communication with each other. We agree to avoid gossip and negative nonverbal communicating. We will practice self-assessment to evaluate our role in difficult interpersonal interactions.

We agree to utilize stillness to increase our ability to make assessments and decisions that are in line with company values.

We accept responsibility for ensuring that our work is aligned with our interests, talents, skills, and highest-held values so that work becomes a source of fulfillment, joy, and contribution. If that isn't possible within our company, then it becomes the responsibility of the organization and the individual involved to find or recommend employment elsewhere.

Questions about self-responsibility in the context of the workplace have sparked energetic and ongoing dialogue at Mani. It is a question that is integral to the understanding of true empowerment. For a company to empower its employees is only half the equation; employees must be willing to accept empowerment and understand what it means in their daily work. The company journey into self-responsibility has at times been difficult but also exhilarating and surprising. It has taken courage to reveal our authentic selves to one another and broach sensitive subjects that are often taboo. Having a purpose, guiding principles, and methods of operation expands our understanding of the core belief, informs our decisions and actions, and assists new employees in their understanding of the values of the company.

ENCOURAGING VALUES

What is our purpose, or reason for being, in the workplace? What forms the core of our actions? Have our addictions, distractions, and ego agendas replaced our sense of purpose? Having a compelling company passion elevates our actions and brings joy and health into all of our moments.

The Mani covenant, beliefs, and operating principles form guidelines that answer these questions. They help alleviate difficulties and offer solutions for team members. They clearly outline most expectations and they are also important for educating new employees to the company culture. Company team members have been part of the process of understanding and writing these, working together to make them meaningful and useful.

The CEO of a Fortune 500 company told me that after reading our operating principles he discussed them with the chairman of the board. They were intrigued, for instance, with the idea of strongly advocating against gossip. "Gossip," he said, "is at the source of most of our internal headaches. I have found it to be one of the greatest drains on our company's resources and feel it has no place in the work environment." He asked how we enforce and police the principles.

We do not police them; we encourage them. We seek their agreement on the principles. Evaluations and bonuses place heavy emphasis on how well a team member understands and operates by company principles. In addition, all company members are expected to be self-evaluating and to pioneer methods of working together that serve our goals; their input regarding difficulties and progress on this is important to the ongoing evolution of the principles by which we operate. When the entire company comes together three times a year, time is frequently devoted to understanding and refining the principles. This all serves to create an environment that helps ensure the integration of the core values. It is these values that outline our group purpose.

There are many thousands of businesses in the world that are successful in meeting their financial goals. Creating another one would add little to the world. It holds no interest for me; if that were all I could do with my businesses, I would close them now and devote myself to personal, creative, and philanthropic endeavors.

What excites me is the idea of building successful businesses driven by and deriving their success from humanitarian values, businesses that live those values daily, each employee learning to embody the principles. The creation of that model is what engages me. It is for that purpose I am involved in business.

21

Values IN THE Workplace

An understanding of values is essential in business operation: not as a semantic discussion about the difference between a value and a principle or a quality, but rather as discussion about what we value. What do we value and how are those values operating in our families, our work, or our communities? Examining what we are currently valuing is illuminating. If we value money, it is a prime operator in our experience. If it is security, then that forms the platform of our life. Consciously choosing our primary operating values and crafting methods that support them bring us into alignment with our own authenticity and integrity.

There are numerous attributes we value and operate by. They constitute the methods and practices that are the cornerstones of our daily operations. Stillness, innovation, peaceful means, creativity, soul-based interaction, authenticity, timeliness, all these are included in our core values. Dignity and equity, justice and wisdom, temperate means and intuition are others that guide this business.

— Mani Management Group

GRACE, DIGNITY, AND EQUITY

On one occasion, a dispute arose with a musician over working credits for a song of Jewel's. Jewel had requested, from the start, that the two of them share the credit equally. The work was completed before a contract was actually signed, which is common in this business. After the work, but during the contract process, the musician requested sole credit. Jewel felt the contribution of each was equal and she wanted the credit line to reflect that.

The industry attorneys typically handle this type of negotiation, so the matter went back and forth between lawyers for a time without good result, growing more polarized. I finally contacted the manager of the other party and suggested a personal meeting between the manager, his artist, and myself. This is unusual and they were hesitant but reluctantly agreed when I told them I simply wanted to have a more complete exchange of the history, feelings, needs, and reasoning of each party.

When we met in a New York hotel room, their trepidation was high. So I began with a calm and humorous overview. My tone and lack of tension helped place us on less volatile ground, dulcifying the atmosphere between us. I asked them to tell me everything they could to shed light on the process. They were initially defensive and their statements involved a lot of the typical "case building" and accusation. After listening, questioning, and understanding them thoroughly I suggested that we mildly debate the various points in the spirit of our mutual interest in working together again. They agreed and we spent some time going back and forth over the divergent points and history.

Following that, I asked for two or three minutes of quiet for us to consider where we were now. They were partially relieved yet somewhat uncomfortable with the idea of silence and were rather fidgety during the five minutes or so that I sat staring out the window, pondering. As I reviewed, I considered the following:

- ❊ It was apparent to me that our own communication at the start was unclear and incomplete, resulting in some of the problem.
- ❊ They had no contractual recourse, so legally we were not under obligation.
- ❊ Several of the points held by each of us could not be

resolved; only our separate and conflicting experiences, opinions, and desires supported them.

- The credit meant far more to the other artist as a career builder than it did to Jewel. It was an important career step for them.
- Jewel had nothing at risk and she would have many future opportunities to receive credit.

I shared my thoughts with them and said that the decision seemed not to rest on the history of the matter but rather on what was timely and just in the career of both artists. It seemed to me that from that point of view the right thing was for the other artist to receive the full credit.

They expressed surprise and gratitude to be recognized in this way. Following the spirit of our gesture, they offered to share a joint credit with Jewel on another point that was clearly theirs. This was a nice surprise for all of us. Most heartening, however, was the shift in the energy. I've learned that, in most circumstances, when people are treated with grace, dignity, and fairness, they respond in kind.

JUSTICE AND WISDOM

Justice and wisdom, as values that inform our methods, have nearly disappeared in many areas of our culture. For instance, information is accessed far more frequently than wisdom. Wisdom, with its combination of experience and the ability to access that deeper knowing, is a vital quality. The lack of it is a great deficit to our society and our personal process. For each one of us can access wisdom and justice within us by forging our connection with the Infinite Source.

The consideration of justice in individual or corporate matters is as rare, and significant, a loss. We can seek wisdom and infuse a sense of justice into all of our interactions and especially our problem solving. To move beyond the difficulties facing our world, both wisdom and justice can and must be brought to the table in all negotiations and interactions. More people of wisdom are needed to step forward and fulfill an obligation to contribute solutions to the difficulties we face in all disciplines: in local, national, and global politics, finance, environment, science, and business. Public officials, educators, business, and other leaders who serve only public opinion without bringing a higher wisdom to bear cannot truly serve the public good.

TEMPERATE MEANS

Compassion, tolerance, and nonjudgment are values I advocate at Mani. They bring temperance to a situation, elevating it above the level of personal agendas and egos. Contrary to common belief, they cost very little and net much. The idea that we understand one another at the expense of our own goals is absolutely false. It is time that we begin to be courageous in this respect.

The key is in holding, indeed valuing, all parts of the picture as necessary to the whole. Others' agendas are of value to them, mine to me. In the area of agenda, it is an even playing field. Not judging theirs or my own keeps me focused on assessing what my needs are, my values, and whether the situation is suitable for me to meet those aims or whether I need to seek another situation.

Even when taking a stand for or against something, the matter can be held in tolerance and nonjudgment. Anything else is futile. The amount of judgment in our lives is a grave factor in creating our current situations. Intolerant and damning views serve only to impossibly polarize positions.

> I know when I have a problem and have done all I can to figure it out, I keep listening in a sort of inside silence until something clicks and I feel a right answer.
> — Conrad Hilton

> The only mistake I ever made was not listening to my gut.
> — Lee Iacocca

INTUITION

On one occasion we were working a very lucrative arrangement with a dot-com company. All had gone exceptionally well — it promised to be very rewarding financially for us and we had a great humanitarian project worked into the deal. We liked the company as well as its people very much. We were close to our final agreement when a few "hitches" came up. The problems, primarily, were internal issues within the other company that seemed to affect our agreement. It appeared that some time would be needed to resolve the issues. As I stepped back to observe this I noticed that I had some new feelings of unease. I could not pinpoint the cause of them; everything seemed in good order. Still, the feelings persisted and the delays continued. Then, during a conference call, I surprised everyone including myself by pulling out of the deal, saying, however, that I was open to being approached at another time when their internal matters were resolved. My team, disappointed that months of work seemed to have come to naught, queried me about the sudden decision. I replied that I felt certain it was the right thing to do, but could not explain fully. It was a strong intuition. Just a few weeks later the technology stock market crumbled and the entire dot-com landscape was imperiled. Had I not followed my intuition we would have been very negatively impacted.

To access intuition, it helps to slow down. In our dealings we generally operate at a very fast pace. Our breath then is usually shallow and rapid. Movement, breath, and thought are all connected. When we slow down and breathe more deeply it slows our thoughts enough to override our chattering and often circular mental process and assumptions. We can then hear the quiet voice of inner wisdom. It is there for all of us if we value it and prioritize opportunity for it.

Intuition is grounded in a deep knowingness. In it is a certainty. There is the certainty of the ego and there is the certainty of the soul. The first is subject to our entire melange of agendas, fears, hopes, desires, beliefs. The second issues forth from the Infinite Intelligence as it expresses in our personal circumstances. Learning to sort out the ego's voice and hear the soul's is the challenge.

An executive at Atlantic Records said of me in an interview, "When we first met, she seemed to have an uncanny certainty about Jewel's career." That certainty stemmed from the day I wrote about previously, when on the beach in San Diego, Jewel understood what she wanted to do and her purpose for doing it. At that time, we had an epiphany in which we "knew" that we would work together to create a platform for good in the world. In that moment I "saw" the path before us, and its outcome. It was from that certainty that I worked; I felt absolutely assured of the outcome. That certainty of vision and purpose becomes a compelling individual prime wave that reverberates back with a resounding "Yes" from the Source.

> What this power is, I cannot say. All I know is that it exists…and it becomes available only when you are in that state of mind in which you know exactly what you want…and are fully determined not to quit until you get it.
>
> — Alexander Graham Bell
>
> It's always with excitement that I wake up in the morning wondering what my intuition will toss up to me like gifts from the sea. I work with it and rely upon it. It's my partner.
>
> — Jonas Salk

PEACEFUL MEANS

Practicing peaceful means is another company value — "being" peace in our interactions. Being peace doesn't mean simply giving in or giving up or always "making nice." It has far more to do with balance, courage, thoughtful action, stillness, self-assessment, preparedness, and patience. It must include compassion, clarity, creativity, and forthrightness as well as justice and wisdom. It is a strong position to take, not a weak one, and it requires great self-discipline and commitment to put forward. We must begin to ask this of ourselves more frequently. We cannot simply continue to stand by, feeling victim to an unsafe world. There are steps we can take. Every day we are faced with countless opportunities to grow in these abilities — in situations at work, challenges within our families, and our friendships.

Yet we hold ourselves hostage to all that we are afraid to say, confront, or expose. The cost is beyond reason: the nearly complete forfeiture of our most authentic feelings, values, thoughts, and interactions. We become unable to recognize ourselves. We become unbelievably restricted by our straitjacket jobs, marriages, and dull routines. It takes courage to change or, especially, to leave a life that little resembles us. It is a vital moment of choice: the moment when we choose to alter a life that is primarily designed to get by, that is designed to work within limitations and darkness. We can choose instead to have a life of meaning and creativity, a life of purpose, a life of service, a life of value. Our lives can change, gradually or even literally overnight, but for the change to occur it means committing to the evolvement of our Soul.

PUTTING VALUES TO THE TEST

When the general manager of Atlantic Records called to say that Jewel was being offered the cover of *Time* magazine, I told him we would need a little time to consider if she would do it. It had been many years since an Atlantic artist was on the cover of *Time*, so they were thrilled to be approached by the magazine. It was understandably difficult for him to imagine circumstances in which one would say no. He likely questioned my sanity. I told him there were many things we valued much more than an opportunity to increase her fame and that one of them was her healthy personal growth. I explained that Jewel was currently in a process of adjustment about fame. She was beginning to see what it was, what the cost and concerns were. She wasn't at all sure she wanted it. It weighed heavily on her mind. I felt that accepting the cover would move her quickly toward the realm of celebrity without the opportunity to consider if it was her choice. If she agreed without exploring it fully it would be based on everyone else's assumptions that it was an automatic "yes" that was desirable or necessary.

That type of process is a decision by default. In a default decision you allow convention, ego responses, others' views, or old programming to be the values that inform and determine your decision. Conscious and fully informed choice is aborted in such a process and you find yourself acting based on the automatic assumptions of the default idea. As they unfold, default decisions result in many difficulties because it is hard to serve them with real satisfaction. They are ego centered and time driven. And they rarely include one's soul values.

The suspense in this decision was heightened by the fact that Jewel was on a much needed retreat for the weekend and I would not be able to discuss it with her until Sunday. It was three long days for the Atlantic team, but to their credit they were gracious rather than hysterical with us, though they told me later that no one slept all weekend. When I spoke with Jewel, she felt obligated to accept — it seemed expected of her. I suggested that she consider what it would mean for her, to review her recent feelings about fame and celebrity, and to consider her values. I asked her not to make a default decision. "A *Time* cover is a wonderful thing if it's truly timely. Be certain you feel ready; if you are not, it would be folly to do it. If you pass on it, your career will not be harmed, you can trust in that. There are no missed opportunities."

She spent two days going into her fear and hesitancy about fame — the change, the security issues, the loss of privacy. She asked herself if she was ready for more, and she asked from a place where she really felt she had choice. She knew I would say no to Atlantic and hold firm through the inevitable pressure that would follow.

She received a wonderful understanding in herself. "I was sort of worrying about the fame issue before and this opportunity has brought it to a head for me. As I meditated and prayed, I examined myself and asked my heart who I was and what I was ready for. I saw I had a strength. I *knew* I was ready. This was a surprise to me," she said. "I hadn't seen it when I was worrying. And I can see where I am vulnerable and what support I will need so that I don't forfeit what I value about me."

By making a fully examined choice, she did not default to assumptions about her career path or what was good for her. She knew she could move forward without forfeiting her core self.

IF NOT NOW, WHEN?

I work with excitement and wonder at what is possible between people. Again and again I am humbled by how willing they are to act outside of their familiar patterns. Given a chance, I find them usually glad to have opportunities to be in more harmonious business and personal exchanges. I am continually heartened by what we can do and how we can be together. It is working from the platform of our common human values that makes this possible.

When the uncomfortable situations, angers, and issues occur, I elevate them to the highest degree that I am able to within myself. I go into them thoughtfully, even prayerfully. I enjoy them, I don't dread them. They are welcome to come to me. Why not? Where else should these matters go? To someone who will perpetuate the same ridiculous old stuff that is fundamental to the serious problems that we are all so very, very sick to death of? Each of us can be the agents of this change simply by acting on the saying, "If not me, who? If not now, when?"

If, in our interactions, some of our exchanges can be transformed, we are making a substantive difference. It is a difference that facilitates transformation — a transformation vital to our very survival.

THROW BACK YOUR HEAD

Throw back your head
       And cry the falcon's cry
       Or the lover's sound in bed
Throw back your head
       And laugh the fool's laugh
       Or that of the saint gone mad
Throw back your head
       And sing your own certain melody
       Or the anguished mourner's song
Throw back your head
       And shout the victor's chant
       Or anger to the Gods
Throw back your head
       And listen to the wisdom on the wind
       Or the guidance from within
Throw back your head
       And chant the story of the people
       Or the litany of your sins
Throw back your head
       Beseech demand revel revere
       Pray despair emote inquire exalt
Throw back your head
       And join the countless legion voices
       Human and divine

Lenedra J. Carroll

THE
Architecture
OF
Health

I CREDIT MY HEALTH TO EVERY MOMENT I HAVE PAID HEED TO
THE VOICE OF MY INNER WISDOM, LEARNING — AS HIPPOCRATES
ADVISED — TO TREAT MY ILLNESSES BY MY OWN JUDGMENT.
SLOWLY AND SURELY I HAVE ACHIEVED WELLNESS AND VITALITY
BY BUILDING FROM THE ORIGINAL BLUEPRINT OF HEALTH THAT
IS EMBEDDED IN MY SOUL.

22

THE Physician Within

*H*er potions and powders spread out all around her. Small brown containers with white lids, stolen from her parents' medicine cabinet, line up tidily on the forest floor; the kitchen cupboards also yielded many promising unguents and liquids. Plants, dried and fresh, lay on the huge tree roots that form tables in her secret laboratory. She mixes up some special healing potions for her dad — he flew his small plane into the side of a mountain in a whiteout during a snowstorm. He hiked to safety in a cabin many miles below, but his foot got frostbite and now everybody says he's going to lose it. Visions of ancient remedies and secret potions obsess her as she imagines herself valiantly struggling against the odds for the cure that will amaze the grown-up world and save her father's leg.

Using a flat rock and a smooth stone for her mortar and pestle, skinny green olive jars for beakers, and tinfoil and matches, she concocts remedy after remedy. She makes careful notes: two ground-up aspirin, the powder from three pink and white pills, one of those blue-coated tablets pounded with the pestle, a tablespoon of vinegar, one teaspoon of baking soda, six moose hairs she found caught on a barbwire fence, and twelve drops of spring fern juice. Moose is for strength. Fern is for new growth. It's one of her favorite potions because it has a most promising fizz. Altogether she has nine different remedies. There are creams for rubbing, powders for sprinkling, liquids for drinking. A few batches are buried underground — one is forty-two days old, she'll dig it up soon! The plants talk to her, they tell her what they are good for: cleaning the blood, skin rashes, or stomachache. None of them say they are good for gangrene, but maybe combined with the other things...

Then one day her parents notice a lot of medicine bottles missing from the cabinet. They ask her if she knows anything about it and she has to tell them. Because the medicine is expensive and Dad isn't working because of his foot, they're angry until she tells them why she needed them. But they don't want to try any of her potions. And they make her shut down her laboratory.

❧ ☙

My father's leg was amputated just below the knee. After nearly two years of trying everything medical science had to offer, he said one day, "I'm sick and tired of all this. I don't need the dang thing anyway; let's take it off and have it over with." So they did. And he was right — it didn't slow him down much. He used to tell us kids about the "ghost" foot that was still there, and how he could scratch the missing big toe (which itched a lot) by scratching a certain place on the stump. He used to keep money in the prosthesis, the "Bank of Hollow Leg" as he told me once. Mom admitted finding fifteen thousand dollars in it when he died, many years later.

When I was young I was passionate about healing and medicine. In my outdoor "lab," I learned two important things. One was that nature is a pharmacy: plants are good for medicine and we can communicate with them. I also learned that the body "remembered" itself as whole even when a part was cut off. At eleven we still feel "all powerful." I really believed I was a healer; I thought I could heal Dad. I wasn't wrong about the first part — we all have an internal healer; I have called on mine many times.

Healing Is

Over the years I continued to follow my interest in the innate healing ability within; there were many times that I called on this source.
On one occasion, in 1969, when I was beginning the fifth month of
my first pregnancy I suffered a miscarriage that resulted in serious
hemorrhaging. My husband found me lying weakly in a pool of blood
on the floor of our tiny living room. I felt certain I would live and
that the bleeding would stop if commanded, but I was too weak to
do it. With the doctor some distance away, I told my husband, Atz,
to get Jerry, the Mormon bishop. He and his wife Nelda were my
dearest friends; he was a man of simple but impressive faith. They
lived a mile away. When he arrived, the blood slowly pumping out
around me was a daunting sight, but he placed his hands on my head
commanding the bleeding to stop and health to flow back into my
limbs and that is what happened. I recovered immediately and fully.
The doctor later confirmed that I indeed suffered a massive hemor-
rhage; he was amazed by my instantaneous recovery.

Mormons have a wonderful tradition and heritage of miraculous healing, one that built my own belief in our innate ability to
provide healing to one another. There were many times I worked
successfully in a healing way with my children when they were ill. I
learned to diagnose their problems by asking my own body to tell
me where the problem was. One night when my oldest child was
only a year old he woke at midnight in great distress. Nothing
soothed him, not milk, rocking, or music. When I tuned my body to
his, my right hand began to ache; spasms racked my upper arm.
Removing his pajama top and examining his arm, I discovered a
rubber band binding it just above the elbow. The circulation was
restricted and the hand and arm were blue.

Many times I successfully evoked healing for them or myself,
not because I was a healer, but because *we all* possess a relationship
with the "inner physician." Through that relationship we can access
healing and wisdom, we can evoke information to come through
others, we can connect with healing modalities that are right for our

situation, and we can communicate powerfully with our bodies. We do this not by trying to become healers, but by remembering that health lies within; it is simply our natural birthright.

MATTER ON THE HEAD OF A PIN

Over thirty-five years ago, in middle school science class, the teacher slapped his hand down on a desk in the front row making us all jump. "This table," he stated emphatically, "is not solid. It is merely a vibrating mass of gyrating atoms." He paced the room excitedly, enjoying himself, pointing out other "nonsolid" objects — our pens, shoes, the walls in the room. Then he delivered his punch line. "Even your bodies are not solid. They have the same vibrating atomic structure. And they are primarily space. If all the space in your body, the space between the atoms, could be removed, the remaining matter would fit on the head of a pin."

It made an impression. Like me, many of us were taught this concept years ago and we still do not grasp the immensity of its meaning. We are primarily space. Space plus an infinitesimal amount of matter. The body is, quite literally, not solid and there are many reliable reports that demonstrate this. In 1905 several of Iceland's leading scientists conducted well-documented investigations into psychic phenomena. One of their subjects, Indridi Indridason, shocked them when, "during deep trance, different parts of his body would completely dematerialize. As the astonished scientists watched, an arm or a hand would fade out of existence, only to rematerialize before he awakened."

The body is not solid. It is primarily space, though it is not empty space, of course. It is pure energy and as such is vital, pliable, and malleable. In his extraordinary work *The Holographic Universe*, Michael Talbot reports that "when physicists calculate the minimum amount of energy a wave [field] can possess, they find that *every cubic centimeter of empty space contains more energy than the total energy of all the matter in the known universe!*"[1]

---

1. Michael Talbot, *The Holographic Universe* (New York: HarperCollins, 1991).

How can we affect this space, tap this energy that fills our bodies? It is very responsive, especially to sound, light, and thought. Renowned physicist David Bohm believes "there is a deeper and nonlocal level of existence from which our entire universe springs." He sees this deeper level of existence, comprised entirely of waveforms of differing kinds, as the implicate order (the originator and cohesive force) of the cosmos. Bohm's research led him to understand that it is our intention and imagination that affects the creation of form:

> Every action starts from an intention in the implicate order. The imagination...already has the intention and the germs of all the movements needed to carry it out. And it affects the body...so that as creation takes place in that way from the subtler levels of the implicate order, it goes through [all the more subtle levels] until it manifests in the explicate, as what we know as matter.[2]

In other words, he is saying that manifestation in the explicate — or physical — levels occurs by intention, imagination, and thought moving through the subtle levels of the implicate order until it manifests in matter, such as the body. This shows in a very real way how our thoughts create our dream reality.

FOUNDATION FOR MIRACLES

Many doctors and scientists have studied the ability of thought to bring about healing. One, psychologist Jeanne Achterberg, while head of research and rehabilitation science at the University of Texas Health Science Center, helped validate this and develop imagery healing techniques widely used in medicine and with athletes.

Using a group of college students, Achterberg taught them to image a white cell known as a neutrophil. She trained a second group of the students to visualize another type of white cell, the T-cell. Each

---

2. Ibid.

group showed significant increase in the number of the white cells that they imaged but no increase in the white cells they did not image. In her fascinating book *Imagery in Healing*, Achterberg describes many cases of belief, thought, or visualization being the factors in seemingly miraculous healing.

Dr. O. Carl Simonton uses such techniques with patients. While a radiation oncologist and medical director of the Cancer Counseling and Research Center in Dallas, Texas, he suggested to a patient that he could influence his own disease. The patient was a sixty-one-year-old man with throat cancer so advanced that he was extremely weak and could barely swallow or even breathe. He had only a 5 percent chance of surviving. Simonton taught the man very specific visualization and relaxation techniques that he combined with conventional therapy. The results were so dramatic, the recovery so remarkable that Simonton and his colleagues taught their mental imaging techniques to 159 cancer patients considered incurable. Four years later 14 of those terminal patients were disease free and 17 had stabilized. In another 12 their cancers were continuing to regress. All together, an astonishing 63 of these patients were still alive.[3]

Shamanism and similar mysterious areas of research have gained in significance because they postulate new ideas about mind and spirit. They speak of things like vastly expanding the realm of consciousness...the belief, the knowledge, and even the experience that our physical world of the senses is a mere illusion, a world of shadows, and that the three-dimensional tool we call our body serves only as a container or dwelling place for something infinitely greater and more comprehensive than that body and which constitutes the matrix of real life.

— Holger Kalweit

3. Ibid.

THE TERMS OF RENEWAL

The body is a swirling vortex of highly refined energies such as atoms, electrons, and neutrons that are shifting and changing in every moment. And it is always new; masterfully renewing itself regularly. Dr. Paul C. Aebersold of the Oak Ridge Atomic Research Center has become convinced by his study of radioisotope tracings that nearly 98 percent of the atoms in the human body are replaced continually. A liver completely renews itself in less than six weeks; the stomach's lining is replaced every five days. Even the bones, he says, "are quite dynamic," continually re-forming. Donald Hatch Andrews, who is professor of chemistry at Johns Hopkins University, estimates that one's physical body completely renews itself every five years, down to the very last atom.

The body, then, is *constantly* new. It is continually in movement to renew itself. This being the case, why would the stomach lining — while renewing itself — re-create an ulcer again and again every five days? Why doesn't it slough the ulcer with the old tissue and create a healthy lining? To understand this we must realize three things: The body has its own memory and consciousness in the cells. The body is amazingly responsive to our thoughts. Our thoughts move quickly on flashes of light, but the body, being far denser matter than thought, can be slower to respond, and may need persistent thought to affect it.

It is well understood in sports medicine that the body memorizes movements and trauma, among other things. It is now widely accepted that it is the body that holds such memory. This understanding about body memory explains my father's experience that his amputated leg was still there. The phantom limb phenomenon explains sensations of some amputees that missing limbs are still present. "Such individuals often feel eerily realistic cramps, pains, and tinglings in these phantom appendages, but it may be they are experiencing the holographic *memory* of the limb that is still recorded in the wave patterns in their brain."[4]

---

4. Ibid.

BREAKING THE PATTERN

A thought, laid down repetitively in the pliable wave field of the body, creates a body memory or habit, a pattern. Unless this pattern is interrupted at the thought level, it will ultimately manifest in the physical as an interruption of the natural health of the body. Form follows thought. The body is taking information and direction from our thoughts continually. The prime tone of the thought directly affects physical health. That is how thoughts filled with fear, worry, self-hatred, stress — if not contained by our awareness and supported by actions to change — rob us of our health, even creating very specific ailments in our body.

We can, however, change our thoughts much faster than our bodies. Being far denser in its composition than thought, the body can be slower to catch up. This is good. It allows us to recognize and interrupt the thoughts that may create difficulty. But it also accounts for why, when we have understood and corrected an unhealthy pattern, the physical change doesn't appear to follow. The body is slower to respond and that is why the *repetition* of visualization and relaxation is necessary to break the pattern *and* alter the physical situation.

We can become discouraged and give up quickly. Not seeing immediate results, we abandon our practice and settle back into fear or despair or complacency. This is rather like committing to take a car trip from California to New York but upon becoming lost in Las Vegas we say, "Oh, it's no use. I'll just turn around and go home." Rerouting is all that is required to put us on track no matter how many times we lose our way while changing an unhealthy pattern. The constant rerouting is what *unavoidably* interrupts the undesirable wave pattern being laid in the body.

If at first you do not succeed — try to hide your astonishment.

— Harry F. Banks

The body is not solid. The body is always new. The body possesses a consciousness, intelligence, and memory and is extremely responsive to our thought. Combining this knowledge, we have a remarkable tool for our health. By communicating consciously and lovingly with our body there is really no limit to its capability to respond. It can bring about our renewal to full health, heighten our vitality, and even slow aging.

Hundreds of cases have been documented of yogis in India, shamans in indigenous cultures, and martial arts masters who completely control bodily functions, even taking poison without harm, being cut and punctured without bleeding, surviving in good health indefinitely without eating or drinking, and many more "impossible" things. These are not bizarre miracles beyond comprehension or beyond the ability of the majority of people. It is a latent power within each of us. This is simply the natural power of the healer within.

As I have learned to hear that inner physician and implement its wisdom; as I have cleansed my thoughts and body, come to love myself and my life fully; as I have learned to partake of the succor and Light available in the Implicate Order of stillness, and integrate peace in my own being, I have grown healthy, full of vital energy, and noticeably more youthful. In the next chapter I will share what that journey into health has been for me.

> Basically all healing is the intake into the body of eternal sun, the Light. If you can call upon this Light, it will actually control the cells of the physical body. The body is so heavy, material life so strong, that you forget the power of God to re-create tissue, to re-create the living cells of your body.
>
> — White Eagle

23

Journey INTO Health

O f course, everyone wants to be
healthy. The amusing thing is no one's really sure how to do it.

— Jerry Seinfeld

My soul orchestrated a divorce for me in 1982. Deeply frightened
and uncertain about my ability to care for my children and myself, my
situation felt desperate to me. Lacking means, education, or job experience, and with no resources to fight for child support in the courts,
I felt severely handicapped. I questioned what the opportunities were
in this difficult situation. Through my meditations I realized they
were in possessing the vast source of my own unique strength,
becoming reliable and trustworthy to myself, and in becoming
emotionally and physically whole. Thus began a seven-year journey
from the dark of fear into the lightness of personal freedom.

It was a time of great upheaval for me as I submitted to my soul's
agenda to cleanse the old emotional and mental ways of being. There
was much confusion and the deep-welling turmoil of a powerfully
resistant ego thrashing about. Lacking new tools, not clear yet about
where all the old baggage was, and only moderately capable of radical
self-honesty, it was a difficult period. There were many tears. I often
found it difficult to sit still for the process I was in, preferring actions
that would distract me. On one especially difficult morning, I suddenly

jumped in my truck and drove two hundred and fifty miles to the nearest city to see friends, go to a movie, and avoid the issue that was prodding me. Upon arrival I realized what I had done. Seeing my self-ruse and sensing that a breakthrough was near, I got back in my truck and immediately drove home. On the five-hour return trip, I pondered what I was trying to avoid; I examined the pain in my life. What were the new patterns needed? How could I change? I arrived home with many answers that enabled me to move ahead.

LEARNING TO SURRENDER

Into this potent emotional struggle was thrown an intense legal fight. I truly didn't know if I would survive the nightmare that seemed to be my life. I took control of the litigation and grounded myself in the passion of my anger, refusing to become a victim. I determined to assign the necessary energy to the matter, but not more. I refused to let my mind or ego dwell in repetitive regrets or recriminations regarding others or myself. I examined what was needed for my growth, educated myself to the situation, took business courses, and fiercely defended my rights.

Just as I stabilized in my ability to handle that situation, my attention was called urgently to my health. The constant fear, stress, emotional pain, and financial desperation collided with genetics, poor diet, and lack of sleep and exercise. After my heart attack, I realized something was seriously amiss. Though only forty years old, my cholesterol was over 750 and unresponsive to any medications; there were indications of damage to my heart muscle, my fatigue was consuming, and I suffered from angina. The medical advice was drastic. I felt a clear mistrust of it, and besides, I had no money for treatment.

Now that I had come fully to the legal fight, I was being pulled out of the ring. My body and my soul were both giving me a major wake-up call; I had to wonder to what purpose. Having come to a willingness to seize responsibility for my life and dream it differently no matter the obstacles, to do whatever it took to create the change, I was now unable, physically, to take any action at all. I was required to surrender and to relinquish my methods of "doing."

When I sought the advice of my own wisdom, I understood to seek deep solitude and rest. My brother offered me an old cabin on his wife's family homestead. It was remote and, though it had electricity, it lacked plumbing entirely. It was basically one small room and quite rudimentary. I had to haul water from town in five-gallon jugs, and there was an outhouse in back. At this time, Jewel was at Interlochen Arts Academy, Shane was in college, and Atz Lee was with his father, so I retreated to the cabin and invited my soul to lead my life, entirely.

For nine months I lived quietly there in full surrender. My focus was on cleaning house — cleaning out detrimental mental and emotional patterns, and cleansing my body. Medication and diet had failed to improve my health in any way, but this focused communion with spirit and clearing of unhealthy emotional and mental habits brought startling improvements. My cholesterol dropped significantly, and I began to mend.

> Health is a state of complete physical, mental and social well-being and not merely the absence of disease or infirmity. The enjoyment of the highest attainable standard of health is one of the fundamental rights of every human being without distinction of race, religion, political belief, economic or social condition.
>
> — World Health Organization

CLEANSING THOUGHT

We relate to our bodies as babies, children, then teens, adults, and so on until they grow old and die. But throughout this process they are always new, continuously regenerating. They are a generative source responsive to our every thought, awaiting only our *consciousness* to begin to partner with us in creating abundant health. Being conscious, we are utterly capable of dreaming the body to have health in every moment, but this is predicated on having the thoughts be as clear as possible.

In *Health Is Our Birthright*, a fascinating book of case studies from many years of practice, Dr. Ellen Jensen addresses the need to purify our mental processes:

> The body is a magnificent creation of God. It comes equipped with an innate intelligence and powerful energy to heal itself when given the opportunity. Keeping the mind free of debilitating thoughts is necessary to access this energy and intelligence. Feelings such as guilt, worry, fear, or anger can drain us of the vital energy that is so essential for a high quality of health and life.

When our thoughts are a constant babble — when they are filled with guilt, fear, worry, judgment — they create wave patterns that erode physical health. Worry, for instance, is one of the most egregious losses of energy. It takes a situation that is merely an invitation to be creative and funnels it into repetitious, monomaniacal, fear-based thinking. Again and again we traverse the loop of the same defeating thoughts, unable to break the chain of worry about what our boyfriend thinks, the actions of coworkers, or whether we are safe in a given situation.

Such thoughts collide with our wisdom and intuition, our moments of clarity and certainty, and our desire to change and grow. The resulting conflict creates a misfiring in our central nervous system that causes erratic mental activity. This erraticism is not rhythmic or coherent. It does not allow the body to rest in the simple knowledge that we are on track, on purpose, that our life is unfolding as it should and it will continue to do so. It prevents us from knowing that everything is presented for our edification; not as a test or punishment, but for our growth.

To dream abundance, to have ease rather than arduousness requires putting our thoughts in order. Cleaning house in this way occurs through purposeful engagement in activities that assist the thoughts to become more organized. Aids such as meditation, prayer, physical exercise, and journal writing help bring a sense of prioritization and organization. Without this order, the mind tends to go over the same ground again and again with the same fearful or limited thoughts. This creates a tremendous drain of energy and vitality.

I am aware that it can be difficult to interrupt these obsessive thoughts. When I was trying to make strides in my ability to discipline my mind, I found the habit so deeply ingrained that it seemed hopeless. It was at the end of a relationship; my mind replayed over and over painful scenes with my boyfriend and fears about the future. It was so compelling that I could not remember anything else to think about when I asked myself to. To remedy this, I made flash cards for myself. On them I wrote several thoughts it would be beneficial for me to concentrate on. They included dreams that were neglected in my thoughts — my new business, a more satisfactory living situation, my love of music, and so on. I referred to them again and again. My life began to change in positive ways as I patiently but insistently gave my obsessive thoughts *only* specific, deeply productive time while I allotted the remainder of my thoughts to the dreams and needs of the present.

Organizing and disciplining our mental processes clears away the clamor and allows us to hear the inner voices of our bodies' needs and knowledge. During my time in the forest cabin, I helped achieve this by creating visualizations that in turn established consistent communication with my body about health. Because I had difficulty concentrating, I made tapes of my own voice reciting poetry, meditations, and singing; I played them throughout the day. I discovered that the body loves to be sung to, that our voice is unique in its ability to access the healthy blueprint, so I sang a great deal. I made every effort to change fearful emotional and mental patterns. I created ceremonies that facilitated change and celebrated growth, reminding myself that I was safe and whole. All this served to create a quiet, disciplined thought pattern that gave me better access to my soul's guidance.

CLEANSING THE BODY

As a result of our modern lifestyles, we accumulate waste from food additives, pollution, residue from overstimulated adrenal glands and hormone systems. These toxins create a "noise" that overrides the quiet wisdom of the body.

In a dream, I was told to drink large quantities of pure water and go to the produce section of the grocery store and ask my body what it required. When I tried to follow this guidance, I discovered that I was never thirsty; I had no natural urge to drink water because it had been ignored for so long. At the grocery store, I heard no urgings in front of the vegetables, but I felt loudly called to aisles three and four where the potato chips and ice cream were. I could only hear the pestering addictions of the ego, and they were very compelling. When I contemplated how to change this, I knew that cleansing the body was required. I searched for methods of doing that.

I began by eating more simply and consciously, choosing foods that were organic. Herbs from the forest — dandelion leaves, fern, mushrooms, chamomile — became part of my diet, along with nutritious broths, soups, and teas. I determined to acquire a taste for vegetables. I began drinking more water, hydrating the cells and flushing waste. I studied nutrition, supplements, and herbs, read about health, and learned new ways to accomplish my cleansing goals.

> The secret to vibrant health, youth, and vitality is in cleansing the body and mind and then adapting a lifestyle that includes clear thoughts, natural foods, pure water, fresh air, sunshine and exercise. Learning to cleanse the body and the mind is an essential part of healing. When the body is burdened with toxic waste material, it will be tired and have low immune function. When the body is clean, it can absorb the essential nutrients it desperately needs to heal and repair.
>
> — Dr. Ellen Jensen

Dr. Bernard Jensen developed a colon health and tissue-cleansing program that gave me wonderful results. At what is now known as the Eden Center (see page 339 for more information), I experienced Dr. Jensen's cleanse as part of their wellness program. In less than two weeks, I had a vastly expanded understanding of options and a personal program for promoting and maintaining health.

I experienced substantial physical improvement as well. My cholesterol dropped from 750 to 450 during my two-week stay, and in the month following, it stabilized at below 200. My liver and kidneys resumed healthy functioning. The doctors were amazed and encouraged me to continue. A fellow guest at the center with multiple sclerosis became pain free and able to walk without her wheelchair; another released a tapeworm nearly a foot long; and a cancer patient overcame the debilitating edema and aftereffects of his radiation treatments by flushing the chemicals from his body. Working through both the liver and the colon, the program is effective at cleansing the cells of the whole body, not just the colon. A commitment to cleansing is a potent message to the universe that we are sweeping the old wasteland clean and remodeling the habitation of our soul.

HARMONY IN THE BODY

Attention to diet is vital, but it has not come easily to me; I have had to be patient and persistent. Now at every opportunity, I eat fresh organic foods, which have a greater life force and purity than processed or fast foods. I cannot overstate the importance of this. Eating mindfully creates an entirely different relationship between food and our body than grabbing something to quickly fill a need, eating the consciousness of fear and guilt, longing, sadness, or anger with every mouthful.

In clinical studies using Kirlian photography, an orange being eaten with attention and appreciation showed wavelike rays emanating from the fruit in all directions. One that was eaten quickly while the subject thought of events of the day showed minimal, dull wave activity. It is a matter of consciousness. Dr. Leonard Laskow, in his best-selling book *Healing with Love*, compellingly explores the idea that food consciously blessed before eating is measurably different than food that is not. He gives many examples of techniques for using the energy of love to improve our health. Attention to color, beauty, and presentation in our meals has also been shown to add vitality to food.

Engaging in a diet in order to fit society's perceptions of body image is clearly not effective. At the source of many unsuccessful diets are the unhealthy, critical feelings we have toward our bodies and our food. These feelings set up an antagonistic relationship with what we eat. Every mouthful is regretted, judged. In the entertainment industry, I meet many men and women who feel guilty with every bite of food they take. That is not an intent that generates a successful wave — it washes back into the body as a disturbing fear-based frequency.

It is preferable to bring an organized frequency of consciousness to what we are putting into our bodies. What do our bodies tell us they require, what to avoid? We honor our earth and ourselves when we eat the fruit of the earth, the beauty of the earth, with delight rather than guilt. Then eating is a prayer, and we are in harmony with the earth systems we spring from.

Dr. Salila Tewari is an esteemed nature physician from New Delhi, India, whose patients include the current prime minister of India. Her teacher, a masterful yogi and healer, on several occasions drank water laced with poison or infected with cholera without ill effects. He did so, with medical and scientific witnesses, to demonstrate that, when the body is fully harmonized with the cosmic energies, even poison is not harmful to it.

I spoke to a scientist who visited India to study the abilities of certain yogis regarding health. He met one who subsisted solely on numerous daily cups of strong black coffee with three tablespoons of sugar in each. The doctor witnessed the man's every activity in a remote one-room hut in the forest for a month and never saw him taking any other food. The yogi said it didn't matter what he ate because it was the prana, the divine energy, that he "ate" in every breath that sustained him. He had become so adept at absorbing this energy that nothing else was required.

Beginning in 1953, a woman calling herself Peace Pilgrim embarked on a remarkable personal trek devoted to sharing a message about peace. Transversing the United States entirely on foot, she reached her goal of 25,000 miles in 1964, though she continued her journey until her death in 1981. In the book *Peace Pilgrim: Her Life and Work in Her Own Words*, she relates the following about physical energy:

> I usually average twenty-five miles a day walking. . . . I have gone up to fifty miles in one day. . . . Once a six-foot fellow, confident he could outwalk me, walked with me for thirty-three miles. When he gave up, his feet were blistered and his muscles ached. He was walking on his own strength; I wasn't! I was walking on that endless energy that comes from inner peace.

It is important to know what really feeds us, what is available in the life-giving essence we breathe. It is as important to know what is right for us; not for a sage in the Himalayas, but for us now, in our own lives. I may not be able to subsist on coffee and sugar, but my body does tell me what it requires. It asks for simple, pure foods, lots of water, cleansing, and vigorous movement each day; and it craves the sustenance found in stillness.

THE ART OF DISCIPLINE

To achieve a simple eating and exercise routine in a complex life full of travel and stimulation, I must apply discipline. Discipline is a wonderful word because it evokes the status of being a disciple of *our own infinite spirit*. Discipline is required in our lives. It can be engaged by the ego or by the soul. Discipline evoked by the soul is more appropriate and successful.

Every day there is a banquet table laid out for us covered with a myriad of experiences that feed the body, the ego, or the time-oriented self. Discipline is a matter of allowing oneself to be led by the appetites of the soul. The soul knows what we truly hunger for. It does not hurry to fill a hole without knowledge of what that hole is and what is really required. There are many experiences that are not sustaining. They are tempting; they constantly draw the ego into interplay with them. To diminish the inclination to feed the ego's or body's hunger, we can choose a larger perspective than that of either. The ego choices can certainly be enjoyed, but if *all* the choices are made by the ego, we allow it to run the show and set the identity. Choosing to honor ourselves and remember the perspective of our soul allows us to enjoy the other appetites but not be ruled by them.

The soul is a loving master. It is honoring and self-assured. Applying a gentle, persistent discipline from this larger perspective will ultimately break the physical habits that limit our sense of freedom, energy, and health.

THE CONTEXT OF HEALTH

We can improve our health by expanding our context to one that is greater than our problems, greater than our desires, greater than our health challenges. What is the deeper context for who we are? We are spirit, an everlasting soul that has the same cosmic intelligence that can build a body, grow a tree, create an earth, sun, or a cosmos. That is our expanded capability. When we dwell in the minutiae of our daily tasks and problems, it is forgotten entirely.

As we gradually switch from the smaller to the greater context, we become an observer of our dreams. We are still identified as an individual, but one that has access to an identity as a greater self. From this elevated identity, we can *view* the emotion that sets up hormone responses in the body. When a traumatic emotion or memory is triggered, for example, the pulse may elevate, breathing alter, and a chemical response flood through us, affecting all organs and cells. With this operating pattern, our body is forced to process the chemical responses of our emotions and thoughts. The continual overproduction of such chemicals greatly erodes health. But from the higher context, we can be aware of and choose our response instead of becoming engulfed by it. We can remember we are not this body, this personality, our history or future, our projects and creations. We are none of those things; we are the eternal soul. This fact gives us a healthy detachment from the angst and prevents the emotions from being continually run through the body, which greatly serves our physical well-being.

I have not come to health by wishing for it, laying myself in the hands of others, or ignoring the problems that were affecting it. I tried all of these approaches, of course, without success. I count my health today from the moments — when ill, dying, or suffering physically — that I realized I had the wisdom within me for my healing. I count my health from the occasions when I took charge of my path to wellness. I count my health today from the times I looked kindly but unflinchingly at myself and began to change the habits that did not serve me. I count my health from the times spent in silence accessing the original blueprint of health that exists in my soul. I count my health from each moment I have expanded my horizon to include my soul's perspective in life.

We're on the vanguard of a health care revolution as profound as civil rights or feminism. All over, I see an uprising fueled by courageous people, demanding that their spiritual and intuitive voices be honored in the healing process. Attitudes are shifting. I meet medical practitioners and patients everywhere who rail against the icy sterility of technological advances alone — no matter how miraculous — when simple kindness, love, and awe for our inner vision are sacrificed.

— Judith Orloff, M.D.

24

A Legacy OF Health

For two years he had been valiantly fighting for his life with the support of his many loving friends. They were gathered around him now, speaking in positive tones, urging him to keep up his hope and courage. The AIDS virus had decimated his body and he lay, wasted, on his bed. Prayers and chants were spoken: "You know you are going to get well," one woman said; "Believe it and you can do it!" Another reminded him of the many miracles he had received already and predicted that there was one final miracle of healing for him. "Together, we can do it!" they affirmed.

Into this moment walked an older friend of his, a woman he had admired for many years for her great wisdom and forthrightness. She pressed through the crowd around his bed and stood looking down at him; she held his hand quietly in her own. Her eyes, with their depth of peace, communicated all the things there are no words for.

At last she spoke. "You know you are dying, don't you?" She repeated it for emphasis, as a statement: "You are dying."

No one breathed for a long moment. He searched his soul, as her eyes compelled him to do. "Yes," he said at last. "I am dying."

Sharp intakes of breath signaled everyone's shock, fear, even disapproval.

"Then do it with the same passion and joy that you have lived and see what is there for you." With that, she turned to his friends, frowning: "And all of you. Stop this nonsense and help him prepare to go. Live *his* truth, not your own fears and hopes."

She turned back to him with her loving radiance and embraced him. Her tears were cool as they anointed his fervid brow. "God speed you on your journey," she said as she turned to go.

In the stillness she left behind, each one there struggled to come to terms with this dramatic shift. They began to speak quietly together, honoring him, his accomplishments, his work as an artist. They thanked him for including them in his amazing capacity to love. And they spoke tenuously of what might lie ahead.

In the weeks following he lived an exceptional artwork of the passage we call death. He embraced it with his full creativity, examining his life passionately. Gathering together his memories, he skillfully crafted a beautiful album of drawings, poems, cards, photos — all the moments that told the story of his life. His legacy.

In it was evidence of his multitude of well-loved friends, the healing with his father, his travels and lessons, the movement through his fears, his growth in spirit. Though he became weaker in his body, he was surprised to find that he became fearless about the process of dying. Much was communicated to him in dreams and visions that he shared with those near him. All of these, his legacy, constituted his healing.

◦═◦

Vibrant health is found in every moment that we embrace the truth of our soul. This man came to know, beyond doubt, the purpose of his life. He knew it was fulfilled and his legacy secured. It was with this peace and satisfaction that he died late one evening as he had planned — with his friends in ceremony and celebration around his hospice bed.

There is a broad range of choices available to us regarding the legacy that we leave behind. It can be one of chaos, worry, unconscious blundering, destruction; it can be one that we craft with awareness — one of love, health, and the conscious intention of our spirit. Achieving the latter requires us to clear away patterns that prevent it.

BREAKING THE CHAIN

In the first two months after my divorce, separated from my children, I began to wonder what legacy I was leaving them. I saw that they had a rich spiritual life as well as a strong intellectual one. Importantly, they also had a deeply grounded legacy of love. But I saw areas of their emotional inheritance that I did not feel proud of. Fears and unhealthy habits of mine were being handed down to them. I thought of the passage in the Bible regarding the sins of the parents being visited upon the children for seven generations. Our patterns are handed down, parent to child, generation to generation. I wanted to break that chain.

Sin is a word that actually means "lack of consciousness; disconnection from God." When we are unconscious of Spirit we are disconnected from our potential and our wholeness. We lose consciousness in times of fear, denial, worry, blame, and so on. I didn't want my children to inherit the burden of habits I was afraid to understand and change — the "sins" of my unconsciousness and disconnection from the Source. If I didn't change, they would inherit my fear of taking care of myself, childhood trauma, and patterns hidden in denial or manipulation; I would be leaving them poor tools for life. I began to look more closely to see what was there that I could free myself from, and free the children, too.

A new emotional legacy, a healthy one, was what I wanted to pass on to them. And when I began to do so, it changed our relationship. I became someone in their lives who saw, understood, and talked about what was *really* going on. I dropped the party line, the small talk, the unconsciousness, and began to fully grapple with what it meant to be human — all of it. I stopped hiding from myself and pretending to others that everything was fine.

The body is a mirror of our process. When we look into that mirror without judgment, our health provides physical feedback about the journey we are taking. The body does not randomly betray us with confusing and mysterious symptoms. It is communicating with us. What is it saying? It is not hard to find out, but it requires that we be still, ask, listen, and act on what we hear. I was able to facilitate my own healing because I listened, without flinching, to the messages. But there is only one way this can work: we *must* set aside our self-judgment. If not, the wise messages from our body become lost in the litany of our sins. Gentle, loving, unflinching self-honesty combined with a voracious curiosity about who we are and what is showing up for us can garner the information needed for growth into health. Then, with persistent application of this wisdom, our outcome is assured.

What Did I Do Wrong?

Midway through Jewel's Spirit Tour we were both worn out, badly in need of rest and recuperation. I heard about a beautiful lodge in northern New Zealand and booked a few days for our respite. We looked forward to the downtime, with walks along the lake, outdoor hot springs, and the delicious cuisine. I showered quickly at the hotel, mentally preparing for the trip. The phone rang as I stepped from the shower and I dashed to answer it. The next thing I remembered was hearing a frighteningly loud, guttural cry that seemed to be some distance away.

"Someone help her," I thought to myself, "she's hurt." I did not realize the sound was coming from me — I had fallen on the wet tile floor, bashing my right temple against the doorknob. Slowly regaining consciousness, it was some time before I knew what I was, let alone who or where. Then the phone rang again. Jewel was saying something, but I couldn't make it out. Nor was I able to speak or control the crying moan I was making. My next clear recollection was of her holding me as my injured body attempted to overcome the effects of the trauma.

The fall left me with quite noticeable difficulties. In addition to a severe concussion and lateral whiplash, I suffered frequent episodes of ringing in my ears, followed by blackouts. There was damage to a blood vessel above my right ear, which affected my balance. Suffering chronic spasms in my right shoulder and arm, I lost 80 percent of their range of movement.

We often wonder what we did *wrong* when such things occur in our lives, feeling guilty, thinking we did not "get it right." We ask why we fell, got cancer, caught a cold, had a toothache. The question "Why?" can have the nagging inference that we did something wrong. As we become more conscious of the connection between our emotions, our living habits, and our bodies, we may add derogatory judgment to the process. There is the chance that we have gone from making no connection, taking no self-responsibility, to *blaming ourselves*.

We feel that if we were more conscious, more spiritual, then this "bad" thing would not have happened, that there was something we should have done better. We feel it is our fault. This is self-disparaging judgment. When we hear someone else is ill, we may even assess what *they* need to learn, what they did wrong. It is all deprecatory judgment and it gets in the way of the clarity and wisdom that are available.

Balanced and conscious assessment of an experience is helpful. It is important to connect our thoughts and feelings with our actions and our body. It is valuable to ask questions. However, being unduly critical or shaming ourselves keeps us looking back at the past. We can find the benefit, lesson, or plan of action without this type of judgment. Rather than assessing blame, we can look for what will bring the desired movement, the shift, the healing. One of the best questions we can ask is, "How can I bring myself back to what I know to be true — that I am whole, I am safe, I am more than my body; how do I get to that understanding again?"

Naturally, I wondered about my injury. When I asked my body, I understood that it was a simple matter of being out of balance. We had just been through a long and intense work period. I was tired and hard-pressed to find time for rest or recreation. I began to seek knowledge for my recovery. Throughout the nearly three years of the healing process, my focus was not on the difficulties. I did not overlook or deny my injury, pain, and frustration — I experienced and moved through them when I felt them — but my *focus* was on what could be done to recover. The injuries were serious, but I knew my body could regenerate.

With cranial-sacral and chiropractic work, reiki, deep-tissue massage, and Ayurvedic sound treatments, I corrected the whiplash and slowly regained use of my shoulder and arm. Additional cranial-sacral work as well as intensified nutritional supplementation repaired my venous and nervous systems, healing the damaged vein and ending my blackouts. The incident served as an impetus for me to commit to a more active life, strengthening my body for the extensive travel and activity I participate in. I also restructured my schedule to allow for more rest and personal creativity. Two and a half years later, due to these efforts, I was actually in far better health than before I fell.

> A wise man ought to realize that health is his most valuable possession and learn how to treat his illness by his own judgment.
>
> — Hippocrates

AUTOMATIC REFLEXES

Much of my life, I had been caught in negative, repetitive patterns — doing things in the same old way while expecting different results (remember the definition of madness?). For example, I had a tendency to take random action as a first line of defense. During my heart difficulties, I was asked to sit down and stop *doing* and come into my *being*. This was difficult because of deep-seated beliefs that if I didn't take action, any action, all would be lost. As I grew quiet, I began to more fully see my many unhealthy, automatic reflexes.

Manipulation

One was manipulation. I was not consciously manipulative, but I was indirectly so. Still afraid to fully *deserve* my life, I took circuitous routes to satisfy my needs in work, relationships, and communication. I didn't realize that my needs could be easily met, that they were already provided for. Instead, I believed that I had to *arrange* and *strategize* to make everything happen. This belief results in a subtle but pervasive pattern of manipulation. It is one that permeates our human interactions, greatly complicating our relations with one another. This pattern demands much more energy; it is an enormous relief when we become free of the nearly constant indirect strategizing, arranging, and overseeing. I achieved relief from it by being willing to recognize and change the myriad ways in which I manipulated. It became a game to see where I could catch myself in the act. I delighted in ferreting out this unconscious pattern that robbed me of so much energy. Each time my ego tried to protect me from looking at myself — by being defensive and denying the truth — I asked it to grow, to become more healthy.

Stress Response

Another automatic reflex was my stress response. The incessant call to the adrenal glands to pour adrenaline into my system to fuel me, save me, or boost my energy is a habit many of us share. Of course stress is unavoidable; there are stressful situations in each day, but it is how we perceive and respond to them that determines their effect on our bodies. Challenging my beliefs and physical reactions regarding stress brought tremendous gains. Meditation, solitude in nature, writing poetry, singing, and conscious and persistent repatterning were the tools that helped me with this.

Energetic Martyrdom

Another juicy bit I discovered was a propensity for energetic martyrdom. The tendency can be so insidious it may seem genetically based: it is like a family curse passed through the generations as a message dictating that we must live for others. The great danger is that it can rob us of our vital energy. We have an energetic core that must be maintained. If we are constantly drawing from that place, the body soon signals distress; difficulties and disease develop in vulnerable areas. I had exhausted myself to the core; I was heartsick about the litigation. I come from a long line of women who "give their hearts out." The connection is obvious. Learning to receive from others, to nurture myself, to serve my own life and to drink deeply from the wellspring of silence assisted me in becoming self-generative.

Forfeiting Choice

Forfeiting choice was another automatic response. There were many areas in which I co-opted my power to choose because of feelings of responsibility and guilt. It is necessary to consciously make our choices — consciously choosing our work, our habits, choosing each moment. There is health in this. Undercurrents of feeling trapped or victimized, without choice, create immensely disturbing waves in the body.

Ungroundedness

Another pattern I found that contributed to ill health was ungroundedness. I had a great need to become more aware of my body, to learn to feel it, listen to it, inhabit it, breathe into it; be present in it. So much of my world was mental — planning, talking on the phone, meeting. I learned to check in with my body in the course of the day — during phone calls or in a difficult moment. I paused to notice how I felt physically, where tension was held, to relax, and expand my shallow breath.

I began to pay great attention to what I ate, to ride my bike, sing to my heart, practice yoga. Exercise grounds the body, as do breath and a healthy diet. Massage is also nurturing and grounding. I noticed that most of the dialogues I had with my body were not healthy ones; they were most often pejorative, critical, guilt-ridden. Altering this tendency is probably one of the most crucial changes I made in grounding myself in healthy body awareness.

BREAKING NEW GROUND

While recovering from my health challenges, I spent long hours in quiet, contemplation, prayer, and meditation. After becoming aware of the impressive documentation on the ability of transcendental meditation to calm erratic thought patterns and increase physical health, I learned this technique. Though I now practice other, less formalized methods of meditation, it was amazingly helpful in the two years following my heart problems.

Quieting the mind is not easy, but it is rewarding. We are accustomed to giving preference to the linear mind trajectory. When you find yourself following the path of the linear mind, stop. Give yourself space to *feel* what you are facing, whether it is a project, goal, crisis, relationship, or even balancing your checkbook.

Allow yourself to move off the linear mental path. The linear mind memorizes and rehearses formulas and equations. It memorizes groups of thought and analyzed experience. It is not adept at breaking new ground. Breaking ground is a landscape better inhabited by intuition. To access the intuition, leave the linear mind for a bit; it is a good tool, and you can always return to it. Hone the intuition by repeatedly taking yourself out of the linear methods of figuring things out. Pause, instead, to hear your intuition for the needed guidance. Notice how your body feels; it will give you clues. Do you feel uneasy in your gut about an issue? Tight in the throat? What are you afraid to say?

The linear mind will interrupt. I call it babble mind because babble and confusion often arise when I am trying to become still. The babble is simply the cleansing of the palate — clearing all the different voices that compete for preeminence in the thought process when settling into contemplation.

It can be a frustrating practice, but gentle discipline and patient persistence will bring the desired results. As an aid, take one issue or person, one question or topic that you want to illuminate. Write it on a piece of paper; lay it in front of you. Rather than actively thinking about it, let your thoughts drift and become more abstract. Each time the matter becomes prominent or causes agitation, go to a place in your mind where the matter can exist in a state of great possibility and peace. In that place, you can experience the soul of the person or question on more subtle levels. Sit no longer than ten to fifteen minutes in this exercise. Then ask yourself to leave it for a time. Let a day pass before you sit with it again. In the meantime, train your mind away from the thought each time it comes up. If it is an obsessive thought, it will loop back many times at first. Say to yourself, for instance, "I will visit that again tomorrow, during my morning meditation." Then think of other things.

During this process, it is necessary to be patient, knowing we are in a phase of laying in a new pattern. Establishing the new pattern requires us to slow the body and thoughts down; the linear mind tends to make them speed into action, always faster and faster. It is the slowing that allows space between the constant input of formulas from the linear mind. That space allows us to break new ground; forge new patterns, new ideas, and new ways of being in the world. Becoming still, you can hear the body's input.

Mindlessness is not a vacuum or a state in which nothing is being accomplished. It is a shift into another state of mind, a slower one. I read of a woman executive who let it be known she was not to be interrupted when staring out a window or off into space. She had learned that this "daydreaming" allowed her to come to some of her most important business insights. This is a form of mindlessness. And mindlessness allows for moments of quiet sowing and germination in our mental process. Continuous, rapid mental activity and restlessness without respite are akin to trying to achieve constant growth and flowering. For healthy growth and flowering, there must be moments set aside for sowing and germination.

PURPOSE AND HEALTH

Early in the process of recovering from my health challenges, I was guided to clarify my purpose in life and connect to my passion. In purpose there is joy. When we feel we are serving our purpose for being here, that joyfulness provides an environment in the body in which a virus or bacteria cannot take hold. True, we are constantly bombarded by germs and pollutants, but they are pliable, responsive to our thoughts. They have specific wave frequencies. In a healthy body in which we are utterly joyous because we are purposely engaged in a creative expression — one that tells us we have reason to be alive — the wonderful sense of joy sets up a vibration. That vibration creates a wave that acts as a shield, so the constant bombardment has no effect.

Grounding ourselves in the knowledge that we are here on purpose provides an anchor for bringing rhythm into our lives. This assists the body to go through our growth and changes gracefully. It is that sense of purpose that creates joyousness.

When we are in transition, our purpose becomes less defined. At such a time we are more vulnerable to illness. When our job or our marriage no longer serves us, when the children leave home or we drastically change our context — at such times our purpose comes up for review. It is wise at such times to be aware, to be gentle and conscious, and to fully examine our choices. Health can fail when we lose our sense of purpose for being alive. If our purpose wavers, we can even lose our will to live.

It is well known that the will to live plays an important role in recovery. A few years ago, when my dearest friend died, I was with her. In that sacred moment, I witnessed her leave her body. The beauty of that moment held all the glory and wonder of birth. As the veil was pierced by her passage through it, I glimpsed a realm so desirable that I rushed toward it eagerly. It caused me to remember, to remember what we come from and what we return to. I remembered the ease of that place and felt the density of this earth plane.

For the first time in my life I wondered, "Why stay?" I longed to go "home." This feeling was intense and lasted for months. As I struggled to recommit to my life, my health reflected this profound indecision. I got a serious infection in my heart, my immune system weakened, and I lost my vitality. Illnesses plagued me and I knew I was at risk. Eventually it became necessary to retreat into communion with my soul, to inquire what time it was for me. I asked if I could choose to go. In this communication, I was given a renewed knowledge of my purpose here, and I knew that it was time to stay, not to leave. I made a covenant to live. Over the next weeks, the longing to leave dissipated and my health began to return. Passionate commitment to our life's purpose is one of the surest steps toward abundant health.

Fulfillment of purpose creates our legacy. Studying the work of such pioneers as Elisabeth Kübler-Ross and reading the countless stories of near-death experiences, I am struck with a consistency that runs through the case studies. Again and again, people relate that after leaving their bodies and traveling into light, they enter into a life review with a loving guide. In the telling of these reviews, it is apparent that each person assesses the purpose of their life and understands their legacy. Loving review coupled with discipline, silence, self-nurture, and cleansing are the tools to wholeness and health, no matter the circumstances.

> We're the keepers of our own healing. We're keepers of an intuitive intelligence so powerful it can tell us how to heal. The time has come for each of us to claim it again. Never forget: It's your right to heal. It's your right to look inside yourself for the answers.
>
> — Judith Orloff, M.D.

I AM THAT

When you are compelled to startle awake
 I am that impulse
When you long to join with love
 I am that longing
When you fall into that brief but potent pause
 I am that silence
When your wisdom surprises you
 I am that knowing
When you are bathed in light
 I am that sun, that moon, the stars
When your heart swells beyond containment
 I am that bursting
And when your pain and fear, at last, completely fall away
 I am that sweet release
When the deep calm enfolds you
 I am that peace
When you suck air sharply in wonder
 I am that awesome breath
When your laugh is belly deep and permeates your all
 I am that flowing joy
When you glimpse the incomprehensible magnitude
 I am that beneficent vastness
I am that I am

Lenedra J Carroll

THE
Architecture
OF
Love

IN A DEEP PLACE IN US WE MAY FEAR THAT WE ARE A DESTRUCTIVE,
UNREDEEMABLE, AND UNLOVABLE HUMAN RACE. BUT IN FACT, WE
ARE LOVED BEYOND OUR ABILITY TO UNDERSTAND. LOVE IS NOT
OUTSIDE OF US AND IT IS NOT BEYOND OUR REACH. IN ACTUALITY,
LOVE IS THE COMMON HERITAGE OF OUR HUMANITY. IT IS BOTH
OUR BIRTHRIGHT AND OUR LEGACY. COMING TO KNOW THIS AND
BE THE EXPRESSION OF IT IS OUR MOST NOBLE CAUSE.

25

Esteeming Self

H er mother called her by name, adding, "Where are you?" The little girl saw her mother silhouetted in the doorway at the top of the stairs. When her name was spoken, the little one saw swirling colors. "How did you get down there all by your-self?" Again her mother used the name sound. Again the swirling colors.

"Is that me?" she wondered, "those swirling colors with that sound? Is that who I am?" It was the first time her name had sepa-rated out from all the sounds her mother made to her. The colors were beautiful and very familiar. A third time her name was called, and the colors floated through the air and tinkled delightfully. The child realized, "Yes, that's me! It's so pretty!" She felt happy.

~ ~

OUR VIEW OF SELF

Listening to our daily patterns of conversation, we hear ourselves speaking frequently about self-esteem. We say things like: "I have high self-esteem." "I have low self-esteem." "When I lose weight, I'll have better self-esteem." "If I had better self-esteem, I'd be more successful."

We talk about it a great deal. We read about it in the self-help literature; we take classes and seminars about it. We spend a lot of time, energy, and money in pursuit of it. There seems to be some uncertainty about whether we have enough of it. Why does it seem so ellusive, so hard to come by?

The prevailing idea is that self-esteem is how we feel about ourselves or view ourselves. But what determines how we see ourselves? Parental ideas? Television? The concept of self-esteem leads us to compare and judge ourselves against a standard. But what standard? Society's? God's? Each other's? Such standards demand that we monitor our behavior to know when we have achieved them. There are a lot of "shoulds" involved. It may be time to question the model we have created for thinking about this, and for achieving it.

> **self´-es-teem´ n.** 1) belief in oneself 2) undue pride in oneself; conceit
> (from *Webster's New World Dictionary*)

This is very confusing. The first definition requires qualifiers like good or bad, high or low, less or more, or too much. These are judgment words that lead us to think about ourselves from the standpoint of judgment and comparison. The second brings in the noxious idea that maybe it isn't good to think too well of oneself.

Self-esteem is a noun; a specific thing, a done deal. By this definition, it seems to be something to arrive at; something that, if you missed out on it, you have to *try really hard* to recover. There will be a lot of pain and a lot of missed opportunities from such an attempt. You might want someone to blame.

> **es-teem´ vt.** 1) to value highly; respect

Esteem, by itself, is a verb. It's very interesting as a verb. Verbs are action words. They have on-goingness. They reflect process, like life. Life is not the one big event that you are waiting to arrive at, and it's sure not a done deal; it is what is happening now. Life *is* the process.

esteeming self (not in the dictionary)
1) placing high value on self; the act of respecting the self; honoring self

Self-esteem is a rather foggy plateau we try somehow to reach. It seems to require constant journeys into the past to try to "get better," and it is hard to find your way. But as you begin to think of esteeming yourself, a very simple action reveals itself: Begin to honor yourself. Be in the process of valuing and respecting yourself. Begin now. Honor and value what has been. Value what is. A clearer, more loving sense of self will emerge.

FORFEITURE OF SELF

Who do we think we are? Why do we think so? As a child these questions fascinated me and led me on a quest to understand more of myself. From the time we are born, we begin to collect ideas about who we think we are. Our parents give us information about who we are. Our society gets heavily into the act. Our churches put forward lots of ideas for us, as does our educational system. Friends and lovers all get involved. They provide us with someone else's ideas about who *they* *think* we are or *should be*. Everyone is very busy projecting ideas and expectations onto everyone else. We all do it. They are merely the result of social conditioning, but we accept these ideas as our identity.

Why do others think that they know who we are? Why do we believe it? *The "self" we spend most of our time trying to love and improve is primarily a product of the ideas of others.* Most of our available energy goes into endeavors meant to uphold this externally derived self-definition. These external ideas give us an identity. We become attached to our opinions, insecurities, pain, joy, experiences, and history — all wrought from others' notions of who we are. Then we think we know who we think we are:

I am the kind of person who always...
I will never understand...
I'm the one you can always count on...

I could never forgive...
I just don't get over things...
I always get what I want...
I don't like to get my hopes up...
I'm just not the affectionate type...
I will never be happy without...
I don't ever trust...
I'm good at...bad at...

Most of our ideas about who we are and what we are like come from outside of ourselves. We react to these ideas, accepting or rebelling against them, acting them out. We get so attached to these projected attributes that we don't leave room to change and grow. It is wise to examine who we think we are, where we got that idea, and to question whether it serves us to continue with the idea. We have a choice.

> We forfeit three-fourths of ourselves in order to be like other people.
>
> — Arthur Schopenhauer

The personality naturally strives to be individual, separate, unique. This is good. It is desirable to have a well-individuated personality; it is an important stage of development. The variety of individual gifts, methods, and traits is the strength in any group. Difficulties arise whenever our sense of self has been molded more by others, in which case we might want to simply create our own composition more consciously.

How do we do this? Investigating, challenging, educating, and allowing change of our current opinions, actions, understandings, and interpretations bring about our desired results. The process allows our horizons and awareness to expand more and more.

When we have a new awareness, it changes us in many ways; if we change our consciousness, form will follow. As we let the understanding of our self evolve, the world around us changes.

DEFINING THE SELF

Personality, psyche, soul, body, mind, emotions, spirit — we use these terms to describe ourselves. They are all aspects of the self. We interface with the world particularly through our personality and ego. The personality is our costume, our "shark suit" for example. We assemble it from our life experiences. We can put it on, take it off, add to it, remove parts of it. Our personality is the public image we project, much like a celebrity's public image. This personality image is, however, a costume, a façade.

I once saw Isabella Rosellini in a television interview. She related that fans often stop her to say how much they loved her mother, actress Ingrid Bergman. They mention qualities or preferences they attribute to Ms. Bergman that are, in fact, not at all true. Isabella said she initially tried to correct the false impressions, but she found that people would actually *argue* with her and emphatically refuse to change their ideas, even telling her she was wrong. She concluded that they knew, and were deeply attached to, another Ingrid Bergman who was a composite of their own impressions from roles she played and press interviews.

The personality is an image crafted by ourselves and others. It is important and useful. Indeed, a well-defined personality brings breadth and strength to our expression and our creativity, much like an actor adopting nuances to flesh out a character, to take on an angry persona or project a sense of kindness. Personality expresses much of the tone, the coloring and shading of our individuality, but we are more than this expression of ourselves.

Our bodies, of course, are an important part of the costume; we focus on them, changing, molding, loving, hating them, but they too are really only a façade.

The mind, intellect, psyche, and emotions are important aspects of self as well. They serve as receivers and interpreters of information and experience. They are necessary and wonderful tools, but they are also not the essence of the self; nor are the ego, personality, or body — they are parts of the costume. And we are not our costume; we are much more: we are also the soul. We cannot understand the self without grasping this.

LOVING THE EGO

In a recent business meeting, my ego went on a little rampage. It was highly offended that a television producer was casting aspersions on my expertise as Jewel's manager; he seemed to be treating me as a "mere" mother. This sparked my ego's protection of my personal and professional dignity. My ego ranted dramatically and loudly in my head, replaying the little movie *The Moment of Affront* in case I had missed it or was forgetting. It built a strong case and brought intense pressure to bear to incite me to action. "Let him know! Brag a little. Drop a hint or story that will impress him and get him off his high horse! Don't you know it's necessary to toot your horn a little so people will appreciate your abilities? If you don't, you're going to be overlooked and you'll lose your effectiveness." These were the urgent communications my ego whirled furiously around me. I initially got caught up in the spin and fear of it, my adrenaline output elevated and my heart rate increased.

Then I noticed what was going on; I thanked my valiant ego for sharing and asked it to stand aside and trust me. It has little choice these days, but it still tries. A day later, someone mentioned that my "offender" told them that when he met me, he was so impressed that he felt a bit intimidated and uncertain of what to say. The affront was an utter illusion, 100 percent fabricated. There wasn't even a grain of deprecation to take umbrage at. I had to thank the ego for acting on behalf of my soul to alert me to an area in which I felt defensive. I was able to experience my defensiveness, my fear, and the old ideas surrounding them. It was quite instructive. How glad I was that I didn't — as I certainly have many times in the past

— go charging forth after phantoms only to return eating crow. Eating crow is no fun whatsoever, and entirely lacking in dignity!

EGO

Notes blast. Shake bones.
Announcing
The rigid guardian of fears' agenda
Boastful ringing in the ear
Mischievous mirror
Separated self
Soul's servant —
Ego

Lenedra J Carroll

In my view, the ego has been somewhat maligned. Its primary urge is to fiercely guard the gates of individual identity in general, and specifically those attributes we most highly value. It does this magnificently. If we value our power or security, it will be tireless in attempting to preserve them. If it is our religion or country we most closely identify with, it will serve them to the death. It will work tirelessly to spare us any disturbance in our perceptions. The ego will fabricate, bully, brag, lie, trick, or deny in order to maintain its perceived agendas because it does not judge method, only outcome.

The ego was initially intended to serve to preserve and develop the soul's housing. Over eons of time, as we became more and more separated from a remembrance of our Source, and more associated with physical identity, the ego became increasingly prominent. It is the ego that hears the sirens' song of power, fame, and wealth. The soul is immune, but the ego is easily seduced. In response to the call the ego may overstep its bounds, causing us to become irritable and brittle or demanding and bullying. Or it may seek to protect us from our fears and thus prevent us from moving forward, telling us we are not worthy of the task. The ego requires, therefore, the steadying influence of the soul's voice. The ego has value, not as a master, rather in its service to the soul.

Consequently, the goal is not to get rid of the personality or ego. The ego is a creation that is entirely franchised by Spirit. There is no need to fear, dislike, suppress, or eradicate the ego. Such attempts can never quiet it; love is the only thing that can. Love your ego, come to see it as dear and entertaining. Observe its shenanigans with the understanding and discipline of a loving parent.

EMBRACING CHANGE

As the saying goes, the only two things that are certain are death and taxes. Yet, the certainty of death is becoming increasingly arguable, since there is compelling information that raises the distinct probability that there is only ongoing life. Taxes have not always been with us, and it is certainly conceivable they will not always be so. Change, however, *is* one constant in this universe.

The ego is strongly committed to keeping change to a minimum. It has a deep-seated preservation impulse that can be as resistant to reasoning as a petulant child, and as destructive if given rein to dictate reality. It consumes enormous amounts of energy in resisting the desire to change and grow and can, in fact, render change and growth unattainable; and, as science can attest, a system that is forced to be static begins to decay.

Fear of change is a common trait of a personality over-identified with the physical. This personality fears a loss of identity. It does not want to change what it identifies with. This fear is mitigated, however, if we remember that we are not our bodies; we are the indwelling soul, and the soul is pure energy that cannot ever be destroyed. The soul is whole and needs no change or healing. It contains an original blueprint that is built into the foundation of our being. The underlying impulse of our life is to mirror, integrate, and align with that original blueprint to greater and greater degree. To accomplish this, we are called by the soul to change and grow, to bring awareness to places where we recognize that we deviate from that blueprint. We can *intuit* that blueprint, that authentic soul-self to elevate the question "Who am I?"

> We do not have fault, weakness, sin. These labels are only the judgments of our ego. Such pejorative language does not serve us; it keeps us struggling to be good, to conform to outer ideas and rules. They are merely qualities that do not match our original blueprint. We all have them. They are not permanent; we can change them.
>
> *Lenedra J Carroll*

UNFAILING KINDNESS

The cabin walls were closing in around her. Her heart seemed harnessed to the falling dusk, and her mind, too, filled with the impending gloom of night. Despair settled in as she experienced the weight of her faults; she didn't like herself very much right now. Over the past months she had begun to notice how much she judged herself, how she remembered the sins of her past, even of her childhood. She saw the energy that it took to continually keep the secret loathing at bay. She passionately longed to be free of the judging, to feel proud of herself, to fully appreciate her path to now. But in recent months ill health and financial troubles had wrought deep changes in her: she could no longer pretend; she could not maintain a façade or gloss things over anymore. The searing light of self-honesty shone frequently now. In it she saw the smallness, the unworthiness of many of her actions. She shrank away from herself as she contemplated what she saw. Her heart cried out for relief, for the love she sought.

Her soul heard the cry and spoke gently: "Shhhh, it is all right. You will see. Look fearlessly at yourself, yes, but learn to do so with unfailing kindness. Then you will find a way to bring the change you so desire."

As she rallied to this, she began to feel hope. She thought of an exercise she had heard about from a friend's Alcoholics Anonymous group. She left the bed and went to the table. As the last of the day-light drained away, she picked up a pen and began to write in her notebook. She wrote intently, almost furiously, making a litany of her sins and secrets. Every word, deed, action that she was not proud of, the wrongs she remembered — all these, both weighty and small, filled page after page of her journal. A tentative relief approached her as she set the book aside. It was good to see the whole picture at once; the second step could wait.

A few days later she committed herself to the difficult next task. She set up a meeting with someone she trusted. When they were together, she explained that she wanted to make a confession before a witness, with the intention of admitting and releasing everything she held against herself. They sat quietly together for some time before she began. Slowly, all the character faults, the wrongs to oth-ers, all the secrets began to be revealed. She felt remorse, embar-rassment, fear. Her heart pounded sometimes in shame; sweat beaded on her chest and brow, and tears filled her eyes. The emo-tions often choked her voice. Finally coming to an end, she looked up. Reflected in the steady, kind gaze of the human being in front of her, she saw herself as she was: a human being, with a human story, not so much different from other stories. She began to see that her "sins" were only those of self-separation, and that no guilt, no fear, were required. There were simply course corrections to make. With her friend she made a plan to make what amends she could.

Over the next weeks she called or wrote to those on a list she had prepared — where it was wise and not harmful to do so. She expressed her regret, taking responsibility for her actions or words. It was hard, but people were respectful of her process and courage. Much was renewed. On the day she reached the end of her list, she had a private feast and celebration, and then stood in self-gratitude and love out under the stars, cleansed before herself and the Creator of All.

THE HOUNDS OF HELL

The hounds of hell
fall upon me
Tearing at my throat
Revealing throbbing dark blood of vein and artery.
Snagging my lies
Ripping them back, laying bare the bone.
Exposed innards glisten.
         Bile rises. Stench of what is past.
Feeble protest.
My eyes roll back.
I lower into terror and despair.
I know these hounds
I know them well.
My own carrion voice calls them out upon me
to devour all that binds.
         Dead flesh, old ways.
Pulsing red hope rises.
Latent veins of strength surge.
Heat of the Soul
Infuses heart and marrow.
The snarling dark falls back.
I thrust forth new into the bright new world
Glistening with naked truth.
         Health in the navel. Ambient core.

Lenedra J Carroll

The preceding experience was a turning point for me in bringing my harsh ego under the reign of the soul. I felt my soul's love; I heard its suggestions and followed through with them. I gained the practice of unfailing kindness to accompany my self-assessment. I began to grow in my ability to be generous with myself while being honest.

EXPERIENCING CHANGE

During the course of change, we may experience turmoil — this is natural. It is the collision of the old world — our economy of fear and lack — with the new world we are creating for ourselves. They cannot coexist. In this process of the old falling away, fear and guilt may arise and a great upheaval be felt. That is the time to be gentle and loving, to honor our choice to change and know that the change will inevitably come about.

One of the most potent tools we have for gaining loving kindness is simply to be still. When a fear or an old negative pattern is activated, ask nothing more of yourself than to be still. Hold your speech, your actions, conclusions, and responses.

Recognize that the old patterning has been activated; allow yourself to simply be still, and in that stillness express your desire and your request for the old patterning, the old "wiring," to be changed. Do this again and again, steadfastly and assured of the outcome. The mental, emotional, and physical grids in which you have held your relationships and patterns will begin to shift, and the process will become easier and even exciting. The wave tone laid down by past unhealthy patterning will yield to the repetition, which will lay in the new tone being patterned. More and more you will come to resemble your most authentic self and you will know yourself to be whole.

> There is as much difference between us and ourselves as there is between ourselves and others.
> — Michel de Montaigne

THE FOUR GREAT LIES

Throughout the ages we have been fed misinformation that is ultimately fatal to our individual and group growth. It is information that has separated our ego from its source, the soul. These false ideas have led us to believe that we are destructive by nature, evil, unworthy, perhaps even a hopeless humanity. These lies have led to the loss of our authentic self-knowledge and thus to a mass crisis of identity. We have been taught these lies to serve the agendas of individuals and organizations whose own separation from the Source led them to develop fear-based relationships with power, greed, and God. And so we have been taught:

> We are bad.
> We are not enough.
> We have limited potential.
> We are alone and separate.

When in reality the profound truth is:

> We are intrinsic goodness.
> We are whole and complete just as we are.
> We have the potential of our divine heritage.
> We cannot be separated from our divine Source.

The negative and false beliefs have seriously eroded our esteem and even convinced us that we are not lovable. In fact, we are loved beyond our ability to comprehend it. Love is not outside of us. Love is not our mother or father or lover. Love is not our family or community. Love, in truth, simply is. Love is. Love is the essence of the life force surrounding us; it is what allows everything to have cohesion. Love is both our birthright and our legacy; it is in the original blueprint of our Soul.

26
Loving Others

*M*ay those who love us, love us . . .
And those that do not love us, may God turn their hearts;
And if he doesn't turn their hearts, may he turn their ankles
So we will know them by their limping.

— *Old Gaelic Blessing*

THE SOUL'S AGENDA

The quiet isolation of growing up in an alcoholic home accustomed me to silence, sent me into nature for my solace and companionship, and gave me the recognition of stillness and knowledge of the implicit order of that which is God. An emotionally abusive boyfriend taught me, finally, to channel my abilities toward my own support. My legal problems and the loss of my business caused me to rethink my entire dream, building a new one based only on my own values, my soul's agenda for my life, and connection to my Source. Failure of health brought back my remembrance of the divine physician within me and forced me to activate that infinite wisdom to become whole.

Each of these periods of growth was sparked by difficulty. The intensity of the difficulty was of my own making. The soul will knock gently at first, and we often do not hear, then insistently, but we may not answer, then very loudly. Most of the situations I cited were harsh because I ignored the quiet voice of my soul. I lingered in fearful inertia until the drama fully captured my attention and gave me few choices but to grow. I do not believe we grow only through difficulties, but the soul does not hesitate. It uses the means necessary to move us out of stasis. As I have grown in my ability to hear the soul, the curriculum has become a gentle and joyous one.

It is the soul's agenda that forms the infrastructure of everything that occurs in our lives. Its intention is for us to grow, moving inexorably toward a higher and higher potential. It has this curriculum always: consciousness, self-knowledge, and growth.

When you have been fired from your job, or are trying to recover from your sixth painful relationship, ask yourself what your soul's agenda is for you. It may be to resolve an ancient fear or to take responsibility and embrace power. Perhaps it is to understand illusion, gain the freedom of surrender, or grow more peaceful. Whatever it is, you may be certain that it will serve the highest in you if you rise to meet it. If you do not, you may be sure the soul will call again.

WHO IS IN CONTROL?

We may believe our lives are dictated by our relationships, that we are subject to spousal demands, or that we do not have freedom at work to express our values and more authentic selves. For instance, I sometimes feel controlled by my obligations to my business; the jobs and opportunities I provide my team members seem a responsibility that restricts my freedom of choice. We may feel this way about our children, that we cannot pursue our own passions until they are grown because we are locked in service to them, which consumes all of our focus and energy. We may feel an abusive parent controlled our life, that they are controlling it still. We feel controlled by time and by lack of money.

Insecurity comes in many guises: financial difficulties, a troubled child, an unfaithful spouse. Having a tyrannical employer can make each day one in hell. But imagine that you realize you have a choice about your work, that your soul is actually offering you a chance to change, that everything you need for that change is available to you. In that case, you do not feel the same entrapment and fear. You are still afraid, certainly, but you have a sense of there being choices that can be made, action that can be understood and taken with courage.

Brian is one of the most loving and unusual men I know. Yet his history is a truly heartbreaking story of childhood abuse. His is the kind of story that horrifies, that seems impossible to comprehend. It relates physical and emotional torture, mental cruelty, sexual abuse, shocking neglect. But Brian's life now is full of love. He has a large family of loving friendships and a vast global network of people who support his creativity and work.

When I asked Brian how he survived his horrible childhood, how he healed, his reply was startling. "Lenedra, my childhood *made* me who I am. I absolutely believe it was my own choice, before I came into this life, to have that experience. I know what it is to be oppressed and for reasons I can't fully articulate, I *know* it was important to my soul that I experience this.

"Beyond that," he related, "I learned that the body doesn't have to feel pain, that there is a 'self' which nothing can efface. I spent days tied up in closets, and that gave me my unique creativity as I plumbed the wonders of my mind to keep from losing myself to the fear and pain. Many, many insights came to me in the darkness and despair. Something beyond myself comforted me and loved me even there in that closet, and I became familiar with that loving presence. Something deep within taught me. Entire worlds of meaning and possibility opened to me."

I struggled to comprehend Brian's perspective in the face of such damaging experiences. "I am not damaged," he continued. "As I moved into adulthood, I learned that, ultimately, I control my well-being. I found I could call to myself the healing I needed, the nurturing and family. It is all here for me. It was up to me, really, to love myself; no one could do that for me, and as I offered the gift of love to me, my life became full of love. I do not regret my childhood in any way. My parents played the role of tyrant so I could learn to become utterly free of tyranny."

Why would the soul place a being in such a situation? Brian would answer, "to grow."

Jack Swartz, a Dutch-born author and lecturer, might say the same. In studies conducted at the Menninger Foundation, the University of California's Langley Porter Neuropsychiatric Institute, and at other institutions, Jack astounded doctors by his ability to be pierced with six-inch needles without bleeding, be burned with cigarettes without pain or harm, and to heal immediately. He held hot coals in his hands for extended periods without damage. Throughout all these events, he produced none of the beta brain waves that are normally present when a person is in pain. He explained that he acquired the ability to be able to control the pain of severe beatings he received while in a Nazi concentration camp. He believes anyone is able to learn such control and thus gain responsibility for their own health. He lectured and taught tirelessly to help others learn, feeling it was his life purpose.[1]

Why would the soul place anyone in a Nazi concentration camp? Or give them an abusive childhood? Brian and Jack have their own answers. Brian feels it was vital for him to become utterly free of his fear of tyranny. Jack felt he learned the secrets of freedom from physical pain and an awareness of consciousness beyond the body. He felt it was well worth his experience to gain them for himself and to demonstrate them to others. Both Brian and Jack felt not only undamaged by their experiences but also a sense of *purpose* in them.

This is not an idea we can easily embrace. It is a discussion we cannot fully bring ourselves to because we are so deeply terrified by the heinous acts in our world, confused by and afraid of the pain

---

1. Michael Talbot, *The Holographic Universe* (New York: HarperCollins, 1991).

and injustice and danger. Yet in a larger context, we must at least ask, "Could there be meaning and purpose in them?"

We fear that if we allow that there is purpose, it means we must accept the gross inequities and exonerate the people who perpetuate them. But this idea defies reason. It is a "victim" mentality. Feeling, on the other hand, the situation is unredeemable and beyond our control leaves us without options. But recognizing the purpose or opportunity in such chaotic events, we can then utilize them to bring change. When we see the larger purpose underlying an event, our understanding aids us in healing the pain and bringing about growth. When we act on that understanding, we learn to trust ourselves.

SELF-TRUST

We waste a lot of energy wondering who we can trust, what we can trust them with, and recovering from being betrayed. But you are the person you really need to trust. *You can trust everyone if you can trust yourself.*

We lack self-trust because of the countless times we sold ourselves out, abandoned ourselves, ignored our intuition, refused to take appropriate action, forfeited our power. So, lacking self-trust, we are left to the hopeless device of trying to make everyone and everything conform to our need to feel safe.

What are the things we need to be able to trust ourselves? We must each know that we will courageously and creatively understand and take the action required for our growth and wholeness. We must feel that we can be trusted to truthfully see our underlying agendas. We need to know we can count on ourselves to intuit whether or not a situation is healthy for us. Having perhaps chosen poorly, can we trust ourselves to change a situation? Can we trust ourselves to give up limiting patterns or addictions? To delve for the truth about our participation in recurrent negative scenarios? To live by values that bring growth and joy?

During my time in the remote cabin in Alaska, I realized that if I could trust myself, then trusting others would be easy; I would be free to see who people really are, instead of what I needed them to be. At the time, there was one person I was very mistrustful of. He had betrayed me in a horrible fashion. But when I examined the matter honestly, I saw that I had been given many warnings about how he was; I just didn't want to believe them. In truth, I could trust him to continue being how he was. But I could not trust myself to see the truth of a situation and take the right action for myself.

I stopped fearing and obsessing about what he had done to me and began to seek what I needed to know and do to change my situation. This is the crux of the matter. People will be *who they are*. We can count on it. They will always be acting out their fears, limitations, hopes, and dreams. If we trust our own judgment, choices, healing ability, and self-honesty, we become free of the need to make others "behave" so we can feel safe.

In the silence of the cabin, I came to know something even more valuable about trust. I was asking the question "What can I trust?" when I heard, in reply, this from my soul: "You can trust that your life is on course, that you are exactly where you should be, in every moment and situation." I realized then my life was not a series of accidents; it was managed by my soul with great purpose. Coming to know that deeply, I understood that I could trust the Source of my life, in all things.

> "Falling in love" is conditional love, a projection onto our loved one of our own idealized image of him or her. In effect, our attraction to the other person is primarily our attraction to our own projection.
>
> — Leonard Laskow, M.D.

✥ THE SOUL TALKING STORY ✥

The man had been hounding me for weeks. After my heart attack, I was forced to change my diet. Now, at restaurants, at parties, at the movies, there are many things I can no longer eat. There are many times I have to make special requests for the dressing oil to be put on the side, not on the salad, for the butter to be left out of a recipe. I have to inquire about ingredients and take great care. By some quirky coincidence, this man was often there, listening. He is behind me at the movie concession, at the next table in the restaurant, or at the community potluck. Each time he rolls his eyes and makes a rude comment. He grows more and more bold in this, until it becomes quite annoying. Naturally, I wonder what difference it makes to him if I eat butter or not. Is it any of his business?

One evening at a party, the dessert tray goes around the room, and I pass it on without sampling. Who do I turn to as I pass the tray? My constant critic! He speaks in his booming voice, filling the room. "Yeah! She won't have any. She won't have this, she won't have that," he says in a punitive singsong. "She might as well not eat at all." It was one of those moments when all conversation stops in a room and everyone turns to see what is going on.

I have a look on my face that my friends recognize: an eyebrow raised, my eyes narrowed somewhat, my mouth forming a slight smile. It is a look that says, "Enough! Now I'm going to put an end to this."

My friends are thinking, "What fun! She's going to put him in his place; she'll cut him off at the knees."

And in fact I lean in with just the little turn of phrase to do the trick, to shut him up for good. After all, I've known him for years, we all have, and he is no favorite in the little town.

I take a half step forward and draw a breath to deliver my well-timed, clever little remark, when something rather unusual happens. Time suspends, the moment extends, no words come out of my mouth; his face swims in front of me. And there, from his face, is the depth of his soul shining out at me. It is a wondrous soul, breathtaking in its beauty. And that lovely soul reveals this man to me. I seem to have stepped inside of him. I know his life, the weight of his pain, the extent of his despair, his unrelenting loneliness and unworthiness. I feel his tired, beaten-down body, heavy and numb with its pointless posture. And I feel the grandeur of the soul that loves and guides him. I see my own blessed life; I see my harsh judgment of him and its effects on us both. It is a long moment as I stare, transfixed, at his face, with everyone in the room staring at me. No one breathes, it seems.

Then a gush of wind fills my lungs and I speak: "I have wondered why it matters to you what I eat. I don't know the answer. But standing here in confrontation with you, what I am really struck with is my own deep despair that we cannot, as humans, see eye to eye about such a small matter. In my heart I ache to have a greater peace. But I don't know how. How can we ever end the continual wars on our planet if such inconsequential things keep us from it every day? That's what I am feeling," I say.

The platter passes along, people shift positions, small talk begins to fill the space, and the party goes on. But a week later the man makes a beeline for me at the drugstore; I feel uneasy as he approaches, but he surprises me when he speaks.

"I want to apologize for what I said the other night." He shuffles self-consciously in the aisle. The words are foreign to his rough voice. "I had to wonder, too, why I cared what you ate. And I remembered that mealtimes when I was a kid...well, they were hell. Pure hell. The ol' man came down on us for everything. One wrong move then — watch out! Funny, it's the first time I've thought about any of that in many years."

And this man begins to reveal his story to me. It is the story you might imagine, a story of abuse and fear and pain. The pain still fills every pore of his body, which is worn with carrying it. As I listen, I hear also his hopes and dreams, some of them still alive. I find there, too, his passion for his work and the love he feels for his son. He talks; I hear the soul "talking story." I hear a human story and I know what it is to be a human being.

To love is to live in God. Loving is activity in God, so that every thought and action is in God — not in the world. When a man loves he no longer responds to the vibrations of destruction and death, but to those of the more abundant life.

— White Eagle

SEEING THE SOUL OF ANOTHER

Each time we hear a human story, we learn more about what it is to be a human being, having a human life here on this planet. This is one of the ways in which we discover our humanity. It is important to honor one another's stories when possible, for we each inhabit an individual universe. And within that universe we are always in relationship with ourselves. Even when apparently interacting with others, we are really in relationship to ourselves. Because of this, when we hear or observe another person, we will misunderstand much of what we see and hear: Because the experience is filtered through our own perspectives, beliefs, experiences, and needs. Some studies suggest that less than half of what we "see" is based on information entering our eyes. The remainder — the majority — of our sight perception is the piecework of our expectations and context.[2]

That is why, when a friend gets new glasses or shaves his beard, we often do not notice. We are so accustomed to relating to them within the frame of our usual context, that we don't see what is actually there. We filter it out so that our context remains unaltered. There is evidence that suggests that the percentages regarding what we hear are even lower. As you are listening to others at work, home, or at the grocery store, remind yourself that the chance that you will actually grasp their full meaning, let alone their reality, is quite small.

---

2. Ibid.

To most accurately and fully relate to another, we *must* relate to their soul or we will only be in relationship to our own context. Gracie taught me this fifteen years ago. Gracie was in her seventies when I first knew her. She lived in a charming old log cabin next to my art gallery. In fact, my gallery occupied property that was once part of the "stake" she and her husband Niles had settled in their early days in Alaska. Over the years, the city grew up around them, until Gracie's log cabin was the odd note in a jumble of bustling commercial properties. Niles had died a few years earlier, and I used to keep company with Gracie from time to time and share stories.

She told me that one of Niles's dreams as a young man was to travel around the world for a year. When he married and children began to arrive, that dream got tabled, but the longing stayed. Gracie told me she was acutely aware of this and finally told Niles he had to "go off on that trip, children or no." And she sent him packing for a year. She said she didn't want him having that kind of regret when he was old; she knew "it was something very important to his soul."

Gracie tells it that she was unhappy about being left behind with four children but soon stopped moping about and feeling sorry and wondered what the change allowed her to do. She discovered a dream of her own. She had always wanted to spend time in Hawaii, so she "up and left with those four kids to bide my time in paradise. There wasn't much money," she said, "but you don't need much if you're in paradise."

Nine months into his trip, Niles called from someplace foreign and said he was satisfied that he'd seen what he wanted to of the world. He was coming home — which was good because Gracie was tired of paradise by then.

It delighted me to hear that Gracie listened to the soul longing of Niles instead of imposing her fears and needs on him by tying him to his obvious responsibilities. She didn't ignore his deep desire in favor of her own security. And she listened to the voice of her own dream and created the perfect situation for herself as well.

LOOKING FOR LOVE

The urge toward union, the longing for love, is innate in us. But what is the longing really for? What do we want union with? Why? Is there a hole we are trying to fill? Is the longing for union based on a need for security? Can anything truly make us secure? The ultimate answer is that the underlying cause of our great insecurity is the absolute, inculcated belief that we are our body. We are not our body; we are the indwelling soul. As long as our context is primarily the physical side of ourselves, we will feel fear and anxiety about our well-being. Ego, disconnection from source, and abandonment of self derail most of our relationships. The root of peace and security is in the blueprint of our soul. Accessing that understanding opens us to myriad realms of possibility and stability.

Instead of looking to others for love, become love. Inhabit it. Love your divine soul, love who you are, love the dream you have manifested. When you do, what manifests in your dream? Love. It comes in on the incoming wave and engulfs you.

Moving into a life in which the experience of loving is the only thing you will accept, there are many feelings of vulnerability; and there may be awkward stages. There are many graceless moments in which you struggle to involve yourself in a new economy, the economy of love, yet you are still struggling to use all of the old tools of intimidation, humiliation, withdrawal, and others. This is a natural part of the process. By listening to the voice of our soul, we are guided to new tools and experiences and new relationships with others.

To develop access to that voice of the soul, I have found it necessary to return repeatedly to the silence, refining my ability, honing it with discipline and patience. I have learned that, while failing and succeeding to varying degrees but insisting and persisting over time, we can achieve communion with that great I Am, the animating principle of this world.

Divine love, unutterable and perfect, flows into a pure soul the way that light rushes into a transparent object. The more love that it finds, the more that it gives itself, so that as we grow clear and open, the more complete the joy of loving is. And, the more souls who resonate together, the greater the intensity of their love, for, mirrorlike, each soul reflects the others'.

— Dante

27

Divine Love

The day will come when, after harnessing the ether, the winds, the tides, gravitation, we shall harness for God the energies of love. And, on that day, for the second time in the history of the world, man will have discovered fire.

— Pierre Teilhard de Chardin

The little girl watched the woman in church with the new baby. They were right next to her. The baby snuggled in a soft white blanket, dressed up in a beautiful long white gown that was all lace and ribbons. The lady cradled her little one in her arms, beaming down with a beautiful smile, cooing quietly. Her glossy black hair fell across the snowy blanket, touching the baby's cheek lightly. After a while the baby began to fuss and squirm. "Shhhh," the woman crooned, rocking the babe carefully. Her eyes were so gentle. "Shhhh." Her voice was soft and soothing. Rock, rock. "Shhhhh, shh, shh . . ."

As the baby quieted, the little girl felt a deep longing. "I want that," she said to herself. "I want someone to hold me just like that."

She sat very still for a long time, pretending she was the baby. It felt so safe and warm there, next to the pretty lady.

☙ ❧

People often feel unconditional love toward a newborn child. The child's nearness to the realm from which it so recently came may help evoke this pure expression from us. I recognized that feeling as a small child and longed for it. Most of us long for it still. We are taught to value and strive for unconditional love, but we are taught that it is an unattainable ideal. It is attainable. As an internalized quality, it is the foundation for abundance in every arena of our life. When our primary experience is that greater Love, it does not confuse, wound, or elude us. It stabilizes and heals, filling our deepest longings as nothing else can.

What is it? Why would I want it? What would my relationships — with myself and others — look like if they were unconditionally loving? What kind of commitment would it take? These are some of the questions that have expanded my understanding of love.

LOVE WITH A BIG "L"

Big Love, unconditional Love, Divine Love, greater Love, Spiritual Love, Christlike Love, infinite Love. There are many terms for Love, but when we dwell in an ego-, security-, and fear-based existence, it is difficult to understand such Love. The love that we typically experience is romantic love, familial love, or carnal love. Romantic love is in the domain of the physical. It is the seductress and seducer. Combining the experience of Spirit with seduction does not diminish it, but heightens it. Confining Love to romance, or sex, is limiting.

Sexual love is not really love at all. Rather, it is woven into and closely related to love — not separate, though we realize that it can be. Sexual expression is the energy of the seed; it is not the flower. It is the impulse and energy of germination, not the flowering. Sexual and romantic love are confused with Love because, at their essence, they contain an expression of joy, an exultation of life. Divine Love certainly does not exclude sexual or romantic expression, though we sometimes fear that it does.

Without a greater understanding, without knowing that Love is about the expansion of the very universe, whether individual or cosmic — without this knowing, love can become polluted as expressed through the security-seeking context of body and ego. We can choose our experience, whether the limited body-based or the greater Love. Each context serves different purposes and life lessons, but infinite Love moves us beyond the boundary of the purely physical and adds divine potential to it.

Coming to distinguish within ourselves the romantic form of love and the sexual expression of love, we can then further identify familial love, and we can identify love that is based on love of humankind. From there we can go on to identify Love as an energy that does not have a specific object or behavior pattern nor does it have a specific mood or outlet but is more like stillness — a place of sitting, a place to reside; a place of having one's *beingness*. Practicing unconditional love elevates the quality of the feeling. Going into silence to experience Divine Love can cause profound moments of overflowing communion. In it is the peace, certainty, and power that allow an individual to access it as an antidote to their fear. We can be the Love in the world in the same way and through the same process that we can be peace.

> The desire and pursuit of the whole is called love.
>
> — Plato

SURRENDERING TO LOVE

One of the reasons we have difficulty shifting to the context of this greater Love is our clinging so tightly to what we believe will keep us safe — to our beliefs about how it should be in our life, in

others' lives, in the world at large. Very often, we have rigid stric-
tures built into a formula for sanity — for what we *believe* to be our
sanity — and we fear to relinquish, even for a moment, the way
that we have it structured. How we do fear for our sanity. Even
the promise that beyond those restrictions is a life-giving essence,
a celebratory presence, an exuberant, exultant intelligence —
even that promise is typically not enough to let us relinquish our
rigidity.

Socrates declared that his so-called wisdom merely showed him
how little he knew. In fact, the adage, "The older I get, the less I
know about how things really are" is spoken as wisdom. It refers to
the *beginning point* where we finally come to a place within where we
know nothing. We do not know how a relationship is supposed to
be. We do not know what a family is supposed to look like. We do
not know what a life is supposed to be built on, what we are supposed to strive for, what we are supposed to achieve. We do not
know good and evil, right and wrong. We do not know. We relinquish. We surrender, and in this surrender we become, in that
moment, a force of nature like the rain on the sandstone canyon
walls or the inexorable shifting movement of the expansion and
contraction of the earth's crust.

And then, for a long moment, we allow ourselves to be that.
Just for a moment. And perhaps another moment. For in that
moment, there wells up within our being a sense of the order that is
cosmic, the knowing of our place in that order and clarity about its
place in our individual life. And then grace begins to flow out and
inform all the things we no longer know. It informs our relationships, our work, our purpose, our knowledge of good and evil. From
that moment, we sense the order that is filled to bursting with
Love's energy, the energy to express the Divine.

The falcon, in its fierceness, does not fear for its retirement; it
does not fear for the wound it may sustain when hunting its food,
nor does it judge the life that it has taken to feed its young. It is exu-
berantly, exultantly itself; as is the ocean rising and falling on the

shore. The ocean does not judge whether its tide brings gentle waves of life to the seashore or comes crashing in as stormy destruction. It is, it simply is. It does not judge. It celebrates its essence and, in its essence, gives itself up to the infinitely organized expression of the Divine. That is Love.

To love is to unreservedly seize Life, and not to do so is to choose death. The ego, thinking itself separate, has whispered to us of death, and prompts us to try to possess life, and love. It insists that we hover over our children, exact promises from our lovers, cling to our small morsels. The soul smiles and urges greater courage. It knows Love and Life are free and omnipresent.

> Joy, exuberance, exultation are foundational energies of Love. In Love is the sound of glory, of all things singing the praise of Life. Love is the impulse toward celebration. The Universe, being most purely Love, is celebrating this instant. The sun is celebrating. The earth is celebrating. The trees, the plants, all creatures are glorying.
>
> *Lenedra J Carroll*

ACHIEVING LOVE

We may yearn for this experience, we may deeply desire unconditional Love to be the defining element in our lives, but how do we achieve it? What would it look like if we had unconditional relationships?

Rather than being surrounded by relationships in which the primary context is insecurity, fear, and need, we can have intimates whose love is unconditional and associated with the consciousness of their soul's expression. The unconditionally loving relationships in my life are not free of fears or misunderstanding. In fact, precisely because they are filled with openness and a passionate zest for life and Spirit, they challenge old ways of relating, and many uncomfortable feelings may rise within us. But a hallmark of the relationships is a fearlessness even in scary places.

These friendships are typified by self-responsibility and commitment to growth, authenticity, and grace. They are playful, healing, deeply satisfying, and phenomenally creative, and they are infused by our pioneering spirit and with ceremony. All of these are the qualities that uplift our expression of love. Making them our undeviating goal, becoming them, draws into our lives others who share them.

Pause for a moment and think of the most difficult person in your life, past or present. Feel them very clearly, until you recognize their "tone." Experience the emotions that linger around you. Remember the person fully: close your eyes and see them clearly, standing or sitting in their surroundings. Now step into their body. Feel their life, their longing. Feel their stress. How does their body feel; where is it tense or hurting? Experience their breath. From inside them, know why they are the way they are. Find their hope, their vulnerability. Sit quietly in their life. *Commune with their soul.* Know that instead of resisting, judging, or hating them, you can, if you choose, love them unconditionally. Explore this option, seeing how it feels to you. Hold them in the same understanding in which the Divine Source holds them. Let that understanding permeate you, and them. In it, feel your own safety and strength. When you are ready, bless them and wish them well on their journey. Repeating this exercise from time to time, you will find that the fear you hold about them will dissipate.

Fear is a frequency; it can and has been measured. I met a scientist in Los Angeles who studies frequency and waveform. He told me that the frequency of fear happens to correspond to the musical note G in the Western scale. It would seem that tone is the prime note, or wave, that the human group is singing: we sing the song of fear. We fear that we are alone, fear we will destroy ourselves, fear there is not enough, fear for our life, fear.

Love is the antidote to fear. It is the exact opposite of fear, the opposite pole. And fear dwells within the Ocean of Love. Seeing the Love, knowing we dwell in it, being the Love, the fear dissolves into the ocean. When Love is engaged, fear cannot exist because Love — as the purest energy that exists — is the energy that allows a sprout to become a great oak. Here is our safety and security. Here is the safe haven, here the means to create heaven on earth, to transform.

Understood and purely experienced, Love's vastly elevated wave will transform the song of humanity, for it is the essence of the space that fills us and surrounds us. It holds our atoms and the planets in their unique orbits. It is the blackness of the cosmos and the cohesive thread of all life therein. This Love is ours. It does not need to be searched for, worked at, won, or held on to. It is in us, around us. It simply is.

LOVE IS

It is common among us at this time to grow in Love as we grow in knowledge of persons. This is good, but the knowledge is not necessary. Love is not based on knowledge, though this is one way to come to know it.

Love is not really an emotion, though it is often experienced through the emotions. Emotion is like touch and smell, a sense through which we interpret our world. So Love is sensed through emotion, and this is a purposeful phase, a way to begin to know Love, to notice it and become familiar with it. But it can also be sensed and expressed by other means, by the physical body, through the chakras, through the individual and group light fields. Love can also be experienced through the Soul as a divine communion.

(continued)

Love Is. It has its own is-ness. Love is God. It is and moves through all things. It surrounds us. To be in Love is to be in the body of the Creator. Love *is* the One in whom we live and move and have our being. It connects, binds, integrates, nourishes all that is. It is omnipresent.

Love expresses through us. As we increase in our capacity to receive and express Love, we become capable of being fuller expressions of a higher and more complete spectrum, increasing the breadth of the frequency we are in interplay with. The divine Source then has its expression, through us, into the world of form, changing, vivifying, uplifting all that it comes into contact with.

When one is in Love, one is in God. One knows then that one *is* God, one with God; at one. At*one*ment. Human beings are uniquely evolved to be conscious receptors and transmitters of this pure Love. To become this unconditional Love in physical form in our world is to fulfill the highest purpose of human life.

Lenedra J Carroll

THE GLORY OF LOVE

Love, in this elevated way of thinking and accessing, is the most profoundly balancing energy in the universe. It is the cohesive factor that allows everything, all of life, to be held together. It is the potent creative force sensed in our more common love. It is latent in most of our expression, but it is there to be elevated and become a transformative force unlike any other, as the platform on which our dream can take place.

Being an expression of this immensely loving force does not mean we become weak, nor does it mean we never experience "nonloving" emotions. Think of those most often associated with this Love. Christ was passionate, active, powerful, angry, and impatient. The stories of most "saints" also show the gutsiness, sharpness, and decisiveness of fully embodied Love. There is great strength and power in this refined expression. The nature of Love is to both defend assertively and embrace completely. Think of the hands of Siva, one thrusting out to destroy, the other outstretched in loving welcome — they are representative of the epic *force* implicit in Love. It moves through the body and changes the molecular, cellular, and genetic structures when wholly and completely engaged as a pure energy. This Love creates a light of such brilliance and profound magnetism, that one who is able to access it is granted, in that moment, access to all riches, all accomplishment, all knowledge without any vestiges of fear.

Love is the essence of the mysterious "empty" space, the prana, plenum, life force, the breath of life of our universe. It is the source of healing and miracles. Christ, Buddha, and many others have *shown* us it can be achieved in human form. They taught that it is fully available, not out of our grasp. When science develops technology to measure the highest frequencies of Love, as well as the frequencies of "empty" space, it will discover what the sages have declared throughout time: they are the same; it is all Love.

Love, Love, Love...Love is all you need.

— John Lennon

TOLERANCE
The conscious effort to overcome
habitual separateness
by practicing allowance and respect
for the nature, beliefs, and behaviors of others
Becoming willing to gain knowledge of another
with this knowledge leading to
SYMPATHY
A consequence of willingness and knowledge
allowing the heart to be touched
promoting growth into
COMPASSION
Loving action expressive of the
commonality of human experience
that strikes the chord of
HARMONY
Not the elimination of differences but
the organization of differences
Along the line of
LOVE
All inclusive judgeless love, embracing
individuals and groups of individuals but
moving beyond families and friends and countries
Active love, working always
for the uplifting of the greater whole
and achieving
UNITY
Which is not uniformity but
Individuated integration
For in unity there is diversity
in the understanding that
each part is vital to the
integrity of an emerging whole.
Unification at the level of the soul is
the action that promotes

THE
Architecture
OF THE
Soul

SYNTHESIS
The inspired gathering together of
the separate elements
that form the whole
And the bringing of the whole
into the active Divine expression of
TRANSCENDENCE
The ultimate doorway
through which all of life passes
to merge with the One infinite life
wherein the highest of promise and purpose
is brought to fulfillment and
GRACE

Lenedra J Carroll

28

THE Psychology OF THE Soul

They were driving to the Hopi reservation. She relaxed back in the comfortable front seat, gazing out the passenger window, enjoying the arid beauty of the New Mexico high country, and contemplating the unusual gathering of nations she had been called to attend. Thinking of the wisdom of the Elders she would meet and of their prophecies, she drifted mindlessly, listening to the soft voices of the other women in the car.

Suddenly the windshield in front of her shimmered, altered, and vanished, replaced by the inky expanse of deep space. Confused, she shifted about to get a bearing and discovered before her the breathtaking vista of planet earth. As she stared in wonder at the suspended green and blue jewel that was her home, a shadow began to move across the planet. It traveled across the face of the earth, obscuring the colors in darkness. She looked sharply to her right, wondering what had cast the shadow, and as she did so, a voice spoke: "It is the dream of the Great Spirit."

Turning back, she saw an edge of light rim one side of the globe, advancing slowly. The light began to illuminate the darkness, and in the areas of shadow, she saw many people scrambling to get out of the light, looking for places to hide. They were placing secrets under rocks, finding bushes and caves to conceal projects and agendas in the shadows. The light, however, continued along its path, leaving less and less room for these clandestine activities. The movement in the shadow increased to a frantic pace. But the light moved on without ceasing. The voice spoke again: "What is hidden shall be revealed."

She turned again to see the source of the light and was told, "It is all the dream of God." The light drew her again, and she gazed at her planet as it began to effervesce, seeming to take on new life. Staring into the light, she discerned movements that seemed to draw the light forward. Peering closely, she saw thousands of people, then hundreds of thousands, then millions of people tending their light, joining until a great flash consumed the planet in a wondrous glow.

"It is humanity that moves the light forward in the dream of the Great Spirit. You are the light." With these words the scene faded and she became aware of the jolt and drone of the vehicle as they turned onto a dirt road.

We have our life within that Supreme Life that is also dreaming: it dreams the dream of the Universe, of the Cosmos, of the transformation of consciousness into light of transformation. Within that life, we are the Soul dreaming its individual dream within the group dream. And within each of us is the light of transformation. It is expressed through the soul, and as we become familiar with our soul, as we bring stillness into our being, this light grows, and we emerge from the dim, penumbral world of form.

In one of Plato's wonderful allegorical stories, he tells of a number of prisoners in a cave, the entrance of which is so brightly lit that the shadows of those that pass outside are cast on the inner wall. The prisoners can face only the inner wall to which they are chained. Having been there all their lives, they think that the shadows are what is real. There comes a time when they are led out of the cave into the light, and, at first blinded, gradually they come to disbelieve. The light seems so much less real to them than the shadows on their wall.

Our world is the world of shadow. It is a shadow world cast by the light of the soul within the dream of the Divine Source. We often move through this shadowy dreamworld relating to it as though it was not shadow, and so missing all that is real. But the real is all around us. And the real is within us.

THE SHADOW AND THE SOUL

Modern psychology has focused entirely on the personality and its mind and emotions, on understanding and healing the individual's accumulated experiences. What of the psychology of the soul? The psychology of the Soul is the evolution or transformation of consciousness.

The ego is strongly identified with the physical world and body. Because of this, it experiences an exaggerated sense of vulnerability. The soul perceives the body as the form through which it expresses in the physical world. It loves and recognizes, enjoys and uses the physical, but knows it is not the physical form. It knows its existence is not dependent on the body; the soul is secure in its knowledge that it is everlasting. As humans, we live in the shadow reality of social consciousness. As souls, we know ourselves to be the source of the light. We are the shadows of our soul.

The physical self is motivated to become individualized; it is concerned with separation and self-definition. The intellect and ego prefer concrete information and carefully constructed, well-defined realities. They are strongly identified with the world of matter. They are driven by instinct and highly motivated toward self-preservation. The physical self is the shadow.

The mind is a receiver, an interpreter, and a transmitter of thought, but the soul is an originator, a source, of thought. The soul deals more in abstraction than in concrete information. The soul's "mind" is far more conscious than what we call our conscious mind.

The unknowable, the abstract, the intangible, the great mystery, the domain of all wisdom, all realities, all truth — these are the realms of the soul's psychology.

The soul self moves always to integrate and unify; it is group oriented. It is both our expression of and our means to understand the intangible and abstract. Intuition is implicit in the soul self, and life purpose is expressed through it. The soul self is the individual expression of divine consciousness.

While the narcissistic ego self clamors to be seen, the conscious, centered soul self, peacefully and with certainty, knows that it does exist, eternally.

What do we know of our own soul? It is time we each became intimate with this self, allowing it to grow in prominence in our lives. How? By loving our soul, honoring it, seeking it out, listening, and following its guidance. Come to know your soul and it will reveal your light.

> The reward for recognizing and developing our souls is freedom from the handicaps and limitations of a demanding ego.
>
> *Lenedra J Carroll*

THE VALUES OF THE SOUL

Within our being is a divine intelligence that cannot be denied, altered, or destroyed; it cannot be harmed or separated from itself, for it is permanently whole. And that self is always guiding us, always. It is our soul.

Our soul cannot be held captive; neither can it be abused or harvested for its emotions. Our soul is divinity incarnate, it is forever. Death means nothing to the soul, for it knows no death or pain. It only knows ongoing eternal life and growth. The body's experience of pain or death is already understood by the soul; if necessary for growth, it embraces them, knowing they are only more of the ongoing flow of life.

It is the personality, the limited self, the ego self that loses touch with the soul's knowledge and begins to value such things as greed, fear, and power in order to feed the desire to be safe. But the soul knows only love, creativity, sharing, nurturing, caring, generosity, heroism, and life — and the eternal abundance of the Source. These are the things that the soul values and builds upon.

Our highest purpose in life is expressed through the soul. Without understanding this, we are cut off from our soul's higher purpose and left to the more limiting satisfaction of personality agendas. In coming to understand our purpose fully and profoundly, we may discover that we are not here for our careers; we are not here only for our family — our husband or wife or children. We may learn that we are not even here for service to the disadvantaged, our community, or the needs of our planet.

We may see, moving into deeper and deeper communion with our soul, that beyond the wondrous and right purpose we find in all of those goals, there is another purpose designed indelibly into our original blueprint. That purpose is to be an expression of the fullest potential of the Divine, to be compelled upstream like the salmon, ceaselessly climbing the waves of our soul's curriculum to match and hold and express the essence of the Infinite frequency in our being. That is our most profoundly satisfying purpose. It is the journey we all are on, without exception. It is the source of our most meaningful commonality. The former lover we no longer speak to is on that journey. The leader or businessman that we fear is also on that journey. All are. There is nothing outside of the purview of the Divine Intelligence, for we have our existence in the infinite mind of God, and the mind of God is not stagnant. It is the animating principle of the world, continually expanding, as are we.

✺ THE FULFILLERS OF PROPHECY ✺

After three days of prayer and ceremony, she sat in the talking circle with the Hopi Elders and experienced the shared satisfaction of a group that had found unity where there had been none. As the talking stick moved from person to person, many dreams and prophecies were shared. Some were visions of hope, others were dire predictions and doomsday warnings holding little hope for the human race. As the feathered wand was handed to her, she paused at length to consider all that had been said.

Then she spoke: "We have heard many prophecies, and there are countless more from other cultures that have gone unspoken today. But who fulfills a prophecy? We are the fulfillers of prophecy. Therefore it would be wise for us to choose carefully those that we wish to fulfill. It is our choice. It is our dream. All that is our combined history we have dreamed. And the dream is the Creator dreaming us." She shared the vision of the light moving inexorably to fill the earth — the dream of the Great Spirit — that came to her on her journey just three days before.

Following the closing ceremony, three of the Elders sought her out quietly. "We have had the same vision," one said. "We understood the dream and the movement of the light as you did. The same voice of the dream spoke to us the same words you heard."

They told her they shared silence together to understand how that vision would be fulfilled in humanity. "We learned," said the oldest man, "that it will be through the light of the Soul of humanity that it will come to pass."

✺ ✺

THE TRANSFORMATION OF A SPECIES

The evolution, or more accurately, the *transformation* of humanity over eons of time has been the purposeful dream of the Source, each stage having apparent drawbacks but also vital gains. During the Age of Form, the *physical* body developed and we became increasingly focused on it and felt ourselves to be separate from our source. But we survived and thrived, and a wondrous housing for consciousness, for the soul, was refined. No matter how we prod and change our bodies, molding them this way and that, it is mere playful vanity. For the fact is, that stage is finished; the body is sufficiently refined to serve the purpose it was designed for. It is the magnificent housing for the flame of Divine Consciousness.

Then came the evolution of *mind* and *emotion*, the Age of Mind and Psyche. The ego, seizing these tools, galloped through time, wielding greed, fear, and power like a naughty child unaware of its strength. Nonetheless, the equipment was honed, the mind becoming capable of awareness, of pure reason, consciousness, and creativity; and the emotions capable of grand passion and glorification.

Now we come to the opening of the heart, the door to the soul, and the evolution of *consciousness* into light. This transformation will change the face of humanity, of the planet. It will occur as surely as did the development of the body, the mind, and the emotions. It will occur as we become familiar with our spirit, our soul's nature, which is the breath of life that moves through each one of us in every moment.

This transformation is occurring within each individual and humanity as a whole. As the jellyfish in the story in the first chapter of this book, humanity is moving together toward a destination sensed by our souls. In that movement into the Age of the Souls, we are evolving — transforming, becoming conscious aspects of the mind and the dream of the One Life that informs us. This is our group destiny, and we are dreaming, dreaming the coming of that day.

DAYBREAK SONG

I will give this breath to the rising sun
To the day that follows and the night to come.

May I work with Spirit, knowing all are one
And I will that Thy will be the will I've done.

May my pace be steady and my aim be true
Let right action guide me in the things I do.

May my mind be humble and my body strong
Fill my heart with loving, fill my lungs with song.

May I serve the people, dancing hand in hand
May I serve all creatures, may I serve the land.

To my ears come whispers on the winds of change
And the witness ripples 'cross the mountain range.

I am soil of mother, I am soul of fire
I am cell of ocean, I am breath of sky.

I will give this breath to the rising sun
To the day that follows and the night to come.

And I will that Thy will be the will I've done.

Lenedra J Carroll

To receive a complimentary CD of Lenedra Carroll singing "Daybreak Song," see page 337.

29

THE Transformation OF THE Soul

I f you assume that there's no hope, you guarantee that there will be no hope. If you assume that there is an instinct for freedom, that there are opportunities to change things, there's a chance you may contribute to making a better world. That's your choice.

— Noam Chomsky

Consciousness is sparking the evolution of the family of human "being." And the context for this transformation is the arena of individual change. This individual change is the method by which we evolve as a group. Our efforts to change and heal our families and communities are the dynamic that will heal the discord between countries. The world is filled with our conflict: Tibet, Macedonia, Northern Ireland, Bhutan, Afghanistan, East Timor, Peru, Lebanon, Israel, Pakistan, Palestine, Senegal, Colombia, Honduras. Why is this so?

Of one thing I am certain: it is not a capricious, angry, controlling, or indifferent God who creates the horrors of our world. It is humanity — feeling separate from all that is God — who orchestrates the horror. We visit our wars upon ourselves — each injustice, each holocaust, and each inhumanity.

We forfeit our freedoms and resources. We refuse our power.

Again and again we have dreamed the same limited, painful existence. Why doesn't the Creator or the angelic being intervene? Ultimately, can you enter the nightmare of another and alter their dream for them? No. Only the dreamer can awaken to see it is a dream, and dream anew. It is all the dream of humankind; therefore it is only *we* who can dream it differently. This has vital implications for each of us. If world conflict is to cease, *we* must commit ourselves to the evolvement of our souls.

We are not alone on this earth; we have a responsibility not just to ourselves, our mates, or our own communities. We have a responsibility to the family of humankind. Realizing this and making a commitment to it, we will be able to bring ourselves to challenge our fears, challenge our addictions; we will be able to come to a place where the anger is transformed into Love, where the dissonance is transformed into peace, where the prayers are lived into being. That is the true context of change and transformation.

> The door to transcendence, to transformation and enlightenment, is a door that leads into a hall of mirrors. Wherever you look, there is only you looking back.
>
> — L. D. Thompson

THE GENIUS OF THE SOUL

The story is told of an impregnable city. It was a city of wondrous treasures, but it was a closed city; no one from the surrounding countryside was allowed in. A large group of peasants from without the walls wanted the city opened to everyone. Insistent that the city be changed, they engaged in a siege to break down the barriers and get in. Ceaselessly they battered the gates, finally exhausting themselves. In despair, they held counsel to determine what to do. One peasant asked, "Why do we want to go there? It is polluted and crowded. Let's build our own city."

Acting on this wisdom, they turned their focus from the futile battle to enter the old city and founded their own fortress on a beautiful site some distance away. They built a city of such magnificence that the entire countryside was transformed and even the old city opened its gates to allow exchange.

For too long we have been obsessed with the old city, all that is wrong with the world. We study crime, write books, and produce specials by the thousands that delve into the criminal mind, theorize about the evil that surrounds us, focus on the corporate and government wrongs that exist, and so on ad infinitum. Billions of dollars have been poured into this effort because *we fear* that if we do not, "they" will overpower us.

It is time to build a new city, to become fascinated with the transformation of our species. It is time to devote our resources to understanding genius. It is time to study the realm of the Soul. Within our soul lies genius. It is available to everyone.

Walter Russell was a genius, an extraordinary painter, sculptor, architect, businessman, and spiritual master. In the book by Glenn Clark about Russell's fascinating life, *The Man Who Tapped the Secrets of the Universe*, there is the following quote from Russell regarding genius:

> I believe sincerely that every man has consummate genius within him. Some appear to have it more than others only because they are aware of it more than others are, and the awareness or unawareness of it is what makes each one of them into masters or holds them down to mediocrity. I believe that mediocrity is self-inflicted and that genius is self-bestowed. It is available to all. Every successful man I ever have known, and I have known a great many, carries with him the key which unlocks that awareness and lets in the Universal Power that made him into a master.
>
> Every successful man or great genius has three particular qualities in common: they all produce a prodigious

amount of work, they never know fatigue, and their minds grow more brilliant as they grow older, instead of less so. The geniuses have learned how to gather thought energy together to use for transforming their conceptions into material forms. The thinking of creative and successful men is never exerted in any direction other than that intended. [1]

There are many thousands like Walter Russell who have understood the power of genius in the omnipresent Soul and harnessed it in their lives. If we can understand their path, the development of their capacities, their knowledge of a Universal Power, we can begin to access the potential of that force in our own lives. Imagine the undiscovered gifts that lie in the untapped genius within. Imagine what will happen to the world as we begin to bring them forward. The potential of that power to bring about an extraordinary evolution in humanity lies within the reach of each person reading these words, each person yearning to know the secrets of abundance.

THE SOUL'S LEGACY

Our task is simply to *be* more fully. To be more fully within each thought, within each breath, within each interaction. This will grant unto us a grace that allows us not to stumble, not to get caught up in pettiness, not to be hard on ourselves when life seems overwhelming. This will be possible because we are activated from a deep place of remembrance in our being. There lie the power and opportunity of the legacy that we can embrace in order to simply be the more loving world, the more peaceful world that we long for; to be able to live in peace in every moment of our existence, to become a being of unconditional love. This is a legacy that we are uniquely qualified to create. It is a legacy of hope, of change, of validation to the hearts of humanity. It is the legacy of the soul.

---

1. Glenn Clark, *The Man Who Tapped the Secrets of the Universe* (Univ. of Science and Philosophy, 1989).

We create this legacy by courting stillness, committing to being creative, evoking our courage, asking better questions, challenging our context, and remembering that it is a dream. We create it by living our values, by grounding ourselves in actions that uplift and transform, by becoming one with the systems of natural order, and by growing intimate with our souls. In this way we create an inheritance of abundance for ourselves, our planet, and our species.

Each of us leaves behind a legacy. That is assured. Each moment that we live affects and molds it, for it issues forth out of each relationship, each decision, each action. There is the opportunity to create a generative legacy by empowering ourselves to become active participants within the Mind of God, which contains all potential. In all potential anything is possible: greatness or obscurity, riches or poverty, beauty or the lack of beauty, genius or limitation. In the Divine Mind, *all* is potential, all is grace.

What each of us can do, in our own unique way, is to allow ourselves the understanding that this potential is the very ocean that we swim in every moment, that this is not merely air but *energy*. As energy, it can be made into anything. All abundance. It requires *knowing* — not trust or faith, though both are steps along the road — but *knowing*, completely, that we are One. Therefore, the infinite abundance of the Universe is the same infinite substance that is ours, and that we are.

This is the legacy we inherit as our birthright. It is the knowledge of the soul: there is no exterior source. The source is in our divine being. That is the source of the goodness of life, the source of love, the source of passion, of safety, of health, knowledge, or wisdom. It is the source of all abundance.

THE NEW CITY

We are entering into a time on our earth when we will see changes occur that we have only imagined. They will render our planet unrecognizable. Many of us will witness these changes in our own lifetimes. We will see sweeping developments that will affect our travel and play, communication, healing capabilities, education, and the arts.

They will affect our ability to recognize and accept what spirit is. Science will gain the ability to create human life. It will acknowledge the existence of the soul. Life spans will greatly expand; decrepitness in old age will not be the norm. Our relationship to death will change. We will learn to provide a high quality of life for every being on earth.

Recovered records and new information will shed light on many mysteries of Spirit. New prophecies and scriptures will come forth. People will cease to war upon one another in the name of religion. A new people will step forward, by the millions, fiercely determined to be the change that the world needs. Forces that have ruled the planet for ages will begin to give way. Our interaction with the time and space continuums will be vastly altered, and "time travel" will be understood. Communication with interplanetary relatives will not be uncommon.

Ahead is a time of vastly accelerated change, and it will challenge and shift much of what we have held to be our security and our methodology. Are we ready for such a time? Will we grapple, with integrity, with the responsibilities and opportunities? If we listen to the wisdom of the soul and follow its course of change, we will pass through the transformations with grace.

The human family is moving together on the ocean of consciousness. Led by our Soul, we are re-forming our individual and group consciousnesses, and with them our dreamworlds of form. This transformation is what we are here for.

My life has been one filled with the passion to know the Source, to tap its extant excellence, to remember and to access the power within us to move mountains. The growth toward the highest that is possible is leading us into a new revolution, that of the transformation of the Soul of humankind. We all have our part to play.

We are the architects of change. The greatest and most heroic sacrifice we can make to change the world is to sacrifice fear, guilt, and judgment, to sacrifice the habits, behaviors, and qualities we possess that no longer serve our world or us. There is no greater thing we can do to change the world than to change ourselves.

THIS BREATH

We are the elements of this mother earth, the space of the cosmos, the water of the great ocean of being, and the fire of Spirit. Pause a moment and know fire. It cannot flame without space. Space brings air — there cannot be fire without air, without breath. The breath of life is literally that. We can live more than a month without food, less than a week without water, but only minutes without air. That is because it is not empty air; it contains vital nourishment, full of the energy of the Source. This breath is filled with the life of the everlasting Soul. Breathe.

Lenedra J Carroll

Acknowledgments

*E*xultation is the going
Of an inland soul to sea,
Past the houses — past the headlands
Into deep Eternity —

Bred as we, among the mountains
Can the sailor understand
The divine intoxication
Of the first league out from land?

— *Emily Dickinson,* Poem 76

At 6:33 A.M. PDT on Friday, June 15, I completed the final chapter of this book. Removing my hands from the keys of my computer, I felt a rush of exultation — it was finished! I was then immediately overwhelmed by a wave of feeling that engulfed me with such force, I had to lie down on the rug in front of the fire. It was the force of my gratitude for the countless lives that have lent their dreams to mine. I felt deep gratitude to the Source of my inspiration, and to all those in the etheric realms who have guided me. And I experienced the all-encompassing gratitude that the Divine has for me. I lay in silence, in the warmth of the hearth, as my tears flowed on the tide of such swelling thankfulness.

Throughout the writing of this book, I have felt gratitude for all those who people my dream. I feel the prayers of my ancestors, those pioneers who journeyed into new lands, new religions, who built new cities, and the strong values that are my heritage. My father and mother, Jay and Arva Carroll, brought me into a new frontier rich with nature — Mom, it is your shepherd's heart that inspired my love of humanity. Jerry and Nelda Tietjen and many others in Homer, Alaska, nurtured the child I was and the growth of my abilities.

I feel, beyond words, the breadth of the partnership I have with Jewel. You are my hero — your personal courage and commitment to being a difference are an inspiration to me. You are an extraordinary presence in my life. I am joyous about the wonderful, creative exchange I have with my sons, Shane and Atz Lee. Your own writings, poetry, songs delight me — I wish everyone could know you. I am also aware of the gift that Atz Kilcher has been in my life, for he gave me music.

Jacqueline Snyder, I have heard your whisperings in my ear. I salute your knowledge and love of the Creator. Your joy in life so blessed mine; your family — Sean, Brandon, Lisa — still do.

There are those people whose efforts have, indeed, made the book possible. L. D. Thompson is one: without your contributions of Spirit, the endless editing, your unconditional love, and your knowledge of my soul, dear one, I would still be on chapter 1! Another is David Owen Kniffen. David, it is your gift for structure and your brilliant way with words that have lent so much to the architecture of the book; and your loving was the haven I rested in.

In Mani Management Group there are many whose support has been remarkable. Colleen Anderson was there every moment during the first weeks and the final weeks. And in between, Beauty, your love and your excellence in the business held the place for me to write. Francesca San Diego, it was your grace and skill that kept the company strongly on course — thank you! Julie Agrati and Thomas Sharkey kept Mani Artist Management running smoothly — thank you both for stepping up. Ken Calhoun, your knowledge of the material and the key points kept me on track; your gift as a writer enriched the content. I promise the same for your book! West Kennerly shot the cover and jacket photos. What great pics, West; they reflect your love of your craft and of me — thank you for both.

Also at Mani are Berne Smith, our art director, Cambria Jensen, team editor, and Shani Gianis, project manager for the book. Thank you for your art and your grace. Jan Sudweeks, my personal wizard: in the middle of the blur, there you are, keeping it all in focus. Bridget Hanley and Keith Anderson are the two who have been with us from the beginning. You are both so important to me. And Kelley Worrall and Marcia Quigley-Neel — you kept hearth and home steady and welcoming with your calming energies. To every one of the team members at Mani: know that your meditations and efforts on behalf of our dream are felt and appreciated deeply. I am so proud to have a company filled with people who are committed to pioneering human excellence. My praises to each of you.

Sandra Martin, my agent, was one of the first to convince me to write. Sandra, your vision and understanding of my story greatly expanded what this book has become, and it was you who determined to make it public. Thank you for the generosity of your spirit. I selected my publisher, New World Library, not only for their excellence in the trade but because, through the vision of Marc Allen, they are a company committed to the values that this book expresses. My editor there, Georgia Hughes, along with Munro Magruder, Marjorie Conte, Mary Ann Casler, Katie Farnam Conolly, Katie Karavolos, and Tona Pearce Myers are a *delightful* team. Ron Shapiro and his extraordinary staff at Atlantic Records have been tireless in their support of our dream. As a record company, you tower above the rest and Jewel and I both love working with you!

While writing the book, I have felt the souls of those of you who read it. I have heard your prayers, your dreams and fears. Your questions have guided me in my writing. I thank you for your path to now, and I cannot express the gratitude I have for your path to come, the changes you are poised to make, the difference you will be to our world.

God bless you all on your journeys.

Permissions Acknowledgments

Grateful acknowledgment is given to the following for permission to reprint quotations in *The Architecture of All Abundance*. Every effort has been made to contact all rights holders of the material in this book. If notified of errors the publisher will correct any omissions or mistakes in acknowledgments in future editions.

Coleman Barks with John Moyne: From *The Essential Rumi*, Translations by Coleman Barks with John Moyne © 1997. Reprinted by permission of Castle Books.

Calvin and Hobbes: From Universal Press Syndicate, Calvin's last words 12/21/95, 1995 United Press Syndicate. Reprinted by permission of Universal Press Syndicate, a division of Andrew McMeel Universal.

Henry Hamblin: From *Dynamic Thoughts* by Henry Hamblin © 1999. Reprinted by permission of Yoga Publication Society.

Willis Harman: From *World Business Academy, Journal on Business and Global Changes*, vol. 14, no. 4 © 2000. Reprinted by permission of Berrett-Koehler, Inc., San Francisco, Calif. All rights reserved. 1-800-929-2929.

Ellen Jensen, M.D.: Grateful acknowledgment is given to Dr. Ellen Jensen for use of her quotations.

Holger Kalweit: From *Dreamtime and Inner Space* by Holger Kalweit © 1984 by Holger Kalweit and Scherz Verlag, Bern and Munich (for Otto Wilhelm Barth Verlag). Translation © 1988 by Shambhala Publications, Inc., Boston, www.shambhala.com.

Elisabeth Kübler-Ross: From *A Grateful Heart* edited by M. J. Ryan © 1994 by M. J. Ryan. Reprinted by permission of Conari Press.

Daniel Ladinsky: From *The Subject Tonight Is Love* by Daniel Ladinsky, 2nd ed., © 1996. Reprinted by permission of Pumpkin House.

Leonard Laskow, M.D.: From *Healing with Love: A Physician's Breakthrough Mind/Body Medical Program for Healing Yourself and Others* © 1992. Reprinted by permission of HarperCollins.

John Lennon: Song lyrics from the album *The Yellow Submarine*, track 6, by the Beatles. Reprinted by permission of Capitol Records.

Wayne Muller: From *Sabbath* by Wayne Muller © 1999. Reprinted by permission of Bantam Doubleday Dell.

Jane Nelson: From *World Business Academy: Perspectives on Business and Global Changes*, vol. 14, no. 4 © 2000. Reprinted by permission of Berrett-Koehler, Inc., San Francisco, Calif. All rights reserved. 1-800-929-2929.

Judith Orloff, M.D.: From *Dr. Judith Orloff's Guide to Intuitive Healing: Five Steps to Physical, Emotional, and Sexual Wellness* by Dr. Judith Orloff © 2000. Reprinted by permission of Random House, Inc.

Alicia Ostriker: From *The Imaginary Lover* by Alicia Ostriker © 1986. Reprinted by permission of the University of Pittsburgh.

Raimundo Panniker: From *A Grateful Heart* edited by M. J. Ryan, © 1994 by M. J. Ryan. Reprinted by permission of Conari Press.

Paul H. Ray and Sherry Ruth Anderson: From *Cultural Creatives: How 50 Million People Are Changing the World* by Paul H. Ray and Sherry Ruth Anderson © 2000. Reprinted by permission of Random House, Inc.

Walter Russell: From *The Man Who Tapped the Secrets of the Universe* by Glenn Clark © 1989. Used by permission.

Jerry Seinfeld: From *Sein Language* by Jerry Seinfeld © 1995. Reprinted by permission of Bantam Books.

Aqeela Sherrills: Grateful acknowledgment is given to Aqeela Sherrills for use of his story.

Michael Talbot: From *The Holographic Universe* by Michael Talbot © 1991. Reprinted by permission of HarperCollins Publishers, Inc.

L. D. Thompson: Grateful acknowledgment is given to L. D. for use of his quotation.

Lynne Twist: Grateful acknowledgment is given to Lynne Twist for use of her quotations.

White Eagle: From *The Quiet Mind, Sayings of White Eagle* © 1972. Reprinted by permission of The White Eagle Publishing Trust.

Margaret Young: From *The Artist's Way* by Julia Cameron © 1992. Reprinted by permission of Penguin Putnam.

Index

If you would like to receive a *complimentary* CD of the author singing "Daybreak Song," you may order a copy at:

www.LenedraJCarroll.com

or call toll free:
(800) 519-2999

or complete and mail or fax the following form to:

Mani Services, Inc.
300 Carlsbad Village Drive, #108A-332
Carlsbad, CA 92008-2999
Fax number: (760) 602-4886

| Name | Phone number | E-mail |

Street Address

| City | State | Zip |

Comments

_____

_____

_____

Please visit our website, www.LenedraJCarroll.com, for further information about Lenedra's schedule of activities:

- ❈ speaking schedule
- ❈ conference and seminar schedule
- ❈ consulting work
- ❈ continued reflections on abundance in our daily lives

For more information about Higher Ground for Humanity and/or the Clearwater Project, please visit our websites at:

www.highergroundhumanity.org
www.clearwaterproject.org

or call or write to:

Be the Difference
P.O. Box 9002
Carlsbad, CA 92018-9022
(866)BtheDiff
(866) 284-3343 toll free

For further information on the Eden Center, please visit:

www.edenctr.com

or call toll free:

(866) EDNHLTH
(866) 336-4584

New World Library is dedicated to
publishing books and cassettes that inspire
and challenge us to improve the quality
of our lives and our world.

Our books and cassettes are available
at bookstores everywhere.
For a complete catalog, contact:

New World Library
14 Pamaron Way
Novato, California 94949

Phone: (415) 884-2100
Fax: (415) 884-2199
Or call toll free: (800) 972-6657
Catalog requests: Ext. 50
Ordering: Ext. 52

E-mail: escort@nwlib.com
www.newworldlibrary.com